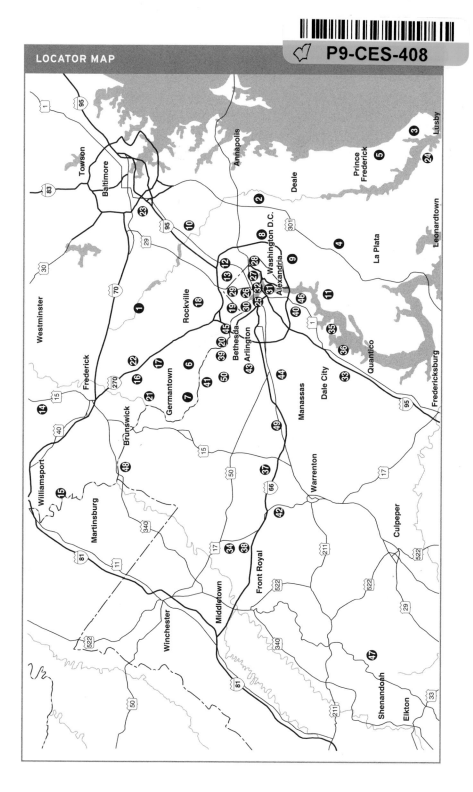

AMC'S **BEST DAY HIKES** NEAR
WASHINGTON, D.C.

FOUR-SEASON GUIDE TO **50** OF THE BEST TRAILS
IN MARYLAND, VIRGINIA, AND THE NATION'S CAPITAL

STEPHEN MAURO AND BETH HOMICZ

Appalachian Mountain Club Books
Boston, Massachusetts

AMC is a nonprofit organization and sales of AMC Books fund our mission of protecting the Northeast outdoors. If you appreciate our efforts and would like to make a donation to AMC, contact us at Appalachian Mountain Club, 5 Joy Street, Boston, MA 02108.

www.outdoors.org/publications/books/

Distributed by The Globe Pequot Press, Guilford, Connecticut.

Front cover photograph © Guy Crittenden
Back cover photographs © (l-r) © iStockphoto, © www.123rf.com
All interior photographs © Stephen Mauro, except for images on pages 35, 36, 40, 44, 58, 83, 87, 97, 126, 146, 152, 154, 200 © Beth Homicz, and on page 106 © Mark Wells
Maps by Ken Dumas, © Appalachian Mountain Club
Cover design by Gia Giasullo/Studio eg
Interior design by Eric Edstam

Library of Congress Cataloging-in-Publication Data
Mauro, Stephen.
  AMC's best day hikes near Washington, D.C. : four-season guide to 50 of the best trails in Maryland, Virginia, and the nation's capital / Stephen Mauro, Beth Homicz.
    p. cm.
  Includes bibliographical references and index.
  ISBN 978-1-934028-39-1 (alk. paper)
  1. Hiking--Washington Metropolitan Area--Guidebooks. 2. Trails--Washington Metropolitan Area--Guidebooks. 3. Washington Metropolitan Area--Guidebooks. I. Homicz, Beth. II. Title.
  GV199.42.W17M38 2011
  917.5--dc22
                         2010050762

The paper used in this publication meets the minimum requirements of the American National Standard for Information Sciences-Permanence of Paper for Printed Library Materials, ANSI Z39.48-1984. ∞

Outdoor recreation activities by their very nature are potentially hazardous. This book is not a substitute for good personal judgment and training in outdoor skills. Due to changes in conditions, use of the information in this book is at the sole risk of the user. The authors and Appalachian Mountain Club assume no liability for accidents happening to, or injuries sustained by, readers who engage in the activities described in this book.

Interior pages contain 30% post-consumer recycled fiber.
Cover contains 10% post-consumer recycled fiber.
Printed in the United States of America,
using vegetable-based inks.

10 9 8 7 6 5 4 3 2 1   11 12 13 14 15 16 17

Mixed Sources

Product group from well-managed forests, controlled sources and recycled wood or fiber
www.fsc.org   Cert no. SCS-COC-002464
©1996 Forest Stewardship Council

FSC

CONTENTS

Locator Map . . . . **iii**

At-a-Glance Trip Planner. . . . . **viii**

Introduction . . . . **xvi**

Acknowledgments. . . . . **xviii**

How to Use This Book . . . . **xxi**

Trip Planning and Safety . . . . **xxiii**

Leave No Trace . . . . **xxvi**

SECTION 1: MARYLAND

1 Patuxent River State Park 3

2 Merkle Wildlife Sanctuary 7

3 Calvert Cliffs State Park **12**

4 Cedarville State Forest **16**

5 American Chestnut Land Trust. **20**

6 Seneca Creek State Park—Clopper Lake **25**

7 McKee-Beshers Wildlife Management Area . . . . . : **29**

8 Watkins Regional Park **33**

9 Cosca Regional Park **38**

10 Patuxent Research Refuge 42
11 Piscataway National Park—Accokeek Foundation 47
12 Greenbelt Park 53
13 Lake Artemesia and the Northeast Branch Trail 57
14 Catoctin Mountain Park and Cunningham Falls State Park 62
15 Antietam National Battlefield 67
16 Sugarloaf Mountain 71
17 Black Hill Regional Park 75
18 Matthew Henson Trail 79
19 Capital Crescent Trail 84
20 Billy Goat Trail at Great Falls 89
21 Woodstock Equestrian Park 95
22 Little Bennett Regional Park 99
23 Patapsco Valley State Park 103
24 Greenwell State Park 107

SECTION 2: WASHINGTON, D.C.

25 Theodore Roosevelt Island and the Potomac Heritage Trail 113
26 Potomac River: Georgetown to Lincoln Memorial 118
27 National Arboretum 123
28 Kenilworth Aquatic Gardens 129
29 Rock Creek Park 134
30 Around Georgetown 138
31 East Potomac Park and Hains Point 142
32 The National Mall 149

SECTION 3: VIRGINIA

33 Prince William Forest Park 159
34 Sky Meadows State Park 164
35 Mason Neck State Park 168
36 Leesylvania State Park 173
37 Bull Run Mountains Natural Area 177
38 G. Richard Thompson Wildlife Management Area 181
39 Riverbend Park and Great Falls Park 186
40 Huntley Meadows Park 192
41 Fraser Preserve 197
42 Wildcat Mountain Natural Area 201

43 Washington & Old Dominion Trail and Cross County Trail 205
44 Bull Run—Occoquan Trail. 210
45 Scott's Run Nature Preserve 215
46 Mount Vernon Trail—Fort Hunt Park to Mount Vernon 220
47 Old Rag. 224
48 Harpers Ferry to Maryland Heights 229
49 Manassas National Battlefield Park. 235
50 Meadowlark Botanical Gardens 241

NATURE AND HISTORY ESSAYS

Saving the Bald Eagle **46**
A Story to Tell: The Piscataway People. **51**
Matthew Henson and the Race to the North Pole **81**
Centuries of Perseverance: The Chesapeake & Ohio Canal **94**
Peace and Long Life: Spirit within a Tree. **126**
Washington's *Sakura*—and Those Who've Loved Them **144**
What's in a Name: Mr. Smithson's Legacy **152**
Under Cover: Spies in the Parks **162**
Far Away in Time: The Geology of Great Falls **189**
Beavers at Work. **193**
Roosevelt's Tree Army: The Civilian Conservation Corps **226**
John Brown and the Assault on Harpers Ferry. **232**
"Firsts" of the First Battle of Manassas. **239**

APPENDIX

Further Reading. **247**

Index **251**
About the Authors. **255**
Appalachian Mountain Club **256**
The AMC Washington DC Chapter **257**
AMC Book Updates **259**

AT-A-GLANCE
TRIP PLANNER

#	Trip	Page	Location	Difficulty	Distance and Elevation Gain
	MARYLAND				
1	Patuxent River State Park	3	Sunshine, MD	Easy	2.0 mi, 290 ft
2	Merkle Wildlife Sanctuary	7	Croom, MD	Easy–Moderate	5.25 mi, 440 ft
3	Calvert Cliffs State Park	12	Lusby, MD	Moderate	4.8 mi, 330 ft
4	Cedarville State Forest	16	Waldorf, MD	Easy	9.2 mi, 400 ft
5	American Chestnut Land Trust	20	Prince Frederick, MD	Moderate	6.8 mi, 400 ft
6	Seneca Creek State Park–Clopper Lake	25	Germantown, MD	Moderate	4.5 mi, 400–500 ft
7	McKee-Beshers Wildlife Management Area	29	Poolesville, MD	Easy	6.0 mi, 200 ft
8	Watkins Regional Park	33	Largo, MD	Easy	2.2 mi, 45 ft
9	Cosca Regional Park	38	Clinton, MD	Easy	1.4 mi, 25 ft
10	Patuxent Research Refuge	42	Laurel, MD	Easy	2.1 mi, 35 ft

Estimated Time	Fee	Good for Kids	Dogs Allowed	Public Transit	X-C Skiing	Snow-Shoeing	Trip Highlights
1.0–1.5 hrs		✓	✓		✓	✓	Total seclusion and easygoing trails along Patuxent River
2.5–3.0 hrs	$	✓					Critical wetlands preserve along Patuxent River
2.0–2.5 hrs	$	✓					Miocene-era cliffs rich in shark teeth and other ancient fossils
4.5 hrs	$		✓				3,500 heavily forested acres
2.5–3.0 hrs		✓	✓				Hiking along pristine Chesapeake Bay tributaries
2.5–3.0 hrs	$	✓	✓				Mature hardwoods, excellent shoreline views
3.0 hrs		✓	✓				Excellent hiking, great birding location
2.5–3.0 hrs		✓	✓	✓	✓	✓	Family fun: farm animals, garden, mini golf, carousel
2.5 hrs		✓	✓		✓	✓	Fun outing rich in natural wonders
2.5 hrs		✓	✓				Hands-on nature center, wonderful array of flora and fauna

#	Trip	Page	Location	Difficulty	Distance and Elevation Gain
11	Piscataway National Park–Accokeek Foundation	47	Accokeek, MD	Easy	4.0 mi, minimal
12	Greenbelt Park	53	Greenbelt, MD	Moderate	5.3 mi, 350 ft
13	Lake Artemesia and the Northeast Branch Trail	57	College Park and Berwyn Heights, MD	Easy	3.5 mi, 20 ft
14	Catoctin Mountain Park and Cunningham Falls State Park	62	Thurmont, MD	Difficult	10.4 mi, 2,200 ft
15	Antietam National Battlefield	67	Sharpsburg, MD	Easy-Moderate	3.5 mi, 400 ft
16	Sugarloaf Mountain	71	Dickerson, MD	Moderate-Difficult	5.3 mi, 1,375 ft
17	Black Hill Regional Park	75	Clarksburg, MD	Moderate	6.8 mi, 320 ft
18	Matthew Henson Trail	79	Viers Mill and Colesville, MD	Moderate	4.5 mi, 235 ft
19	Capital Crescent Trail	84	Bethesda, MD, and Georgetown, Washington, D.C.	Moderate	8.0 mi, downslope
20	Billy Goat Trail at Great Falls	89	Great Falls, MD	Difficult	8.2 mi, 650 ft
21	Woodstock Equestrian Park	95	Beallsville, MD	Moderate	2.2 mi, 100 ft
22	Little Bennett Regional Park	99	Clarksburg, MD	Moderate	6.6 mi, 300 ft
23	Patapsco Valley State Park	103	Elkridge, MD	Difficult	6.9 mi, 1,300 ft
24	Greenwell State Park	107	Hollywood, MD	Moderate	4.5 mi, 290 ft

Estimated Time	Fee	Good for Kids	Dogs Allowed	Public Transit	X-C Skiing	Snow-Shoeing	Trip Highlights
1.5-2.0 hrs	$	✓	✓				Shoreline views, boats for rent
2.0-2.5 hrs		✓	✓	✓			Excellent loop hike through secluded second-growth forest
2.0-2.5 hrs		✓	✓	✓	✓	✓	Birding trail, fishing piers; good for all ages
5.5-6.0 hrs	$						True mountain trails, pristine waterfall
2.0-2.5 hrs	$	✓	✓				Quiet, beautiful farm country
3.0-3.5 hrs			✓				Challenging hike, wildflower-rich trails
2.0- 2.5 hrs			✓				Butterfly hotspot
2.5-3.0 hrs		✓	✓		✓	✓	Peaceful trail with many flora- and fauna-sighting opportunities
4.0-4.5 hrs		✓	✓	✓	✓	✓	Views of C&O Canal, Potomac River, and old railway crossings
4.0-4.5 hrs	$						Spectacular hike to Mather Gorge overlooking Potomac River
1.5 hrs		✓	✓		✓	✓	Rolling farmland, rustic trails, and horses, butterflies, and deer
3.0-3.5 hrs			✓		✓	✓	Rolling hills, historic mills, barns, and schoolhouses
3.0 hrs	$		✓				Tranquil Cascade Falls
2.5-3.0 hrs	$	✓	✓				Pine forests, agricultural fields, tidal creeks, sandy beaches

#	Trip	Page	Location	Difficulty	Distance and Elevation Gain
	WASHINGTON, D.C.				
25	Theodore Roosevelt Island and the Potomac Heritage Trail	113	Arlington, VA, and Washington, D.C.	Easy	4.7 mi, 160 ft
26	Potomac River: Georgetown to Lincoln Memorial	118	Arlington, VA, and Washington, D.C.	Easy	5.7 mi, 130 ft
27	National Arboretum	123	Northeast Washington, D.C.	Easy-Moderate	8.2 mi, 800 ft
28	Kenilworth Aquatic Gardens	129	Kenilworth, Washington, D.C.	Easy	2.5 mi, minimal
29	Rock Creek Park	134	Washington, D.C.	Moderate	6.0 mi, 840 ft
30	Around Georgetown	138	Georgetown, Washington, D.C.	Moderate	6.9 mi, 800 ft
31	East Potomac Park and Hains Point	142	Southwest Washington, D.C.	Easy-Moderate	4.5 mi, 30 ft
32	The National Mall	149	Washington, D.C.	Easy-Moderate	3.7 mi, downslope
	VIRGINIA				
33	Prince William Forest Park	159	Quantico, VA	Moderate-Difficult	7.9 mi, 600 ft
34	Sky Meadows State Park	164	Paris, VA	Moderate	5.8 mi, 1,000 ft
35	Mason Neck State Park	168	Lorton, VA	Moderate	5.4 mi, 250 ft
36	Leesylvania State Park	173	Woodbridge, VA	Moderate	7.8 mi, 650 ft

Estimated Time	Fee	Good for Kids	Dogs Allowed	Public Transit	X-C Skiing	Snow-Shoeing	Trip Highlights
2.0–2.5 hrs		✓	✓	✓			Secluded and woodsy landmass between Arlington and D.C.
2.5 hrs		✓		✓			Georgetown riverfront, iconic D.C. buildings and monuments
4.5–5.0 hrs		✓	✓	✓			15 special collections of flora and fauna from around the world
1.5–2.0 hrs		✓	✓	✓			Artificially constructed ponds teeming with water lilies and lotuses
2.5–3.0 hrs		✓	✓	✓			Natural oasis of 1,700 hilly, wooded acres with challenging trails
3.5 hrs		✓	✓	✓			Secluded, woodsy hike in the heart of Northwest Washington
3.0–3.5 hrs		✓	✓	✓	✓	✓	Memorials of founders, four bodies of water, cherry trees
3.0 hrs		✓	✓	✓	✓	✓	Art spaces and landscaped gardens
4.5–5.0 hrs	$		✓				Protects more than 15,000 acres; numerous trail options
3.0 hrs	$		✓		✓	✓	Incredible blend of pastures and woodlands
2.5–3.0 hrs	$		✓				Stunning array of winged predators, including bald eagles
3.5–4.0 hrs	$		✓				Well-maintained trails on peninsula surrounded by Potomac River

#	Trip	Page	Location	Difficulty	Distance and Elevation Gain
37	Bull Run Mountains Natural Area	177	Haymarket, VA	Moderate	3.5 mi, 810 ft
38	G. Richard Thompson Wildlife Management Area	181	Delaplane, VA	Difficult	8.8 mi, 1,750 ft
39	Riverbend Park and Great Falls Park	186	Great Falls, VA	Moderate	6.8 mi, 1,100 ft
40	Huntley Meadows Park	192	Hybla Valley, VA	Easy	1.5 mi, minimal
41	Fraser Preserve	197	Great Falls, VA	Moderate	2.6 mi, 125 ft
42	Wildcat Mountain Natural Area	201	Warrenton, VA	Moderate-Difficult	3.4 mi, 840 ft
43	Washington & Old Dominion Trail and Cross County Trail	205	Vienna, VA	Easy	12.0 mi, 230 ft
44	Bull Run–Occoquan Trail	210	Manassas, VA	Moderate	7.8 mi, 470 ft
45	Scott's Run Nature Preserve	215	McLean, VA	Difficult	2.8 mi, 710 ft
46	Mount Vernon Trail–Fort Hunt Park to Mount Vernon	220	Mount Vernon, VA	Moderate	8.2 mi, 400 ft
47	Old Rag	224	Etlan, VA	Difficult	8.8 mi, 2,510 ft
48	Harpers Ferry to Maryland Heights	229	Harpers Ferry, WV	Difficult	7.6 mi, 1,670 ft
49	Manassas National Battlefield Park	235	Manassas, VA	Moderate	5.4 mi, 900 ft
50	Meadowlark Botanical Gardens	241	Tysons Corner, VA	Easy	3.8 mi, 360 ft

Estimated Time	Fee	Good for Kids	Dogs Allowed	Public Transit	X-C Skiing	Snow-Shoeing	Trip Highlights
2.0–2.5 hrs		🚶	🐕				Closest mountain range to D.C., ancient quartzite outcroppings
4.5–5.0 hrs			🐕				2,200 feet above sea level; Virginia's best display of trillium
4.0–4.5 hrs			🐕				Dynamic views of the Potomac River
1.0 hr		🚶	🐕				Freshwater marsh supporting more than 200 species, prime birding
2.0 hrs		🚶				🐾	Wildflowers, rushing stream; peaceful and secluded
2.0 hrs			🐕				Scenic hiking in Blue Ridge foothills
4.5–5.0 hrs			🐕		⛷	🐾	Paved hike/bike path, historic Colvin Run Mill
4.0 hrs	$		🐕				Remote trail through rural land
2.0–2.5 hrs			🐕				Strenuous hike overlooking Potomoac River
3.5–4.0 hrs			🐕				Continual views of Potomac River
5.0–5.5 hrs	$						One of area's most popular hikes
4.0–4.5 hrs			🐕				Challenging hike, gorgeous surroundings
3.0–3.5 hrs	$	🚶	🐕		⛷	🐾	Rolling hills, forested solitude
2.0 hrs	$	🚶	🐕				Easygoing trails, wildflowers, wetlands

INTRODUCTION

THE ALLURE OF A HIKE IS THAT IT TAKES US TO A PLACE APART from our everyday, mostly urban and indoor life, where we can breathe deeply and actively engage with the outdoors. Day hikes are especially attractive because they don't require the time, planning, or expense that a longer journey into the wilderness might. They are accessible and close to home, and can easily fit into the course of an ordinary weekend. What's particularly special about the 50 hikes described in this guide is the intense richness of trail experiences available in and around the nation's capital.

There is great variety in the terrain and ecology of the D.C. region, where wildlife abounds and extraordinary vistas and sites speak to our historical roots. Parks, arboretums, meadows, forests, mountains, wildlife management areas, canals, and Civil War battlefields are all within a 70-mile drive.

Based on elevation gain, distance, and estimated time, most hikes in this book are classified as "moderate." There are more than a dozen "easy" hikes, ten in Maryland alone. The "difficult" hikes include Harpers Ferry, Old Rag, Thompson Wildlife Management Area, and Patapsco Valley State Park. Including time for planning, packing, and driving, you'll find a wonderful array of hikes you can complete in less than 5 or 6 hours. Best of all, each hike included in this guide is an opportunity to discover something new.

Let's start in the backyard, with hikes that are mostly accessible by public transportation. Within the District of Columbia, the Around Georgetown hike appears at first glance to be a simple stroll through northwest neighborhoods. Yet it offers an 800-foot elevation gain within a diverse and interesting landscape. There are greenbelts, bridges, sculptures, canals, a quarry, cemeteries, and an amusement park. The East Potomac Park trip visits the founders' memorials, four bodies of water, and D.C.'s famous cherry trees.

Maryland offers hikes in the Appalachian Mountains, in the Piedmont foothills, and on the coastal plain. From Black Hills Regional Park to Chesapeake watersheds to the shores of the Potomac, these contrasting landscapes offer distinct hiking experiences. For example, Sugarloaf is a stand-alone mountain, or "monadnock," with a unique ecosystem. Calvert Cliffs State Park contains 100-foot-high cliffs, formed 18 to 15 million years ago during the Miocene epoch, where 600 species of fossils have been identified. To learn more about the Civil War, hike over the blood-soaked ground of Antietam National Battlefield, where the horrendous losses suffered during that battle are still palpable after 150 years. Or head to Watkins Regional Park for some family fun featuring farm animals, mini golf, and a carousel.

West of D.C., northern Virginia offers tidal marshlands, the Piedmont, and, in the western part of the state, the Blue Ridge and Bull Run mountains. Hikes can be found at Old Rag, Prince William Forest Park, and the G. Richard Thompson Wildlife Management Area. Beautiful meadows, such as at Meadowlark Botanical Gardens, Huntley Meadows Park, and Sky Meadows, are known for their flowers, birds, and butterflies. Fraser Preserve is a peaceful and secluded spot to spend a few hours near a rushing stream and wildflowers.

Closer to D.C., Manassas National Battlefield Park, another Civil War venue, gives you the chance to both relive history and get exercise. Close by among the 19 hikes in Virginia, Riverbend and Great Falls parks, along the Potomac Heritage National Scenic Trail, provide an opportunity to see powerful falls and deep gorges where the river crosses the fall line between the Appalachian Piedmont and the Atlantic coastal plain. Seeing the challenges to canal traffic up close will help you appreciate why the canals failed, though those who tried to make them work are to be admired.

One hike in West Virginia, 60 miles northwest of D.C., goes from Harpers Ferry, the site of John Brown's insurrection, past Civil War camps and to Union Stone Fort, on Maryland Heights. From the confluence of the Potomac and Shenandoah rivers, the trail connects briefly with the Appalachian Trail—which runs 2,175 miles from Springer Mountain in Georgia to Mount Katahdin in Maine—and follows the ridgeline to a spectacular overlook that is well worth the effort.

Whichever hikes you choose, you'll want to savor each one, going backward and forward, looping, lengthening, or truncating as time and weather allow. Whether a short walk or a long adventure, each trip will offer you respite and renewal, and a chance to experience the natural and cultural bounty that surrounds the nation's capital.

ACKNOWLEDGMENTS

I WOULD LIKE TO ACKNOWLEDGE THE INVALUABLE, up-to-date information provided by Elizabeth Stoffel of the American Chestnut Land Trust, Faye McKinney of the Virginia Department of Conservation and Recreation, and Daniel Akwo of the Maryland Department of Natural Resources. The glossy, topographic Maryland state park maps in particular were welcome tools in compiling distances and elevation gains.

A heartfelt and humble thank-you goes to my mother and father, Pamela and Stephen Mauro, who helped me meet tight deadlines by taking notes and photographs of several of these day hikes. Thanks also to friends and hiking partners who accompanied me and made this project such an enjoyable one: Sarah Winnan, Jesse and Megan Mahle, Ryan and Beth McAleer, Gregory Tavormina, and Brian Bowman. Finally, special thanks to my colleague and co-author Beth Homicz, whose enthusiasm for history and hiking rings loud and clear in her trip descriptions and essays; to AMC member Sunny Steadman for her help in editing and fact-checking the trail descriptions; to AMC member and Information Volunteer Richard Hillman; and to Tommy Kankowski.

—Stephen Mauro, 2011

"A labor of love." It hadn't occurred to me, until I set out to work on *AMC's Best Day Hikes Near Washington, D.C.*, that the more I labored on this book, the more reasons I would gain to love its subject matter—that it isn't merely a matter of laboring because of one's love, but also of birthing a deeper love through the labor process. I should have remembered my early tour-guiding days, when master guides with ten or 30 years' experience—Walter Berny, Ruth Croan, Nellie Kerr, and so many magnificent others—helped my nascent enchantment with the federal city blossom into full-fledged fascination. They did so in two ways: first, by teaching me countless facts I hadn't known, then connecting them via human-interest stories to concepts already understood; second, by humbly speaking and honestly embodying the creed that kept them young at any age: "There is always *so much more* to learn about Washington!" I thank them with all my heart, and I hope you too will feel the fascination—and the love—as you read, walk, and explore.

My warmest thanks go out to the true professionals at AMC Books, who clearly love what they do and who made this guidebook a gorgeous reality you now can hold in your hands. Publisher Heather Stephenson invited me to co-author this guide and, with her quiet strength, beautifully led the entire team from glimmer-in-the-eyes to finished product. Dan Eisner, the initial editor for this book, brought wit and humor to our work together; Editor Kimberly Duncan-Mooney took over the project in mid-stride with kind grace and perfect aplomb, never missing a beat. Production Manager Athena Lakri's excellent eye and strong dedication were invaluable. And my co-author, Stephen Mauro, was a rich source of ideas for hikes, essay topics, and research directions...and of some hearty chuckles.

Thanks are certainly due, and gladly offered, to the knowledgeable public servants who aided me greatly in my research, and/or in orienting myself to their parks' offerings: Carole Bergmann (Maryland–National Capital Park and Planning Commission); Angelia R. Collins, Gabrielle Tayac, Ph.D., and Dennis Zotigh (National Museum of the American Indian); Callan Bentley (Northern Virginia Community College [Annandale], Department of Geology); Dennis Hartnett (Patuxent Research Refuge); Kathy Garrity, Don Herring, Carolyn Hyman, Annette Moody, Eileen Niveria, Joseph O'Neill, and Sophie Shiaris (Prince George's County Department of Parks and Recreation); and Kandace Muller (Shenandoah National Park).

I would like to give special appreciation to the following not-for-profit and volunteer associations, whose members' bottomless contributions of love, knowledge, and hard work made themselves deeply felt along all of my hiking and research journeys, both literal and virtual: Anacostia Watershed Restoration Partnership; Anacostia Watershed Society; BikeWashington.org; CCC Legacy; Civilian Conservation Corps Museum; Coalition for the Capital Crescent Trail; Historical Society of Washington, D.C.; National Association for Olmsted Parks; The Nature Conservancy; Potomac Appalachian Trail Club; Prince George's Audubon Society; Rails to Trails Conservancy; Shenandoah National Park Association; and TheWashCycle.com.

During part of the writing of this book, I was living in Arizona, commuting between coasts and receiving welcome aid from friends. Loving thanks to Brian Babb for helping me learn to use his handheld GPS device, for feeding my now-departed cat Seashell while I was off hiking, and for "standing alone together" with me for the years we shared. Harley Cupp Jr. and Dale Thomas hosted me in their home with special style and warmth. Patricia Neimeyer and Lisa Claverie of USA Student Travel/WorldPass Travel Group were of great help in my travel planning. And I'm deeply grateful for the gifts that my parents, Maureen Schultz and Bruce and Michele Homicz, have bestowed: encouragement, love, and support of my work—on this book and in everything I do.

Lastly, a shout-out of gratitude to all the hikers, recreators, fishing enthusiasts, maintenance workers, and volunteers I encountered along the trails—many of whom will always be anonymous, but whose good conversation, contagious enjoyment, and local wisdom were priceless.

—Beth Homicz, 2011

HOW TO USE THIS BOOK

WITH 50 HIKES TO CHOOSE from, you may wonder how to decide where to go. The locator map at the front of this book will help you narrow down the trips by location, and the At-a-Glance Trip Planner that follows the table of contents will provide more information to guide you toward a decision.

Once you settle on a destination and turn to a trip in this guide, you will find a series of icons that indicate whether the hike is a good place for kids, if dogs are permitted, if it's accessible via public transportation, whether snowshoeing or cross-country skiing is recommended there, and whether there are fees.

Information on the basics follows: location, difficulty rating, distance, elevation gain, estimated time, and available maps. The ratings are based on the authors' perceptions and are estimates of what the average hiker will experience. You may find the hikes to be easier or more difficult than stated. The estimated time is also based on the authors' perceptions. Consider your own pace when planning a trip.

The elevation gain is calculated by subtracting the elevation of the trip's lowest point from the elevation of its highest point. It does not account for every dip and rise along the route. Information is included about the relevant U.S. Geological Survey (USGS) maps, as well as about where you can find trail maps. The trip overview summarizes what you will see on your hike.

The directions explain how to reach the trailhead by car and, for some trips, by public transportation. Global Positioning System (GPS) coordinates for parking lots are also included. When you enter the coordinates into your GPS device, it will provide driving directions. Whether or not you own a GPS device, it is wise to consult an atlas.

In the Trail Description sections, you will find instructions on where to hike, the trails on which to hike, and where to turn. You will also learn about the natural and human history along your hike, plus information about flora, fauna, and any landmarks and objects you will encounter.

The trail maps that accompany each trip will help guide you along your hike, but it would be wise to also take an official trail map with you. Maps are often—but not always—available online, at the trailhead, or at the office or visitor center.

Each trip ends with a More Information section that provides details about the locations of bathrooms, access times, fees (if any), the property's rules and regulations, and contact information for the agencies that manage the places where you will be hiking.

TRIP PLANNING AND SAFETY

WHILE THE HIKES DETAILED IN THIS GUIDE aren't particularly dangerous, you'll still want to be prepared. Some of the walks traverse moderately rugged terrain along rocky hills, while others lead to ponds and meadows where you'll have extended periods of sun exposure. Some locations have complex trail networks based on old cart and carriage roads—a number of which are unmarked. Allow extra time in case you get lost.

You will be more likely to have an enjoyable, safe hike if you plan ahead and take proper precautions. Before heading out, consider the following:

- Select a hike that everyone in your group is comfortable taking. Match the hike to the abilities of the least capable person in the group. If anyone is uncomfortable with the weather or is tired, turn around and complete the hike another day.
- Plan to be back at the trailhead before dark. Before beginning your hike, determine a turnaround time. Don't diverge from it, even if you have not reached your intended destination.
- Check the weather. If you are planning a ridge or summit hike, start early so you will be off the exposed area before the afternoon hours when thunderstorms most often strike, especially in summer.
- Bring a pack with the following items:
  - ✓ Water: Two quarts per person is usually adequate, depending on the weather and the length of the trip.
  - ✓ Food: Even if you are planning just a 1-hour hike, bring high-energy snacks such as nuts, dried fruit, or snack bars. Pack a lunch for longer trips.
  - ✓ Map and compass: Be sure you know how to use them. A handheld GPS device may also be helpful, but is not always reliable.

✓ Headlamp or flashlight, with spare batteries

✓ Extra clothing: rain gear, wool sweater or fleece, hat and mittens

✓ Sunscreen

✓ First-aid kit, including adhesive bandages, gauze, nonprescription pain-killers, and moleskin

✓ Pocketknife or multitool

✓ Waterproof matches and a lighter

✓ Trash bag

✓ Toilet paper

✓ Whistle

✓ Insect repellent

✓ Sunglasses

✓ Cell phone: Be aware that service is unreliable in rural areas. If you are receiving a signal, use the phone only for emergencies to avoid disturbing other hikers.

✓ Binoculars (optional)

✓ Camera (optional)

- Wear appropriate footwear and clothing. Wool or synthetic hiking socks will keep your feet dry and help prevent blisters. Comfortable, waterproof hiking boots will provide ankle support and good traction. Avoid wearing cotton clothing, which absorbs sweat and rain and contributes to an unpleasant hiking experience. Polypropylene, fleece, silk, and wool all wick moisture away from your body and keep you warm in wet or cold conditions. To help avoid bug bites, you may want to wear pants and a long-sleeve shirt.

- When you are ahead of the rest of your hiking group, wait at all trail junctions until the others catch up. This avoids confusion and keeps people from getting separated or lost.

- If you see downed wood that appears to be purposely covering a trail, it probably means the trail is closed due to overuse or hazardous conditions.

- If a trail is muddy, walk through the mud or on rocks, never on tree roots or plants. Waterproof boots will keep your feet comfortable. Staying in the center of the trail will keep it from eroding into a wide hiking highway.

- Leave your itinerary and the time you expect to return with someone you trust. If you see a logbook at a trailhead, be sure to sign in when you arrive and sign out when you finish your hike.

- After you complete your hike, check for deer ticks, which carry the dangerous Lyme disease.

- Poison ivy is always a threat when you're hiking. To identify the plant, look for clusters of three leaves that shine in the sun but are dull in the shade. If you do come into contact with poison ivy, wash the affected area with soap as soon as possible.
- Wear blaze-orange items during hunting season. Yearly schedules are available at www.dnr.state.md.us and www.dgif.virginia.gov/hunting.
- Biting insects are present during warm months, particularly in the vicinity of wetlands. They can be a minor or significant nuisance, depending on seasonal and daily conditions. One serious concern is the eastern equine encephalitis virus (commonly referred to as EEE), a rare but potentially fatal disease that can be transmitted to humans by infected mosquitoes. The threat is greatest in the evening hours, when mosquitoes are most active.
- There are a variety of options for dealing with bugs, ranging from sprays that include the active ingredient diethyl-meta-toluamide (commonly known as DEET), which can cause skin or eye irritation, to more skin-friendly products. Head nets, which often can be purchased more cheaply than a can of repellent, are useful during especially buggy conditions.

These measures will help ensure a pleasurable hiking experience for explorers of all ages, and a positive experience will encourage young children in particular to maintain an interest in the outdoors.

LEAVE NO TRACE

THE APPALACHIAN MOUNTAIN CLUB is a national educational partner of Leave No Trace, a nonprofit organization dedicated to promoting and inspiring responsible outdoor recreation through education, research, and partnerships. The Leave No Trace program seeks to develop wildland ethics—ways in which people think and act in the outdoors to minimize their impact on the areas they visit and to protect our natural resources for future enjoyment. Leave No Trace unites four federal land management agencies— the U.S. Forest Service, the National Park Service, the Bureau of Land Management, and the U.S. Fish and Wildlife Service—with manufacturers, outdoor retailers, user groups, educators, organizations such as AMC, and individuals.

The Leave No Trace ethic is guided by the following seven principles:

1. **Plan Ahead and Prepare.** Know the terrain and any regulations applicable to the area you're planning to visit and be prepared for extreme weather or other emergencies. This will enhance your enjoyment and ensure that you've chosen an appropriate destination. Small groups have less impact on resources and on the experiences of other backcountry visitors.

2. **Travel and Camp on Durable Surfaces.** Travel and camp on established trails and campsites, rock, gravel, dry grasses, or snow. Good campsites are found, not made. Camp at least 200 feet from lakes and streams, and focus activities on areas where vegetation is absent. In pristine areas, disperse use to prevent the creation of campsites and trails.

3. **Dispose of Waste Properly.** Pack it in, pack it out. Inspect your camp for trash or food scraps. Deposit solid human waste in cat holes dug 6 to 8 inches deep, at least 200 feet from water, camps, and trails. Pack out toilet paper and hygiene products. To wash yourself or your dishes, carry water 200 feet from streams or lakes and use small amounts of biodegradable soap. Scatter strained dishwater.

4. **Leave What You Find.** Cultural or historic artifacts, as well as natural objects such as plants and rocks, should be left as found.

5. **Minimize Campfire Impacts.** Cook on a stove. Use established fire rings, fire pans, or mound fires. If you build a campfire, keep it small and use dead sticks found on the ground.

6. **Respect Wildlife.** Observe wildlife from a distance. Feeding animals alters their natural behavior. Protect wildlife from your food by storing rations and trash securely.

7. **Be Considerate of Other Visitors.** Be courteous, respect the quality of other visitors' backcountry experiences, and let nature's sounds prevail.

AMC is a national provider of the Leave No Trace Master Educator course. AMC offers this 5-day course, designed especially for outdoor professionals and land managers, as well as the shorter 2-day Leave No Trace Trainer course, at locations throughout the Northeast.

For Leave No Trace information and materials, contact Leave No Trace Center for Outdoor Ethics, P.O. Box 997, Boulder, CO 80306. Phone: 800-332-4100 or 302-442-8222; fax: 303-442-8217; web: www.lnt.org. For information on the AMC Leave No Trace Master Educator training course schedule, see www.outdoors.org/education/lnt.

1

MARYLAND

FROM THE APPALACHIAN MOUNTAINS TO THE CHESAPEAKE BAY, from low marshlands to sheer cliff faces, Maryland's topography is greatly varied. Because these hikes include Maryland's Western Shore, the distance covered may be greater than expected in a small state. For example, from Greenwell State Park in the southeast to Catoctin Mountain National Park in the northwest is 100 miles as the crow flies. The extra driving is worth it, however, because Maryland has beautiful green oases, many in the remote watersheds of the Chesapeake Bay on the Western Shore.

Calvert Cliffs State Park rewards intrepid hikers with its sandy cliffs, which are repositories for Miocene-era fossils. American Chestnut Land Trust—in an area founded by federal scientists searching for a cure for the chestnut blight in the 1930s—has hiking in one of the least-developed watersheds of the Chesapeake Bay. Cedarville State Forest, Greenwell State Park, and Piscataway National Park are also excellent Western Shore hiking locales.

North and west of Washington, D.C., approaching the knobby peaks of the Appalachians, are large preserved tracts along the Potomac tributaries—Seneca Creek State Park, Little Bennett Regional Park, and Black Hill Regional Park. McKee-Beshers Wildlife Management Area, where artists flock to paint and photograph the sprawling sunflower fields, and the Billy Goat Trail, which preserves old locks of the Chesapeake & Ohio Canal, are two premiere

Maryland Potomac River hikes. Maryland also boasts unique anomalies such as the privately owned Sugarloaf Mountain, an isolated outcrop of quartzite that Franklin Roosevelt once coveted for a presidential retreat. He settled for a site within the Catoctin Mountains farther north instead, a range of the Appalachians that is also included in this guide.

Closer to the D.C. metropolitan region, Cosca Regional Park, Watkins Regional Park, and Greenbelt Park in Maryland ring the beltway with green buffer zones that break the monotony of suburban row houses. Maryland has several long trails that can be section-hiked over multiple days, including the C&O Canal Trail, the Capital Crescent Trail, and the Northeast Branch Trail.

The Maryland Department of Natural Resources maintains the system of state parks, forests and wildlife sanctuaries, which are among the best in the nation. All of the state parks listed in this section have well-maintained trails, and most have historical sites and excellent visitor centers. Maryland has detailed, waterproof topographic maps available for its state parks, which can be purchased online at shopdnr.com/alltrailguides.aspx.

TRIP 1
PATUXENT RIVER STATE PARK

Location: Sunshine, MD
Rating: Easy
Distance: 2.0 miles
Elevation Gain: 290 feet
Estimated Time: 1.0 to 1.5 hours
Maps: USGS Woodbine; online map at www.visitusa.com/maryland/
maryland-state-parks-images/Central-Maryland/Patuxent-River-
State-Park/pax_river_map.jpg

Total seclusion and easygoing trails are the main draws at Patuxent River State Park, located along its namesake river in northern Montgomery County.

DIRECTIONS
From I-495 (Capital Beltway), take Exit 31 north onto MD 97 (Georgia Avenue), and continue to where MD 97 crosses the Patuxent River. Turn left into the parking lot. *GPS coordinates*: 39° 14.244′ N, 77° 3.352′ W.

TRAIL DESCRIPTION
Patuxent River State Park straddles 12 miles of the upper Patuxent River, which forms the boundary between Montgomery and Howard counties. Although the park provides many hiking opportunities, the Flowing Free Trail system, at the east end of the park near Georgia Avenue, is the only portion that is marked with signs and blazes. It includes Blue, White, Red and Yellow trails.

Be sure to print out a map from the website beforehand because copies are not always available in the plastic container at the trailhead. Start at the side of the parking lot opposite the Patuxent River. From the trail sign near the kiosk, follow Blue Trail uphill along the moderately steep dirt path that takes you into the woods. The trail is well marked with blue blazes as it curves right and continues uphill through the woods, along the top of the ridge.

Hike through a mix of young evergreens, hardwoods, and thickets with an occasional mature oak. Except near the parking lot and Georgia Avenue, all is

The Patuxent River, swollen with snowmelt, flows through its namesake park on the border of Montgomery and Howard counties.

quiet and tranquil. Just as the trail heads downhill, turn left at the intersection with White Trail. Move along the side of the ridge past vine-covered trees. Look carefully for the white trail blazes as you head back uphill. Continue the loop to the right, crest the hill, then head down to an area of beech and walnut trees where the trail again intersects Blue Trail.

Near the intersection at post marker 5, take the left fork of Blue Trail along the ridge. Hear and—when the trees are bare—see the Patuxent River at the bottom of the gentle hill. At the next intersection, in an area of sycamore and tulip trees, turn left onto Red Trail. Follow the red blazes across the top of a small ridge and downhill across a wooden bridge over a small creek. Follow the red blazes as the trail loops to the right and becomes an old farm road that heads downhill past a pile of white rocks marking a section of an old stone wall or small structure. Cross an old culvert and arrive at post marker 9 near where Red, Yellow, and Blue trails intersect. Turn left following the yellow blazes across a longer wooden bridge over a larger creek into a grove of tall eastern white pines.

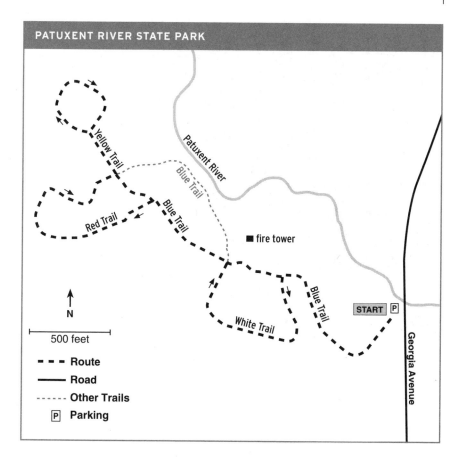

PATUXENT RIVER STATE PARK

fire tower

Yellow Trail

Patuxent River

Blue Trail

Red Trail

Blue Trail

White Trail

Blue Trail

START P

Georgia Avenue

N

500 feet

- - - Route
—— Road
----- Other Trails
P Parking

The trail turns left and then begins a small circular loop to the right through the pine grove. Following the yellow blazes, notice the sentry-like quality of the pines, equally spaced along straight lines, indicating previous government plantings. Several paths cross the grove, so watch carefully for the yellow blazes. Pass a wooden gate that separates the grove from a field and continue around to the right, back to the start of the loop near a large tulip tree.

Turn left back across the wooden bridge past post marker 9 near the trail intersection, then cross the stream at post marker 8. Turn left again onto Blue Trail and follow it across a low ridge and downhill toward the river, passing large trees, mostly tulip trees, on your left. Blue Trail follows a lazy bend in the Patuxent River for a few hundred yards, then moves uphill to the right, away from the river, and rejoins the earlier portion of Blue Trail near the end of the White Trail loop. Turn left on Blue Trail, climb up the moderate hill past the beginning of the White Trail loop, and over the ridge. Follow the trail down the hill across the field back to the parking lot.

Skunk cabbage emerges in early spring at Patuxent River State Park. This wild plant generates heat that enables it to flower even when there is snow and ice on the ground.

MORE INFORMATION

The 6,700-acre park has dense forest and farmlands and offers hunting, fishing, hiking, canoeing, and horseback riding (there is no hunting in the vicinity of Flowing Free Trail). The park is open daily, 8 A.M. to dusk. Access is restricted in the portion that has been designated as a State Wildlands Area. The trailhead is at the parking lot on the south bank of the river where it runs under MD 97 (Georgia Avenue), 6 miles north of Olney, MD. There are no rest rooms near the trailhead. Visit www.dnr.state.md.us/publiclands/central/patuxentriver.asp or call 301-924-2127.

TRIP 2
MERKLE WILDLIFE SANCTUARY

Location: Croom, MD
Rating: Easy to Moderate
Distance: 5.25 miles
Elevation Gain: 440 feet
Estimated Time: 2.5 to 3.0 hours
Maps: USGS Bristol and USGS Lower Marlboro; free sketch map at
visitor center

**Merkle Wildlife Sanctuary was founded as a site for goose breeding
almost 80 years ago and today preserves critical wetlands along the
Patuxent River.**

DIRECTIONS

From I-95/I-495 (Capital Beltway), take Exit 11 onto MD 4 east (Pennsylvania
Avenue) in the direction of Upper Marlboro. Continue on MD 4 and merge
onto US 301 south in Upper Marlboro. Go 1.6 miles, turn left onto Croom
Station Road, and take the next left onto Croom Road (MD 382). Follow it
2.6 miles to St. Thomas Church Road and turn left. The road becomes Fenno
Road; at a sign for the sanctuary, turn left and follow the access road to the
visitor center. *GPS coordinates*: 38° 43.65′ N, 76° 42.50′ W.

TRAIL DESCRIPTION

Merkle Wildlife Sanctuary, astride the Patuxent River in southern Prince
George's County, was an important part of the natural ecosystem even before
Maryland's 1984 Critical Area Act, which protected all land within 1,000 feet
of Chesapeake Bay tidal waters and tributaries. Avid conservationist Edgar
A. Merkle began a goose-breeding program on his farm here almost 80 years
ago. Since the Merkle family sold the 400-acre farm to the state in 1970, the
sanctuary has grown to 1,670 acres. The area now provides winter refuge for
several thousand migrating Canada geese, the largest concentration on Maryland's Western Shore. About 5,000 geese migrate to the sanctuary from mid-
September to December and depart for Canada in late February or March.
About 100 geese stay year-round.

Merkle Wildlife Sanctuary has four hiking trails, all closed to dogs, bicycles, and horses. Poplar Springs Trail is located in the riparian forest buffer

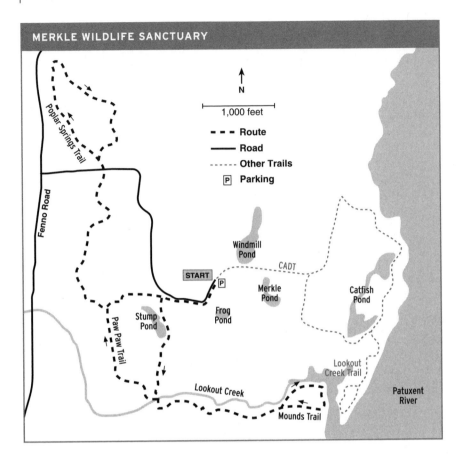

MERKLE WILDLIFE SANCTUARY

zone near the Mattaponi Creek headwater wetland area. Mounds Trail runs south of Lookout Creek along 200-year-old, human-made mounds (more on these later). The short Lookout Creek Trail, accessible only from the Critical Area Driving Tour road (CADT), provides excellent views of Lookout Creek and the Patuxent River. Paw Paw Trail, on which you'll start your hike, features fields, woodlands, and a large pond.

Turn left from the visitor center and follow the asphalt entrance road, passing a kiosk. Just before reaching the woods ahead, turn left into the field on the yellow-blazed Paw Paw Trail. Pass a barn on the left and Stump Pond on the right. Follow the edge of the field and then, at a trail post, enter the woods to the right, following the yellow arrows past a large oak tree, many beech trees, and a bench. At the next trail post, turn left onto Mounds Trail, marked with blue arrows. Hike downhill, cross the wooden bridge over Lookout Creek, and then follow the narrow trail uphill. Turn left at the top of the ravine and pass large yellow poplar, oak, and beech trees, and smaller holly trees.

Zigzag along the top of the ridge with Lookout Creek below on the left. Paralleling the ridge are the long mysterious mounds—4 to 6 feet high and 8 to 10 feet wide. On either side are depressions indicating where the dirt was dug out to form the mounds. Park officials say that these human-made mounds were defensive barriers to thwart British occupation of the area during the War of 1812.

From the ridge top, follow the trail as it takes a sharp turn to the left down the gully to an area of fallen trees, then turns right and climbs the side of the hill above the creek before going down again toward the marshland. Next, you will come upon an eyesore in this relatively unspoiled wildlife refuge—a large pile of junk including appliances, bedsprings, cabinets, sinks, toys, and even a car. Thirty yards past the dump, turn right up the steep hill at the large forked holly tree, then left along the top of the ridge, and then back down toward the marshland to the left.

Where Mounds Trail splits, take the left fork above Lookout Creek and hike through an area of dogwoods, down the side of the ridge to flat marshland, and then back up past a signboard explaining wetlands ecology. Through the trees is a view of the wetlands environment where Lookout Creek flows into the Patuxent River. Continuing down the trail, climb over a section of mounds and return to the start of the loop. Retrace the previous path atop the winding ridge above Lookout Creek, now to the right. Approaching the dump again, look up the hill to the left at a very large oak tree, 7 or 8 feet in diameter and less noticeable when coming from the opposite direction. Follow the trail back down the hill and over the bridge across Lookout Creek.

Turn left at the yellow trail markers and follow Paw Paw Trail downhill across two small footbridges, beneath pawpaw trees that bloom in late spring and bear fruit in early fall. After the second bridge, which crosses the small creek that drains Stump Pond, turn right up the side of the hill. Follow the narrow trail until it comes out into a field. Turn left at the marker post and follow the yellow arrow across the edge of the field to the next line of woods. Turn right at the marker post and walk along the edge of the field until you reach the red-blazed Poplar Springs Trail (the marker at this intersection incorrectly displays a yellow arrow). Turn left onto Poplar Springs Trail and wind through a riparian forest buffer for 0.5 mile before crossing the access road to the sanctuary. In another 150 yards, take the left (west) fork where the trail splits. The sanctuary's champion yellow poplar tree is located just off the west fork. It is part of the Maryland Big Tree Program and stands 154 feet tall.

Follow Poplar Springs Trail down a wide draw and then to the right back up a fairly steep hill. Continue as the trail loops back to the intersection near

Canada geese dot a marshy pond in Merkle Wildlife Sanctuary. These geese were once absent from the Western Shore, but now about 5,000 winter here to feast on marsh and aquatic plants and specially grown corn and millet.

the access road, then cross the road and retrace the previous path, coming out of the woods before returning to the intersection with Paw Paw Trail. Turn left and follow the yellow arrows of Paw Paw Trail along the edge of the field, then enter the woods to the left and hike 250 yards back to the asphalt access road near Stump Pond. Take the road back to the visitor center.

MORE INFORMATION

The sanctuary is open year-round from 7 A.M. to sunset. The visitor center is open Saturdays and Sundays from 10 A.M. to 4 P.M. from Labor Day to Memorial Day, and daily 11 A.M. to 3 P.M. throughout the summer. There is a $2 honor-system service charge for parking at the visitor center. Visit www.dnr. state.md.us/publiclands/southern/merkle.asp or call 301-888-1410.

Besides hiking, Merkle offers excellent bicycling, fishing, and birding opportunities. It provides habitat for a wide variety of birds, including ospreys, hummingbirds, finches, herons, bluebirds, and purple martins. A glass wall at the back of the visitor center opens onto a large pond filled with Canada geese and other waterfowl.

NEARBY

Jug Bay Natural Area is just north of Merkle Wildlife Sanctuary, and offers many more miles of hiking trails that are open to leashed dogs and horses, unlike those at Merkle. Also at Jug Bay is the Duvall Tool Museum, which houses a collection of nineteenth-century farm tools. The 4-mile Chesapeake Bay Critical Area Driving Tour, connecting Merkle and Jug Bay, is open each Sunday from 10 A.M. to 3 P.M. for driving tours, and seven days a week for hikers, bicyclists, and horseback riders.

TRIP 3
CALVERT CLIFFS STATE PARK

$ Ⓧ

Location: Lusby, MD
Rating: Moderate
Distance: 4.8 miles
Elevation Gain: 330 feet
Estimated Time: 2.0 to 2.5 hours
Maps: USGS Cove Point; Maryland official state trail guide

**Calvert Cliffs State Park offers a perfect circuit hike with a halfway
point at a stretch of Miocene-epoch cliffs rich in shark teeth and
other ancient fossils.**

DIRECTIONS

Calvert Cliffs State Park is located on the Western Shore of the Chesapeake
Bay near the mouth of the Patuxent River. From I-95/I-495 (Capital Beltway),
take Exit 11 onto MD 4 east (Pennsylvania Avenue) in the direction of Upper
Marlboro. Travel approximately 36 miles. (MD 4 becomes MD 4/MD 2.) Turn
left onto MD 765 (approximately 14 miles south of the town of Prince Frederick). Follow MD 765 a short distance to the park. Parking is located around
the central picnic area (25 spaces) or at a side lot (40 spaces). *GPS coordinates:*
38° 24.58′ N, 76° 27.10′ W.

TRAIL DESCRIPTION

Calvert Cliffs State Park contains 100-foot high cliffs formed 18 to 15 million
years ago during the Miocene epoch, when a shallow sea covered southern
Maryland. As the sea receded, the cliffs were exposed and began to erode.
More than 600 species of fossils have been identified at Calvert Cliffs, including whale ear bones and skulls, crocodile snouts, pinecones, the dental plate
of a ray, and shark teeth from mako, snaggletooth, requiem, sand, tiger, cow,
and extinct megalodon sharks. The park contains 1,079 acres and has 13 miles
of hiking trails.

Begin the hike on Red Trail (also called Cliff Trail) just to the right of a
pond adjacent to the picnic area. This trail goes 1.8 miles to the cliffs on the
Chesapeake Bay. (Access to the cliff tops is closed because of landslides.)

Cross a bridge over the edge of the pond and follow the trail to the left
that crosses Gray's Creek. Walk beneath white oaks and chestnut oaks. Holly

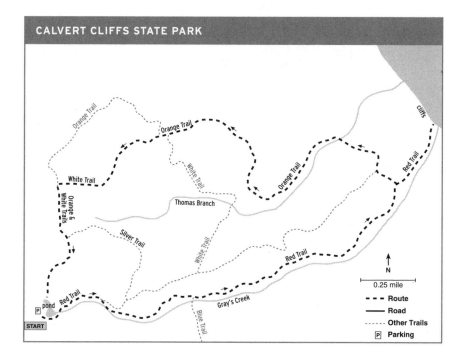

CALVERT CLIFFS STATE PARK

bushes and mountain laurel spread out at eye level, and beach sand dusts the trail underfoot. Turn right onto the gravel service road, and go 50 yards to a right turn back onto Red Trail. Follow the mini rapids of Gray's Creek as it carves its way between ridges. Pass intersections with Yellow Trail (0.2 mile) and Blue Trail (0.6 mile).

At 1.1 miles, the creek reaches an open tidal marsh replete with sunflowers, broad-leaved arrowheads, cold-hardy swamp mallow, invasive arrow arum, spatterdock, and white water lilies. At 1.3 miles, a platform leads out over the marsh to a panoramic (and aromatic) viewpoint and, farther along, fecund pools of arrowhead and water lilies. At 1.6 miles, the trail reconnects with the service road and then passes a network of beaver dams—structures responsible for converting gentle Gray's Creek into a sprawling marsh. At 1.8 miles, reach Chesapeake Bay and the wonderful Calvert Cliffs.

The cliffs are the park's most rewarding sight. Over 100 feet high, they contain the highest concentration of Miocene fossils on the East Coast. Scientists, rock hounds, and children are equally drawn to the cliffs in search of these ancient traces of life 18 to 15 million years ago. Don't be surprised to find people searching with the serious-minded fervor of prospectors! Swimming is allowed at the beach; however, climbing or hiking onto the cliffs is not because the cliffs are fragile and continue to erode at a rate of 3 feet per year.

High tide brings the waves almost to the eroded cliffs at Calvert Cliffs State Park. These cliffs, studded with Cenozoic-era fossils, loom above the Chesapeake Bay shoreline for 30 miles.

Return via Red Trail and turn right onto the service road, climbing 90 feet before a right turn, marked by a wooden pole and Global Positioning Systems (GPS) coordinates, onto Orange Trail. This trail is used much less than Red Trail is. Plunge down the other side of the hill to a 150-foot bridge over Thomas Creek Bog, constructed in 1999 as part of an Eagle Scout project. The bridge affords access to the heart of the freshwater marsh, where sweetgum maples overhead send prismatic sun rays onto a surface ripe with water lilies, arrowheads and, in the summer, swarms of swift-moving dragonflies.

After crossing the bridge, turn 90 degrees to the left and pass through a pine grove, following the edge of the bog as it narrows to a creek bed. Pass a connector trail that comes in from the left (leading to White Trail), and just after it, begin a steep, 80-foot scramble to the top of a ridge. Turn left along the top of the ridge and pass sweetgums and top-heavy pawpaw trees before linking up with White Trail at 3.6 miles. Leave White Trail after a short distance and begin a roller-coaster ride over folded terrain.

Climb the side of a ridge, tracing the hill's contours, and soon enter a grove of monumental yellow poplars and more leafy pawpaw plants. At 4.3 miles into the hike, reach a clearing with cornfields and turn left, passing the intersection with White Trail near a meadow filled with purple milkwort and Queen Anne's lace—the best place in the park to see swallowtail butterflies feasting on the nectar. At 4.6 miles, pass an intersection with Silver Trail and a large fire-warning siren, and then pass some large-leafed paulownia and black locust trees on the left, types not seen anywhere else in the park. Finally, turn right past a gate onto the service road and follow it the final 0.1 mile back to the parking lot.

MORE INFORMATION

There is a $5 entrance fee for the park. Weather-resistant trail maps are for sale at the gate. Dogs are not allowed in the park, and camping is limited to youth groups. There is also a recycled tire playground, probably the ultimate stop for children visiting the park. Portions of Calvert Cliffs State Park are open to hunting, including areas crossed by Orange Trail, so be alert and wear bright colors during fall deer season and spring turkey season. Visit www.dnr.state. md.us/publiclands/southern/calvertcliffs.asp or call 301-743-7613.

NEARBY

Middleham Chapel, an Episcopal church constructed in 1748, is situated just north of the park entrance on MD 765. Also nearby are Flag Ponds Park (farther north on MD 2) and the Battle Creek Cypress Swamp Sanctuary, a 100-acre site that is one of the northernmost habitats of the bald cypress tree.

TRIP 4
CEDARVILLE STATE FOREST

$ 🐕

Location: Waldorf, MD
Rating: Easy
Distance: 9.2 miles
Elevation Gain: 400 feet
Estimated Time: 4.5 hours
Maps: USGS Brandywine; Maryland Department of Natural
Resources Trail Guide (www.dnr.maryland.gov/publiclands)

Cedarville State Forest offers 3,500 acres of forested bottom land as well as access to the largest freshwater swamp in Maryland.

DIRECTIONS
From I-95/I-495 (Capital Beltway), take Exit 7A onto MD 5 south (Branch Avenue) toward Waldorf. After 10 miles, MD 5 merges with US 301 south. Two miles farther, turn left onto Cedarville Road (a brown state forest sign marks the turn). Where the road forks near a factory, stay to the right. Go about 2.0 miles and turn right into the forest entrance at Bee Oak Road. Stop at the visitor center and pay the honor-system fee, and then continue to Forest Road. Turn right and park at the ten-space lot near the picnic tables. *GPS coordinates:* 38° 38.62′ N, 76° 49.02′ W.

TRAIL DESCRIPTION
Cedarville State Forest was established under the auspices of the Civilian Conservation Corps (CCC). From 1933 until 1942, a unit of almost 200 men, mostly African-Americans, built foot and horse trails, fire roads, lookout towers, bridges, public latrines, and charcoal kilns. The barracks and blacksmith shop were located in the northeast corner of the park, where the maintenance complex now stands. Cedarville has five different trails, all color-coded and well marked. Orange Trail leading from the visitor center is the longest, but the trails covered in this hike description include White, Blue, and Green trails. The first half of Orange Trail is a nice walk, but much of its second half passes by campgrounds, playgrounds, picnic sites, and parking lots. The southern trails are more secluded.

Start at Blue (Heritage) and White (Birdwatcher) trails off Forest Road. Examine the charcoal kiln, constructed and operated by the CCC; it is one of three

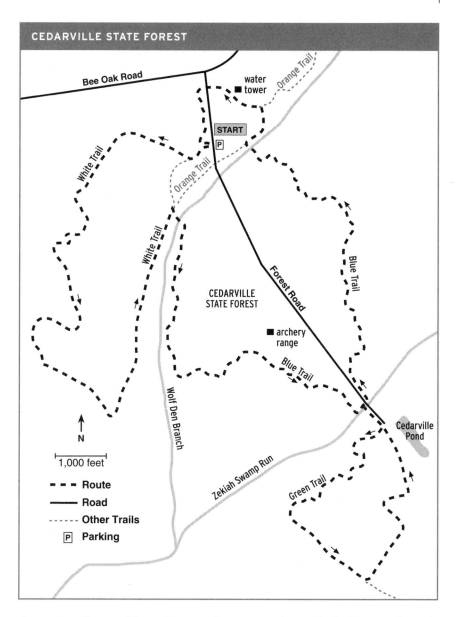

CEDARVILLE STATE FOREST

Bee Oak Road

water ■ tower

Orange Trail

START
P

White Trail

Orange Trail

White Trail

CEDARVILLE
STATE FOREST

Forest Road

Blue Trail

■ archery range

Blue Trail

Wolf Den Branch

N

1,000 feet

- - - Route
——— Road
----- Other Trails
P Parking

Zekiah Swamp Run

Green Trail

Cedarville Pond

that originally stood here, burning the surrounding oak, hickory, and maple on a revolving cycle and producing 3,600 pounds of charcoal per week for the camp. Proceed to the trailhead, make an immediate left turn, and then, after 0.2 mile, a right onto the combined Orange and White trails. Cedarville's prevailing habitat of massive sweetgums, red maples, oaks, willow oaks, and yellow poplars provides canopy, and holly bushes underneath create a natural three-dimensional pavilion. Virginia pines stand as solitary evergreen representatives among the deciduous trees. At 0.3 mile, cross a wooden bridge over a stream. After 0.6 mile, cross another stream, travel up a short incline, and at the 1.0 mile mark, turn left where White Trail abandons Orange Trail.

The trail follows Sunset Road (a seldom-used firebreak) for a short distance before plunging left into a needle-carpeted, aromatic pine grove. At 2.5 miles into the hike, reach an intersection with a sand-and-gravel cut. Turn left, following the cut, then veer to the left and uphill. Here the trail is straight and wide. Over the hill, the pines give way to deciduous giants. At the 3.5-mile mark is a swampland runoff featuring cattails and buttonbush, with water boatmen and dragonflies skidding across water that feeds Wolf Den Branch.

Turn right after 4.0 miles onto Blue Trail where a wooden bridge spans Wolf Den Branch. Undulating humps traverse drainage areas, and the terrain becomes rugged. Shaggy, almost artificial-looking sphagnum moss mixes with bigger, emerald-green fern. While crossing flat bridges over numerous feeder streams, look to the left and right to see giant oaks, yellow poplars, beeches, sweet gums, and oaks with roots greedily lashed into the streambed and the trail. At 5.0 miles, come to an open, grassy clearing. Pass Cross Road and return to the forest. After another firebreak, enter a tournament-style archery range. Continue as the trail follows a feeder stream and then curves left along Zekiah Swamp Run. Follow the path to a CCC bridge and turn right onto Forest Road.

Travel on the paved roadway past Cedarville Pond for 0.2 mile, and turn right onto the 2.0 mile Green (Swamp) Trail, which traverses the headwaters of Zekiah Swamp. This milewide swamp extends southward through Charles County for 20 miles before entering the Wicomico River. Proceed straight for 0.4 mile. Pass a draw on the left marked with a No Hunting Permit Required sign that leads through a managed hunting area. At 6.5 miles into the hike is a trail marker where Green Trail cuts left and Brown Trail goes straight. Stay on Green Trail. It becomes small and overgrown, and then gradually widens into a soft, piney boulevard that returns to the graveled Forest Road. Go left, and after passing Cedarville Pond again, return to the bridge and turn right back onto Blue Trail.

Here the trail is awash in white pebbles. A mud-caked streambed follows your path, then veers away to the right before another stream tumbles into view on the left. Here the trail roller-coasters up and down through some of the park's most undulating terrain. Go straight at the intersections with Cross Road and travel a path lined with hollies over a series of streambeds. At 8.2 miles, cross another firebreak, go over two more streambeds, and finally cross

A North American box turtle takes to a dirt trail at Cedarville State Park.

the large wooden bridge over the Wolf Den Branch. Turn right onto Orange and Blue trails.

At 8.5 miles, turn left where Blue Trail separates from Orange, cross a feeder stream, and pass a big, blue water tower. The road here is basically a large firebreak. Exit through a gate and cross Forest Road. Navigate the curving Blue Trail back to the parking lot near the kilns.

MORE INFORMATION

There is a $4 fee for entry ($3 for in-state residents). Keep in mind that horses and bikers—especially bikers, who come to enjoy the gentle variances in elevation and complete lack of rocks—share these trails. Bikers should yield to hikers, but tread carefully on sharp bends and stand clear on narrower paths. Dogs are allowed on all the park's trails, but must be on a leash. Hunting is allowed in certain areas of the park, and hikers are advised to wear fluorescent orange in season. (There is no hunting on Sundays.) Visit www.dnr.state. md.us/publiclands/southern/cedarville.asp or call 301-888-1410.

TRIP 5
AMERICAN CHESTNUT LAND TRUST

Location: Prince Frederick, MD
Rating: Moderate
Distance: 6.8 miles
Elevation Gain: 400 feet
Estimated Time: 2.5 to 3.0 hours
Maps: USGS Prince Frederick; sketch map at trailhead barn or on
website (www.acltweb.org)

**The American Chestnut Land Trust offers hiking along pristine,
undeveloped Chesapeake Bay tributaries in Calvert County.**

DIRECTIONS
From I-95/I-495 (Capital Beltway), take Exit 11 onto MD 4 south (Pennsylvania Avenue) in the direction of Upper Marlboro. (MD 4 becomes MD 4/MD 2.) Turn left onto Parkers Creek Road, then turn right onto Scientists' Cliffs Road. Go 0.8 mile to the ACLT parking lot on the left. *GPS coordinates*: 38° 30.76′ N, 76° 31.10′ W.

TRAIL DESCRIPTION
In 1935, retired plant pathologist Flippo Gravatt founded Scientists' Cliffs on Maryland's Western Shore. Gravatt had served for 30 years in the U.S. Department of Agriculture's Bureau of Plant Pathology, documenting the slow, sad destruction of the American chestnut tree. He chose the spot for its many surviving American chestnuts, and soon other federal scientists were building vacation homes in the area. Today the American Chestnut Land Trust (ACLT)—founded in 1986 during a period of renewed interest in chestnut preservation—manages the land around Scientists' Cliffs, in the still-pristine Parker's Creek and Governor's Run watersheds of Calvert County, some 40 miles southeast of Washington, D.C.

There are two separate trail systems on the land, one north of Parker's Creek off Double Oak Road, and one 2.0 miles south off Scientists' Cliffs Road. The south system—which is better marked, offers a long circuit hike, and includes several historical sites—is covered in this trip (see the Nearby section of this trail description for hiking the north tract).

From the parking lot, register at the small barn and take a south-side map, as well as the bird and wildflower lists. Start on the combined Swamp Trail (yellow blazes) and Gravatt Lane (red blazes; named for Flippo Gravatt), forging straight ahead toward the woods. Pass bluebird nests and a mini arboretum of marked pines, hollies, sweet gums, black locusts, red maples, dogwoods, and blackjack oaks. After 300 yards, turn right to stay on the combined trail. Pass a rustic privy, go 100 yards, and turn right onto Swamp Trail, where, departing ridge-running Gravatt Lane, it begins its descent to the watershed.

Proceed 0.5 mile over rolling landscape to a small bridge, where the side trail coming from a fallen chestnut reconnects to Swamp Trail. Continue just 50 more yards and turn right to access the first side trip—a 0.3-mile out-and-back that leads to the Percy Howard Farm site. Take the trail uphill to an open area, veer left, and continue upward to a nineteenth-century barn and the ruins of a house. Howard lived on this land west of Scientists' Cliffs Road from the 1890s to the 1930s, tending tobacco fields that were located to the south near the trailhead.

Return to Swamp Trail and continue along the unnamed stream into the shadow of a big hill rising to the left. The dirt trail becomes a boardwalk, 900 feet long and spanning a beaver-created swamp. The walkway is flooded at points under clear, slow-moving rivulets. After passing a steep side trail on the right, you'll reach the end of the boardwalk, which offers a 360-degree panorama of the swamp (0.4 mile from the Howard Farm spur). Eagle Scouts are working to raise 150-foot sections of the walk here to reestablish the Stream Loop.

Reverse course and return to take the left at the sharp uphill, using the hand rope to steady yourself on a 250-yard ascent to a T junction. Turn right here, onto Cemetery Lane. Hike atop the wooded ridge 500 yards to the Hance-Chesley Cemetery, where gravestones date to the 1700s. Take a brochure from the information board. Y. D. Hance, buried here, bought the Taney Place on Battle Creek, 7.0 miles to the west; it's the ancestral home of Roger Brook Taney, the Supreme Court chief justice who wrote the majority opinion in the Dred Scott case. The Dred Scott decision denied African-Americans basic rights as citizens, thus helping to precipitate the Civil War. Hance was buried here near his ancestral home—the ruins of which are just visible in the woods nearby—upon his death in 1855.

Continue downhill on Cemetery Lane for 80 yards to reach Scientists' Cliff Road, go a short distance, and turn right again. Walk downhill 150 yards (on an ill-maintained trail), reach a small side boardwalk and then reach a T junc-

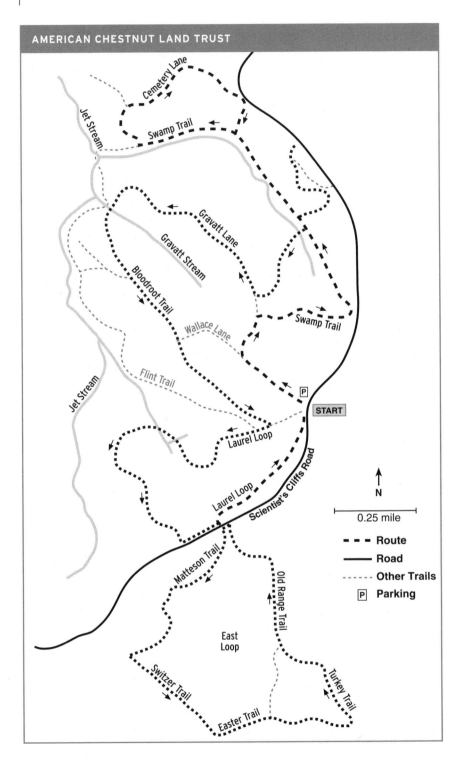

AMERICAN CHESTNUT LAND TRUST

Cemetery Lane

Jet Stream

Swamp Trail

Gravatt Lane

Gravatt Stream

Bloodroot Trail

Wallace Lane

Swamp Trail

Jet Stream

Flint Trail

P

START

Laurel Loop

Laurel Loop

Scientist's Cliffs Road

N

0.25 mile

Matteson Trail

Old Range Trail

East
Loop

Turkey Trail

Switzer Trail

Easter Trail

- - - Route
――― Road
------- Other Trails
P Parking

A four-legged hiker leads the way through a leafy tunnel on the ridge above Jet Stream in the American Chestnut Land Trust. Visitors can find rare hybrid chestnuts among the park's diverse tree canopy.

tion with Swamp Trail (at the main boardwalk). Turn left and hike 350 yards back to the trail at the bridge that leads to the downed chestnut. Pass the remains of the blight-ridden tree, once Maryland's tallest at 75 feet. Turn right and proceed gently downhill. Reach red-blazed Gravatt Lane and turn right (just north of privy).

Travel 0.6 mile, passing through an impressive portal of bamboo and curving along a ridge with a good view of the swamp, before walking 400 feet downhill to Gravatt Stream. Here Stream Trail (yellow) comes in from the swamp and, immediately after the bridge, branches right again. Follow the red blazes left to ascend gently on Bloodroot Trail, where wildflowers—including rare yellow passionflower and large-seeded forget-me-not—bloom in the warmer months. Go about 250 yards and turn left downhill on a small side trail, passing a ravine full of 200-year-old oaks, rare survivors of tobacco field clearance. Turn left onto Flint Trail along Jet Stream, traveling 0.7 mile to a right turn onto Laurel Loop.

Cross a field and skirt an arboretum of hybrid Chinese-American chestnut trees, planted on the site of a 1989 timber harvest. Follow the white blazes through an area rich in scruffy pine trees and mountain laurel, descend to a bridge over a small stream, and then rise to the top of the hike's steepest hill. A bench at the top offers welcome respite. Continue along the edge of private property, travel across a few deep gullies, and reach Scientists' Cliffs Road. Turn left and walk on the shoulder for 100 yards to a parking area (and remember the white blaze and trail sign where Laurel Loop continues).

Cross the road and reach a pair of signs in a cleared grassy area with a large oak tree, one identifying the East Loop and the other asking you to register. After doing so, continue on the easy-to-follow, green-blazed trail through the hilly woodlands. Reach the road close to where you started, cross it and return onto the Laurel Loop for 0.5 mile, following close to the road and passing beautiful, cone-shaped cedars before reaching the starting parking lot.

MORE INFORMATION

Trail maps are available in plastic boxes on the barn in the ACLT parking lot. Beaver activity has flooded a portion of the Stream Loop, which this trail description takes into account, but as of 2010 Eagles Scouts were working to raise the boardwalk and reconnect the loop. Hunting is allowed on both the north and south tracts during the fall season, but not on Sundays (check "Important Message to Hikers" on the website for closures because of hunting). Also note that the ACLT is redoing all the signposts with a numbering system, so signs mentioned may not be up-to-date. Visit www.acltweb.org/explore/trails.cfm or call 410-414-3400.

NEARBY

To reach the north side trails, return to Prince Frederick and turn right onto MD 402 (Dares Beach Road), go 2.5 miles, turn right onto Double Oak Road, go 1.0 mile, turn left at a Double Oak Farm sign, and go a few hundred yards to the parking area and trailhead. A newly blazed, 3.5-mile circuit hike begins here. The ACLT offers guided canoe trips on Parker Creek. For information on amenities and volunteering opportunities, visit www.acltweb.org.

TRIP 6
SENECA CREEK STATE PARK–
CLOPPER LAKE

Location: Germantown, MD
Rating: Moderate
Distance: 4.5 miles
Elevation Gain: 400 to 500 feet
Estimated Time: 2.5 to 3.0 hours
Maps: USGS Seneca, Maryland Department of Natural Resources
Trail Guide (www.dnr.maryland.gov/publiclands/)

**This hike travels underneath towering mature hardwoods, first
following Great Seneca Creek to Clopper Lake and then circling the
lake, and offers excellent shoreline views across open water.**

DIRECTIONS

From I-495 (Capital Beltway) inner loop, take Exit 38 (from outer loop, take
Exit 35) onto I-270 toward Frederick. Take Exit 10 and stay in the right lane to
turn right onto MD 117 (becomes Clopper Road). Travel west approximately
2.0 miles and turn left into the park, then immediately right into the visitor
center parking lot. *GPS coordinates: 39° 9.03′ N, 77° 14.73′ W.*

TRAIL DESCRIPTION

Seneca Creek State Park is a 16.5-mile-long stretch of preserved land along
both sides of Great Seneca Creek. Comprising 6,500 acres, the park starts
just outside of Germantown and continues south to Riley's Lock, the creek's
confluence with the Potomac River, near the McKee-Beshers Wildlife Management Area. The Clopper Lake area is in the northern section of the park.
The park's trail system is extensive—the 25-mile Greenway Trail follows Great
Seneca Creek for its entire distance, and the Schaeffer Farm area has 10 miles
of loops popular with mountain bikers and equestrians. Traveling under the
tall ceilings of old-growth deciduous trees and viewing several crumbling
nineteenth-century mills provides a pleasantly humbling experience.

Start your hike at the visitor center off Clopper Road. The circa-1855
Grusendorf Log House stands nearby on land that was the former estate of
Francis C. Clopper, who along with his descendants built several mills on

Great Seneca Creek. One just to the north near Clopper Road made woolen clothes for Union soldiers in the Civil War, and another near the creek's confluence with the Potomac River cut the red sandstone used to construct the Smithsonian Castle in Washington, D.C.

At the intersection of the entrance road and the parking lot, start on the 1.2-mile, orange-blazed Great Seneca Trail. It immediately descends 100 feet, running parallel to MD 117 through a draw with power lines, a tunnel of dense shrubbery, and between small humps of land that support great sycamores and oaks. Throughout this hike, try to distinguish sycamores (mottled bark with cream-colored under bark) from maples (hard, close-grained bark).

Upon reaching the intersection with Great Seneca Creek, turn left. The 0.6-mile stretch along the creek passes through a lush deciduous forest. The trail is frequently muddy here from floods. The branches of massive oaks, sycamores, maples, and beeches form a lofty, leafy ceiling 40 feet overhead. At a point where a beaver-dammed island splits the water into two channels, the trail bends left under a few large maples and passes through an aromatic pine grove. Enter an open draw, cross a wooden bridge over a seasonal runoff, and return to deep-green pines.

The trail emerges into a second draw, recrossing the power lines encountered earlier. Downy woodpeckers enjoy the poles, and during spring and summer, sprouting wildflowers, with a distinctive woody smell, attract spicebush and tiger swallowtail butterflies. Go past the intersection with Old Pond Trail and over a bridge that spans a trickling tributary. A wide lane runs parallel to the edge of the forest along the power lines for several hundred yards, then plunges back into the woods. Here the moss-covered path winds left and right on a high ridge over Seneca Creek before veering sharply left for an 80-foot ascent to a park road. The road marks the endpoint of Great Seneca Trail.

Cross the road in the direction of Clopper Lake. Turn right on the blue-blazed Lake Shore Trail, which encircles the 90-acre lake. Stream-fed fingers, which you cross via wooden walkway, reach out from Clopper's north and south sides. This hike offers excellent opportunities to see red-shouldered hawks, ospreys, and barred owls fishing for dinner and great blue herons roosting in the treetops. The tree diversity—maples, oaks, sycamores, pines, cedars, hickories, beeches, and yellow poplars—makes for a great variety of reds, oranges, and yellows rimming the lake in autumn. Note that park officials have rerouted the trail away from the immediate shore to higher ground in some areas to restore the natural lakeside environment. Head for higher

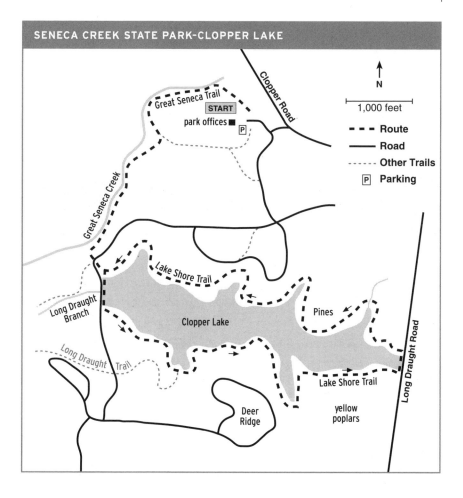

ground whenever the trail forks—the first tree on the correct route is always clearly marked with a blue blaze.

As you loop around the third spur on the north side (after 2.7 miles), continue past the boating center. Stay on Lake Shore Trail until you complete the loop around Clopper Lake. At the intersection with Great Seneca Trail, take a right and retrace your steps along Great Seneca Creek back to the visitor center and parking area.

MORE INFORMATION

There is a $3 entrance fee. The Clopper Lake Boat Center has canoes, kayaks, and paddleboats available for rent, and offers nature tours on the Heron Pontoon Boat in the summer. The center also rents poles, sells bait, and

Clopper Lake in Seneca Creek State Park reflects the sculpted clouds of a brilliant early summer day. Encircling the lake is the 5-mile Lake Shore Trail, and bordering it to the west is Greenway Trail, which follows Great Seneca Creek for 16.5 miles.

offers beginner's classes in fishing. A 32-acre Frisbee golf course is available. Find scorecards and golf discs in the visitor center. Visit www.dnr.state.md.us/publiclands/central/seneca.asp or call 301-924-2127. Check the U.S. Geological Survey (USGS) gauging station on MD 28 for water levels, which should be at 2.1 feet or higher.

NEARBY

Magruder Trail, Black Rock Regional Park, and Little Bennett Regional Park all offer great hiking trails nearby. For an excellent topographical map of the park, visit shopdnr.com/centraltrailguides.aspx.

TRIP 7
McKEE-BESHERS WILDLIFE
MANAGEMENT AREA

Location: Poolesville, MD
Rating: Easy
Distance: 6.0 miles
Elevation Gain: 200 feet
Estimated Time: 3.0 hours
Maps: USGS Sterling

The McKee-Beshers Wildlife Management Area is unique for its alternating fields and woodlands set along the banks of the Potomac River.

DIRECTIONS

From I-495 (Capital Beltway), take Exit 39 onto River Road west. Drive 11 miles, paralleling the Potomac River, to the intersection of River Road and Seneca Road (MD 112). Turn left and continue on River Road for 2.5 miles. Turn left onto Hunting Quarter Road and park in the first lot (a five-spot gravel clearing on the left). *GPS coordinates: 39° 04.79′ N, 77° 22.86′ W.*

TRAIL DESCRIPTION

McKee-Beshers Wildlife Management Area (WMA) has excellent hiking potential. Comprising 2,000 acres and stretching for 2.0 miles along the Potomac River, the carefully managed landscape offers alternating crop fields and woods, and has a large freshwater swamp in the northwest corner with diverse plant life that attracts waterfowl, herons, and egrets. The Potomac-spanning Chesapeake & Ohio Canal National Historic Park (incorporated into this hike) forms the southern boundary of the WMA. Some caveats: Avoid McKee-Beshers in fall and winter, when biologists flood the forests to create "green tree reservoirs" for wood ducks. Steer clear by the start of deer season in late November and during wild turkey season, which starts in April and ends in late May. Also be advised that after heavy rains much of the low-lying area gets wet, so come with appropriate footwear.

From the parking lot, turn left onto Hunting Quarter Road and then immediately turn left past a yellow gate and walk down through a grassy, open

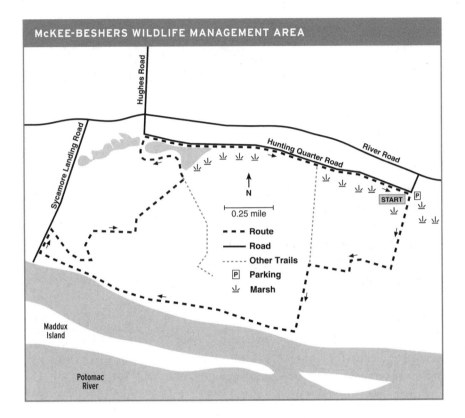

clearing through the woods. After 0.2 mile, the woods give way to an expanse of fields that stretch left and right. In the distance are neatly manicured wood lines that enclose the fields, creating the impression of a giant, open-air coliseum. Eye-catching bird species such as the blue grosbeak, willow flycatcher, red-headed woodpecker, and American goldfinch thrive at this edge habitat. In July and August, a vibrant stand of sunflowers can be seen by walking straight past a large, lone cherry tree at field's edge and continuing past tangles of switchgrass and another strip of woods. At the solitary cherry tree, head west (a left turn if returning from the sunflowers, a right if not), and follow a cleared path through the southern edge of the fields. Go to and through a strip of woods emerging back into open fields and passing a stately pine grove on the left. The trail gently rises before reaching an unmarked gravel trail at 0.8 mile. Turn left to head south in the direction of the Potomac River.

Here the trail alternates between crushed gravel and dirt. On the right, first pass shiny green vegetation that resembles oversized artificial turf and then more natural pavilions of crops surrounded by trees. After 1.3 miles, come to a field, where the trail seems to peter out, and cut straight through to the woods

Acres of sunflower fields attract artists and photographers to the McKee-Beshers Wildlife Management Area in July and August.

on the other side. Continue over a depression that was once the Chesapeake & Ohio (C&O) canal bed and reach the broad, dirt C&O Canal towpath, the elevated walkway from which workers could regulate the canal locks and service the boats. This towpath trail extends for 184.5 miles from Georgetown to Cumberland, Maryland (see Trip 20). Turn right and enjoy a varied canopy of pawpaws, hickories, oaks, black walnuts, pin cherries, sycamores, and elms, along with occasional views of the Potomac River. After almost a mile on the C&O, reach milepost 26 (mileage from the start in Georgetown) and just beyond it the Horse Den Branch campsite, which has a portable toilet and water spigot. Continue for another mile to milepost 27 and, just after a sign that warns of the dangers of the Potomac River, turn right into a circular gravel parking lot.

Pass through the lot and crunch your way north on gravelly Sycamore Landing Road, turning right onto a forest trail just after crossing a one-lane bridge over swampland. This trail bends south and east before veering sharply northward near the headwaters of a small stream. At dusk, the shrill squawks of wild turkeys can be heard as they scramble into the trees to bed down for the night. Ignore a side trail emerging on the left that leads back to Sycamore

Landing Road and follow the main trail as it turns sharply to the right and emerges from the forest at an open, bowl-shaped pavilion of corn. Travel along the edge of the forest, and upon reaching an area where uncut meadow grass rises up on either side near a small sunflower field, turn left toward one of Maryland's largest freshwater marshes. Replete with milkweed, cattail, and water lily, this area has a vegetative but not unpleasant smell, and attracts the Potomac's normal roster of "waders"—great blue herons and egrets—as well as cormorants. The path through the marshes soon connects with Hunting Quarter Road. Turn right and walk for 1.5 miles along the area's northern edge and back to the parking lot.

MORE INFORMATION

McKee-Beshers is part of Maryland's Department of Natural Resources public land system. Its biggest attraction is its wonderfully large sunflower field that blooms in July and August. It is located just off River Road in the northeast section of the WMA, just before the turn for Hunting Quarter Road. Visit www.dnr.state.md.us/wildlife/Publiclands/central/mckeebeshers.asp or call 410-356-9272.

NEARBY

The Kunzang Palyul Choling Buddhist temple, just off River Road between its two intersections with Hunting Quarter Road, has a welcoming gift shop with weekend hours. On the north side of River Road, across from the temple, is Peace Park, a 65-acre park with 2 miles of trails and several sacred structures and meditation gardens, all open to the public.

TRIP 8
WATKINS REGIONAL PARK

Location: Largo, MD
Rating: Easy
Distance: 2.2 miles round-trip
Elevation Gain: 45 feet
Estimated Time: 2.5 to 3.0 hours (including Watkins Nature Center and Old Maryland Farm)
Maps: USGS Lanham; park trail map available online at Prince George's County Department of Parks and Recreation website

Peacocks and pollywogs, owls and llamas, vegetable gardens, good hiking, and family fun await you in this pleasant park. In summer, an antique carousel, miniature golf, and a small-scale train ride add festivity to your visit.

DIRECTIONS
From I-95/I-495 (Capital Beltway), take Exit 15A for MD 214 (Central Avenue) eastbound. Drive approximately 3.0 miles (past Six Flags theme park) and turn right onto MD 193 (Watkins Park Drive). The park entrance is about a mile ahead on the right. Follow the park road toward the nature center, past the playground and farm parking; turn left at a T intersection to arrive at the nature center parking lot on your left. *GPS coordinates: 38° 53.29' N, 76° 47.035' W.*

By public transportation, take Metrorail's Blue Line to the Largo Town Center station. Catch the C26 bus, which will bring you within a quarter-mile of the park entrance. From there, you can walk Loop Trail or Spicebush Trail to the nature center.

TRAIL DESCRIPTION
Watkins Regional Park has *lots* going on—history, live animals (wild and domesticated, from bullfrogs to peacocks), camping, picnic shelters, ball fields, woods and wetlands, miniature golf, a playground, a nature center, lovely nature trails, and even a small-gauge train ride in season. You could easily spend a whole day in the park, and you might decide to do just that once you get here. Created in 1964, the park is named in honor of Robert M. Watkins, a chairman

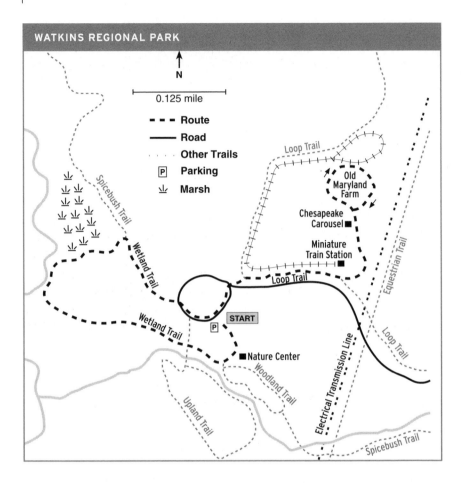

of the Maryland-National Capital Park and Planning Commission, who led efforts to establish open recreational space in Prince George's County.

Begin by walking from the parking lot across the bridge into the nature center, where there are usually several creatures in residence—owls, turtles, and snakes. Baby backpacks and kid-friendly trail activity packs may be borrowed from the nature center (return them here when you depart), and brochures on wildflowers and wildlife are available. You can also ask about Friday night bat hunts and Saturday morning hikes led by park naturalists.

Exit through the rear doors to the trailhead kiosk, crossing over the Frog Pond. At the kiosk, turn right and start to follow the yellow and blue trail markings for Wetland Trail and Spicebush Trail, which run together for a while. A rustic amphitheater will appear on the right, then cross three small footbridges and the green-blazed Upland Trail. The yellow-blazed Wetland Trail curves to the right and climbs a slope, including a couple of steps braced

This curving boardwalk along Watkins Regional Park's Wetland Trail, the Wildlife Overlook, is an inviting vantage point from which to observe beavers, waterfowl, and bald eagles.

with wooden 4x4s. Halfway up the slope, the trail veers left. Now you're on your way into the wetlands. Be prepared for the trail to be muddy if it's rained recently—gravel has been added in some spots for drainage and traction—and take time to search for turtles and tadpoles. Wildflowers of all kinds thrive here too. In spring, look for blue, cream, and yellow violets, wild ginger, and jacks-in-the-pulpit; in summer, look for hyssop and strawberry-like cinquefoil; in late summer and fall, white boneset, mistflower, and Saint-John's-wort.

Cross the curving boardwalk of the wildlife lookout over the marsh, watching for osprey and eagles as well as water critters. Beavers have been known to slap their flat tails for curious hikers too. Watch for a split: The blue-blazed Spicebush Trail veers left, but turn right to continue on the yellow-blazed Wetland Trail. Among the ups and downs of this leg of the trail, keep an eye out for the big, 120-year-old tulip poplars. The trail leads to its terminus at the western end of the nature center parking lot. Continue along the length of the parking area, then, at the eastern end, look for the paved path leading alongside the entrance road to a crosswalk. Take it across the park road and turn right at the Trail to Park Facilities sign, following this paved sidewalk path (which is also part of the park's paved Loop Trail) under a canopy of trees.

Strutting peacocks majestically, proudly—and sometimes rather vocally—guard and herd the turkeys and other fowl at Watkins Regional Park's Old Maryland Farm.

Cross a maintenance driveway, then pass the seasonal snack bar and miniature golf course; the third paved path on the left after the driveway is the narrow Farm Path, and it will curve around to the right (east) of the mini golf area. As you follow it, the big antique Chesapeake Carousel, believed to date from the beginning of the twentieth century and attributed to respected carousel builder/carver Gustav Dentzel, appears on the left, as does the small-gauge train ride. The carousel is considered quite a local gem, brought here and lovingly restored in the 1970s from the nearby bayside town of Chesapeake Beach, a popular summer resort destination in the early 1900s.

As you move along the farm path into the woods, if you begin to hear piercing, agonized-sounding cries, fear not! They're just the calls of the half-dozen or so resident peacocks at the farm, strutting their stuff. There is also a flock of turkeys and chickens, which are vocal at times. Here at the farm are llamas, rabbits, ponies, display gardens, agricultural exhibits and demonstrations, and the Barn Cat Gift Shop—with a very friendly gray cat in residence.

From here, retrace your path back to the nature center parking lot when you're finished taking in the sights, sounds, and learning at the farm.

Note: The latter segment of the trail, from the nature center over to the Old Maryland Farm and back, is an easy-to-follow paved asphalt path. If you are visiting with children young enough to be in a stroller, you might wish to skip the unpaved, rugged, sometimes-muddy Wetland Trail loop portion of the hike (about 1.2 of the total 2.2 miles; its surface includes forest floor, tree roots, gravel, wood chips, and boardwalk), and stick to the nature center building and the out-and-back Farm Path, which is about a mile. The park's Loop Trail is also paved, if you want to stretch your legs a bit more.

MORE INFORMATION

Rest rooms are located in the nature center, which is open Monday through Saturday from 8:30 A.M. to 5 P.M. and Sundays from 11 A.M. to 4 P.M. Old Maryland Farm is open Tuesday through Friday from 9 A.M. to 4 P.M., Saturdays 9 A.M. to 4:30 P.M., and Sundays and holidays 11:30 A.M. to 4:30 P.M., but is closed on Mondays. Visit www.pgparks.com/Things_To_Do/Nature/Watkins_Regional_Park.htm or call 301-218-6700. Attractions are open in season (more or less Memorial Day to Labor Day, plus weekends in September; call ahead to make sure) for visitors of all ages.

TRIP 9
COSCA REGIONAL PARK

Location: Clinton, MD
Rating: Easy
Distance: 1.4 miles round-trip
Elevation Gain: 25 feet
Estimated Time: 2.5 hours (including Clearwater Nature Center)
Map: USGS Piscataway

Cosca Regional Park's Lake Trail and Clearwater Nature Center provide fun and fascination both indoors and out. This easy, pleasant lakeside hike can be surprisingly rich in natural wonders such as herons and owls.

DIRECTIONS

From I-95/I-495 (Capital Beltway), take Exit 7A (Branch Avenue/MD 5 South) and follow Branch Avenue about 2.7 miles (toward Waldorf). Merge right onto the ramp for Old Branch Avenue/Kirby Road and stay in the left lane. Turn left at the light onto Old Branch Avenue and drive 1.7 miles. Go straight as Old Branch becomes Brandywine Road, and continue about a mile (past the Surratt House Museum), then turn right onto Thrift Road. Continue a bit over a mile, passing the main park entrance and group pavilion entrance, and turn right into the Clearwater Nature Center driveway. For the trailhead, park in the small north parking lot section on your right as you approach the nature center. *GPS coordinates: 38° 44.025′ N, 076° 55.047′ W.*

TRAIL DESCRIPTION

Cosca Regional Park—named for former Maryland-National Capital Park and Planning Commission member Louise F. Cosca, who focused her efforts on the well-being of young people—offers plenty of attractions for people both young and more seasoned to enjoy. Camping and picnicking, ball fields and tennis courts, a playground, a seasonal miniature train ride, paddleboating, and fishing are all here, in addition to the hiking and horseback riding trails. Cosca was the first of Prince George's County's three regional parks; its 500 acres opened to the public in 1967, and the Clearwater Nature Center and Cosca Lake were added in 1970.

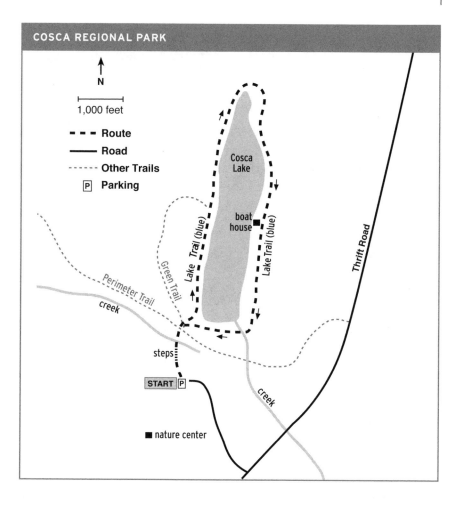

Before your hike, visit the small but charming Clearwater Nature Center, uphill from the parking area. This building, clothed in lava rock, rests in an inviting woodland setting and is accessible for wheelchairs and strollers. It offers a small greenhouse, live animals, and a hands-on exhibit room that's fun for kids. You can lift the bark off a log to see insects burrowing within; try on animal costumes; or visit turtles, hissing cockroaches, chinchillas, lizards, terrapins, and snakes on display. On a recent visit, a rescued Eastern Screech Owl that lost an eye when hit by a car was also resident. Behind the building are birds—eagles, red-tailed hawks, owls, and other birds of prey—as well as butterfly and herb gardens.

Brochures of the park's trails and facilities are available in the nature center. Note, however, that the park map is not to scale nor clearly detailed, and its

Cosca Regional Park's Lake Trail encircles the human-made yet wildlife-rich Cosca Lake, passing by the boathouse where paddleboats and rest room facilities are available seasonally.

trail indicator colors do not exactly correspond with the trail signs you will find "on the ground." So the hike described here differs slightly from what's shown on the park map.

Begin at the trailhead, located at the north end of the three-sectioned nature center parking lot. Walk down the timber steps and across the small creek, looking for wildflowers, such as violets, and ferns as you go. Then, at the trail intersection where four paths face you, take the right-center trail marked with the "Blue" sign. (If you want a slightly longer, more challenging hike, take the trail signed as "Green" straight up the slippery runoff creek bed ahead. Use caution if there has been recent rainfall. Once up the steep slope, the path meanders through sunlit woods and rejoins the blue trail along the western shore of the lake.)

The trail soon opens into a meadowy clearing that can be mucky after rain or thaw. Watch for deer as you walk along the woods of the meadow's western (left-hand) edge. As you approach Cosca Lake at a small inlet, you'll see Lake Trail path. Turn left and follow the path around the lake in a clockwise direction. Watch out for tree roots and muddy spots. More interesting, look out for abundant wildlife. The lake is stocked with bluegill, bass, catfish, and trout, and waterfowl are plentiful, as are aquatic plants. Although human-made, the lake has been in place for more than 40 years and has matured nicely, offering a home to growing wildlife populations. This edge of the lake is said to offer the best fishing too, being farther from the boathouse and other attractions.

Approaching the lake's northern tip, the path becomes rugged in spots, so proceed with caution. You'll cross a footbridge and a zigzag bridge as you round the turn toward a small peninsula, at the top of the lake's eastern shore. Here turtles can be found sunning and swimming in shallow pools, and blue herons are often spotted cruising for their lunch. A large, cheerfully smiling concrete turtle relaxes along the shore (look for its fraternal twin—a Maryland terrapin—a bit farther on). As you approach the boathouse, the path becomes gravel. In summer, the boathouse offers paddleboats for rental and has rest rooms and a snack bar.

Beyond the boathouse, the lakeshore path is paved for a short way. Continue along it, past the concrete terrapin, to the slightly steep slope that climbs the stone berm of the lake's southern edge, which can also be muddy and slippery at times. (Ignore the sign near here for the green trail, which seems to head off toward the campgrounds and away from the nature center.) As you cross the berm, keep an eye on the water: Fishing off the berm is popular, and ducks and geese congregate here. At the berm's far (west) end, descend into the meadow again, and cross the field kitty-corner, following the sign for the nature center to reconnect with the Lake Trail (blue) that leads back through the woods to the five-way intersection. Turn onto the left-center path here to go back across the creek and up the timbered steps to the nature center parking area.

MORE INFORMATION

Cosca Regional Park is administered by the Maryland-National Capital Park and Planning Commission, and the Prince George's County Department of Parks and Recreation. Visit www.pgparks.com/Things_To_Do/Nature/Cosca_Regional_Park.htm or call 301-868-1397. The park is open year-round, 7:30 A.M. to dusk; some facilities such as the boathouse and train ride are open only in the summer season (Memorial Day to approximately Labor Day). Horseback riding is allowed, but no horses are provided on site. Nature programs and special events are offered at the Clearwater Nature Center, open Monday–Saturday 8:30 A.M. to 5 P.M. and Sundays 11 A.M. to 4 P.M. Call the nature center at 301-297-4575 for more information. Rest rooms and water are available at the nature center year-round and at the boathouse in summer.

TRIP 10
PATUXENT RESEARCH REFUGE

Location: Laurel, MD
Rating: Easy
Distance: 2.1 miles round-trip
Elevation Gain: 35 feet
Estimated Time: 2.5 hours
Maps: USGS Laurel; trail map available at the visitor center, and online at the Patuxent Research Refuge website

Grassy meadows and aquatic plants, hardwood forests and holly trees, Canada geese and bald eagles—you'll find all this at the Patuxent Research Refuge, the only national wildlife refuge with a specific mission of wildlife research. Hands-on exhibits help hikers of all ages learn how scientists care for wild creatures.

DIRECTIONS

From I-95/I-495 (Capital Beltway), take Exit 22A and follow the Baltimore–Washington Parkway (MD 295) northbound toward Baltimore. Drive 3.5 miles on the parkway, then take the Powder Mill Road/Beltsville exit and turn right (east) on Powder Mill Road. Drive 1.8 miles, then turn right onto Scarlet Tanager Loop at the brown National Wildlife Visitor Center sign. Follow this one-way entrance road 1.4 miles to the parking lot. When departing, keep right to follow the one-way exit roadway. *GPS coordinates:* 39° 01.628′ N, 76° 47.944′ W.

TRAIL DESCRIPTION

Patuxent Research Refuge, named for nearby rivers in the Chesapeake Bay watershed and established in 1936 as an experiment station, is the only national wildlife refuge with a primary mission of wildlife research. Thanks largely to the refuge's leadership, the bald eagle has been brought back from the brink of extinction and whooping crane populations have grown significantly; their numbers had diminished precariously to 21 birds *worldwide*, but they now number more than 350. Before setting off on your hike, a stop in the National Wildlife Visitor Center is recommended. Say hello to the massive polar bear (taxidermic, of course) and other wild critters on display, a reminder that the U.S. Fish & Wildlife Service manages preservation nationwide in more than

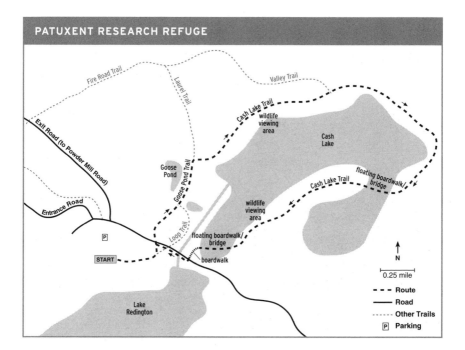

500 National Wildlife Refuge locations, representing very different climates and habitats. Enjoy the 8-minute introductory video, then pop into the glass-walled "viewing pod" to try your hand with its scopes and radio tracking equipment. Check out the exhibits such as the live-scale "Habitats" (enjoyable for kids) and the endangered-species hall "On the Brink," as well as the Hollingsworth Gallery of wildlife art.

Exit the visitor center through the northeast doors and step out onto the paved Loop Trail to begin the hike. You'll immediately see the first of numerous wayside signs focusing on aspects of wildlife management. This one discusses conservation landscaping and invites you into a small, wild garden; others farther along the trail explore utility line right-of-way open spaces, meadow management, and habits of wild birds. Just past two benches, at the first fork, bear to your left to continue on Loop Trail, and cross the tram roadway. At the next intersection, turn left onto Goose Pond Trail (which begins with a wood-chip surface and will become rugged later on) and continue straight until you reach Goose Pond, which will be on the left. Look for nesting boxes atop poles, protected by conical predator guards to keep eggs and young birds safe in the nests. Nesting baskets of straw-filled netting for use by Canada geese can be seen suspended over the water during nesting season (generally mid-March to mid-May).

This bench welcomes hikers at a wildlife viewing area along Patuxent Research Refuge's Cash Lake, where water levels are managed by scientists to support the balance of local wildlife species.

Just past the pond, turn right onto Cash Lake Trail, which veers off into a forest of mainly hardwoods. The tree trunks aren't blazed, but the pathway is well maintained and easily visible. Several good-sized American holly trees are growing in the understory along the trail here. Soon you'll reach the wildlife-viewing area for this shore of Cash Lake, just off the main trail to your right; make a detour to enjoy a quiet spot by the water's edge, where aquatic plants abound. The lake, created in the late 1930s by President Franklin Roosevelt's Civilian Conservation Corps, is one of more than 40 impoundments (artificial bodies of water) on the refuge. Like Goose Pond, its water levels can be managed; in just a bit, as you approach the fishing pier, you'll cross one of the spillways that drain water when needed. Look for beavers, bald eagles, great blue herons, osprey, and the ubiquitous Canada geese.

Continuing along the trail, you'll cross several footbridges, one of which was built as an Eagle Scout project with the support of local sponsors. After going down two sets of wooden-braced steps, you will see a sign for Valley Trail to your left—stay right to continue on Cash Lake Trail toward the fishing pier. A steel bridge here takes you over the drainage spillway mentioned earlier. A rest room is available on the pier. At this point, you can choose to take the boardwalk along the fishing pier or cross the concreted berm. Fishing enthusiasts in season pull largemouth bass, bluegill, black crappie, the colorful pumpkinseed, chain pickerel, and even American eel from the waters. Whichever route you chose, the two will merge beyond the end of the berm. Follow the gravel path straight ahead (there's a service road off to your left, also gravel) to regain the trail as it winds back into the forest.

After a short woodland walk, with many varieties of moss and lichen beckoning you, a floating boardwalk takes you over the calm waters onto a grassy meadow peninsula, edged by a wide variety of lush aquatic plants. Watch the marshy waters for beavers and turtles, listen for the bellowing of frogs, and be sure you've got some sun protection handy. The trail will then wander back into woods and to the south shore viewing area, a favorite haunt for raptors. When you rejoin the main trail after pausing to take in the view, it will lead you toward what was the second floating bridge, which is out of service until further notice because of winter storm damage and a lack of funds to repair it. In the meantime, follow signs for the short land detour leading over the dirt-surfaced tram tour road to the paved road leading back to the visitor center.

When you reach the paved road, turn right; Lake Redington will be on the left. To the right, a permanent wooden boardwalk wildlife lookout (which will eventually reconnect with the damaged floating walkway) offers a good view of Cash Lake. Cross the road bridge over the south spillway, then take the first paved path on the left to finish your hike at the visitor center. Check out that wild garden, rest your legs for a few moments, and savor your visit to one of the largest forested areas—more than 12,800 acres on the North and South tracts—remaining today in the Mid-Atlantic states.

MORE INFORMATION

Trails and grounds are open daily (except for holidays) from sunrise to 4:30 P.M. The National Wildlife Visitor Center building is open daily (except for holidays) 9 A.M. to 4:30 P.M. Call 301-497-5898 or 301-497-5763 for details about the many special-interest programs and tram tour availability. Phone 800-877-8339 to reach the Federal Relay Service for the deaf and hearing impaired. Website: www.fws.gov/northeast/patuxent/NWVCTrails.html.

To preserve the refuge's trails and its habitants, bicycles and skis are not allowed. Dogs must be leashed (10-foot maximum length). Note that very few rest stops or benches are available along the lake portion of the trail. Fishing is by permit only, in season; call the refuge for details.

SAVING THE BALD EAGLE

Not long ago, and not far from the nation's capital, the bald eagle bounced back from the brink of extinction. In 1969, staff at the Patuxent Wildlife Research Refuge, located between Washington, D.C., and Baltimore, published data linking the pesticide DDT to thin eggshells among ducks living in the refuge. The research demonstrated that DDT was a major factor in population losses suffered by fish-eating birds such as bald eagles. The majestic raptor's numbers had dropped to an estimated 487 breeding pairs nationwide in 1963. Thanks in part to Patuxent's work, the federal government banned DDT use in 1972.

Great harm had already been done, however, and human intervention was urgently required. Patuxent became involved in this phase too, initiating a captive-breeding program to incubator-hatch each eagle pair's first clutch of eggs. The parents usually produced a second clutch to raise naturally in their nests. This approach worked so well—124 eaglets were hatched at the refuge, earning it international attention—that Patuxent supplied eaglets to many states for their recovery efforts.

States such as New York, using a technique called "hacking," placed incubator-hatched eaglets in elevated, isolated, human-made nests where biologists fed them until they matured. Another conservation technique recognized that, while eagles can hatch up to three eggs per nest, only two eaglets are likely to survive. So some of these "surplus" hatchlings were transferred to foster-parent eagle pairs, who readily adopted and raised them. Viability rates jumped for both eggs and live birds.

The Patuxent breeding program wound down in 1988, when eagle populations, and their reproduction in the wild, were clearly on the rebound. By 2006, breeding bald-eagle pairs were present in all 48 contiguous states, and total breeding pairs had increased twentyfold, to more than 9,700 nationally. The Chesapeake Bay area in particular enjoyed great success, increasing from 32 pairs and 18 annual young in 1977 to 151 pairs and 172 eaglets in 1993. In 2007, the bald eagle was taken off the federal list of Endangered and Threatened Wildlife—a major milestone.

Bald eagles have survived, with a little help from their friends, but vigilance is needed for their continued protection. Clean water, habitat preservation, and the enforcement of laws against toxins and other threats will always be vital to the support of this noble national bird.

TRIP 11
PISCATAWAY NATIONAL PARK–
ACCOKEEK FOUNDATION

Location: Accokeek, MD
Rating: Easy
Distance: 4.0 miles
Elevation Gain: Minimal
Estimated Time: 1.5 to 2.0 hours
Maps: USGS Upper Marlboro; NPS map

The Accokeek Foundation trails in Piscataway National Park traverse a riverside forest with views of Mount Vernon, and travel through a colonial tobacco farm.

DIRECTIONS

From I-95/I-495 (Capital Beltway) outer loop, take Exit 2A (or from inner loop, take Exit 3) onto MD 210 (Indian Head Highway). Travel about 9 miles. After you pass Farmington Road, take the next right onto Livingston Road (a B&J fast-food restaurant is on the corner). Drive one block and turn right onto Biddle Road. At the stop sign, turn left onto Bryan Point Road. Follow it 3.5 miles, and turn right into the Accokeek Foundation parking lot. *GPS coordinates: 38° 41.635′ N, 77° 03.946′ W.*

TRAIL DESCRIPTION

Piscataway National Park, named for the native Piscataway Indian inhabitants, is located in Prince George's County, Maryland, directly across the Potomac River from Mount Vernon. Congress founded the 5,000-acre park to preserve the view exactly as it had been in George Washington's time, when the president boasted, "No estate in the United America is more pleasantly situated than this." Piscataway stretches for 6 miles along the Potomac, from Piscataway Creek in the west to historic Marshall Hall in the east, but the entire park is not connected by a trail system. The Accokeek Foundation manages 200 acres jointly with the National Park Service (NPS), and the hike described here covers this complete area, which includes a historical colonial farm, an experimental organic farm, a native tree arboretum, and many fine views of Mount Vernon.

Begin the hike at the visitor center just to the north of the parking lot. Behind the center is a gravel path that splits north and east. Follow the path

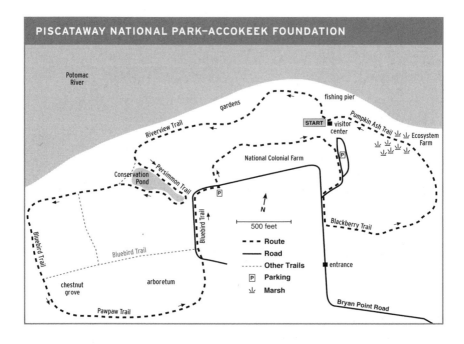

PISCATAWAY NATIONAL PARK–ACCOKEEK FOUNDATION

north to see a popular fishing pier with a view of Mount Vernon, a pleasant bonus while relaxing and reeling in catfish. Continue back to the split and turn right, and then, just before a line of evergreen cedars, turn right onto the 0.8-mile Riverview Trail. Follow the mowed swath of grass to a forested area along the Potomac River and then travel westward along the forest's edge. This 6-acre riparian zone (an ecosystem along the bank of a river) was planted between 1999 and 2002, and includes 60 species of trees and shrubs that protect 3 miles of Potomac shoreline from pollution, erosion, and nutrient runoff. Keep going, passing a blocked side trail that leads to the boat dock, currently unusable because of weather damage. Farther on the left is National Colonial Farm's Museum Garden. Walk around to the front gate and enter for a look at colonial-era crops native to the Americas (zucchini, beans, squash), to Africa (sorghum, okra, yams), and to Europe (potatoes, beets, cabbage).

The trail is unmarked in this area, so walk to the gravel road on the northern boundary of the Colonial Farm and turn right, passing in front of the caretaker's residence. A posted sign on the right points to where the trail returns to open fields. After a short distance, turn left onto the 0.4-mile Persimmon Trail, which encircles a small pond. After traveling the loop, turn right back onto Riverview Trail and enter a larger section of riparian forest. Cross a wooden bridge over a tributary and leave the trees, staying to the right where the trail branches and again where the trail branches a second time. This is

An eighteenth-century tobacco barn (rear), farmhouse (right), and out-kitchen at the National Colonial Farm in Piscataway Park evoke a time when hardscrabble was the norm.

now Bluebird Trail. Bluebird nesting sites line the path here, little habitats with entrances too small for competitors such as starlings and house sparrows. These maintained nesting zones are responsible for increasing once-declining bluebird populations in the eastern states.

Continue, and watch out for the electrified fences on the left side. On the right is a grove of chestnuts, in the midst of which is an intersection. Leave Bluebird Trail where it forks left on a roadway, and turn right onto the 0.5-mile, white-blazed Pawpaw Trail. It winds uphill through the type of mature hardwood forest held sway across the Potomac watershed before the intensive introduction of European farming methods. Exiting the woods, the trail ends at the upper edge of the native tree arboretum, where it reconnects with Bluebird Trail. You can see 128 documented tree species, all extant in the Chesapeake region in the eighteenth century, before continuing north on a paved road through the National Colonial Farm complex. Bluebird Trail officially ends near a barn that houses rare native breeds such as Milking Red Devon cattle, Ossabaw Island hogs, and Spanish turkeys. Continue through the farm, and pass an original colonial tobacco barn before coming to a farmhouse, kitchen, and smokehouse, where guides in period garb provide historical interpretations to visitors on weekends in the spring, summer, and fall.

Exit the farm between two zigzagged split-rail fences and head south past the parking area along the access road that connects with Bryan Point Road. About 50 yards down, near a difficult-to-spot trail marker, turn left onto the

0.8-mile, purple-blazed Blackberry Trail. Follow this to the edge of the Robert Ware Straus Ecosystem Farm. Turn left along the fence line and continue until the fence ends. Turn left onto the 0.5-mile, yellow-blazed Pumpkin Ash Trail and cross the open field, traversing a freshwater tideland area via a wooden boardwalk. Continue through a quiet patch of woodland and on to a picnic area and the parking lot.

MORE INFORMATION

There is a $2 entrance fee for the park. The visitor center has free self-guided education kits for children and birding kits (field guide, binoculars, spotting scope) on loan for adults. On Saturday and Sunday, the foundation offers tours of the Robert Ware Straus Ecosystem Farm (11 A.M.) and Colonial Farm (1 P.M.). There is a canoe and kayak launch point on the Potomac River, just to the east of the fishing pier. Historic Marshall Hall sits to the west; built in the early 1700s, it was the centerpiece for the Washington, D.C., area's first amusement park in the early 1900s. The park is a stop on the 27-mile long Prince George's County Potomac Heritage Trail On-Road Bicycling Route.

A STORY TO TELL: THE PISCATAWAY PEOPLE

They have no land reservations, no federal or state sovereign tribal recognition, no large numbers or renown. But hundreds of years ago, the Piscataway had power and population. They had the courage to welcome strangers to their native place. And they still have a story to tell, of a proud people long ignored, marginalized, wounded, and separated from home and family.

When Captain John Smith arrived in their world, the great chiefdoms of the Piscataway and Powhatan–weakened by recent tribal wars but holding firmly to their lands–stewarded the Chesapeake Bay's western shores. The Piscataway were mainly found north of the Potomac River, in present-day Washington, D.C., and central Maryland. The Powhatan lived to the south, in Virginia's tidewater. Smith referred to the northern group by the name they gave their hereditary high chief's house: Moyaons. The high chief (*Tayac*) was advised by local chiefs (*werowances*), wise elders, and shamans, and could demand tribute from villages or send their warriors into battle.

The Piscataway were descended from Algonquin peoples, who were probably driven south by earlier periods of cooler climate. They were cousins to the nearby Nacotchtank (Anacostans), Tauxenent (Dogue), Mattawoman, Nanjemoy, and Portobaco, whose names still color the region. In their palisaded villages, the Piscataway built longhouses shaped like loaves of bread, with sapling frames and bark or mat coverings, much as their Powhatan neighbors did. Piscataway cultivated the "three sisters": squash, maize, and beans; they also hunted, fished, and gathered. But even their rich organic diet couldn't promise immunity against white people's unfamiliar diseases: smallpox, cholera, and measles.

English Catholic colonizers of Maryland in 1634 found the Piscataway willing allies. The Tayac–who, with his wife, converted to Christianity–offered them land to found St. Mary's City. The Piscataway hoped to benefit by using the settlers as a buffer against other tribes. But as the English population grew, relations between the colonizers and the native peoples deteriorated. By 1668, the Piscataway were confined to two small reservations. In 1675, colonial leaders forced the Piscataway to permit rival Susquehannock, defeated in war by the Five Nations Iroquois (Haudenosaunee), to settle in these reservations as well. Conflict ensued, then the Susquehannock headed north again and joined with the Iroquois against the

Piscataway, making repeated incursions southward. The English were of no help—they too coveted what lands remained to the Piscataway.

In 1697, the Piscataway relocated across the Potomac to Fauquier County, but Virginia colonists sought to send them back. In 1699 they moved again, to an island in the Potomac near Point of Rocks. By 1700, a chiefdom that likely had boasted 8,500 individuals a century earlier had dwindled—through war, disease, and loss of land and sustenance—to about 300. Some of these moved north into Iroquois territory, and eventually into New France (Quebec) and Ontario. Some may have moved south, joining the Meherrin.

Evidence indicates that a number of Piscataway remained on or returned to their ancestral lands. In the 1800s and early 1900s, however, the Piscataway, like African-Americans, suffered widespread discrimination under Jim Crow-style laws. Their identity as a native tribal people was ignored, leaving them void of American Indian treaty protection. The Catholic Church, however, maintained records that more accurately described Piscataway families as native peoples. Anthropologists in the late 1800s also interviewed Piscataway who claimed descent from the chiefdom.

Phillip Sheridan Proctor began a Piscataway revival in the early twentieth century, claiming the old title of chief through his family lineage and taking the name Chief Turkey Tayac. In 1944, he invited Smithsonian scientists to examine an ancient carving of his people's revered forest guardian spirit above Piscataway Creek in Maryland. But in attempting to remove the stone for further study, researchers shattered the precious artifact.

After Turkey Tayac's death in 1978, the Piscataway fractured into three distinct communities: the Piscataway Indian Nation and Tayac Territory, the Piscataway Conoy Confederacy and Subtribes, and the Cedarville Band of Piscataways. Today, they disagree at times over issues such as whether they should seek tribal recognition. In the 1990s, a Maryland panel acknowledged the validity of Piscataway descent claims, but state sovereignty recognition has twice been denied the Piscataway Conoy. Meanwhile, Piscataway-hosted gatherings, such as the annual spring powwow and Awakening of Mother Earth Ceremony, the Green Corn Ceremony, and the Feast of the Dead, are helping to bring about the cultural revival that Turkey Tayac sought.

TRIP 12
GREENBELT PARK

Location: Greenbelt, MD
Rating: Moderate
Distance: 5.3 miles
Elevation Gain: 350 feet
Estimated Time: 2.0 to 2.5 hours
Maps: USGS Washington East; sketch map in National Park Service brochure

Greenbelt Park, situated just inside the Beltway, offers an excellent loop hike that traverses a secluded second-growth forest.

DIRECTIONS

From I-95/I-495 (Capital Beltway), take Exit 23 to MD 201 (Kenilworth Avenue) south, and exit immediately onto MD 193 (Greenbelt Road) east. Go 0.3 mile and turn right at a traffic light onto Walker Road, which enters Greenbelt Park. At the T intersection, turn right and then immediately left into the Sweetgum parking and picnicking area. *GPS coordinates:* 38° 59.64′ N, 76° 53.70′ W.

By Metrorail, take the Green Line to the final stop at the Greenbelt Station. Then take Metrobus C2 for a short ride, getting off at the park entrance at the intersection of Greenbelt Road and Walker Drive.

TRAIL INFORMATION

Greenbelt Park is located just 12 miles northeast of the National Mall. This urban oasis is bounded by the Baltimore-Washington Parkway to the east, the Beltway to the north, and Kenilworth Avenue to the west. Once denuded farmland, since the early 1900s the land has been recovering and now supports a forest of mixed pine and deciduous trees. The small creeks in the park flow into the Anacostia River, which in turn feeds the Potomac River and Chesapeake Bay. The park was initially part of a never-finished "green belt" separating Greenbelt, Maryland—the first federally planned community—from Washington, D.C.

The 5.3-mile Perimeter Trail described here hugs the park boundaries, sometimes running close to the highways and dwellings, but mostly cutting through green spaces and alongside gentle watercourses. There are benches

GREENBELT PARK

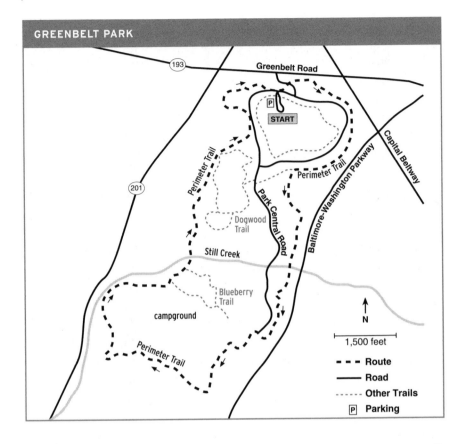

Greenbelt Road

193

201

Perimeter Trail

Perimeter Trail

P

START

Capital Beltway

Baltimore-Washington Parkway

Park Central Road

Dogwood Trail

Still Creek

Blueberry Trail

campground

Perimeter Trail

N

1,500 feet

- - - Route
———— Road
------- Other Trails
P   Parking

along the way at least every half-mile. From the Sweetgum Picnic Area, walk north past the start of Azalea Trail and across the road to the beginning of the yellow-blazed Perimeter Trail. Turn right to follow it clockwise, and note the first of many mile markers indicating distance traveled. In 50 yards, cross the road near the park entrance. Notice the many fallen and cut dead evergreen trees, mostly loblolly pine. Continue past oak and beech trees, as well as maintenance sheds behind the park headquarters. At the 0.2-mile marker, head up a slight hill past a jumble of fallen pines. At the 0.4-mile marker, traffic comes into view on I-495 below and to the left.

Follow the trail along the shoulder of the park road, back into a wooded area of beech, laurel, and oak trees, and then downhill to an intersection. Turn left; a sign indicates Dogwood Trail parking area is straight ahead, and double yellow blazes and a sign on the left mark Perimeter Trail heading left. Continue down the hill along the north branch of Still Creek, where large oaks grow near the streambed and large tulip trees, some with trunks 40 inches in diameter, dot the area. Throughout the park during most of the year are more than a

A quiet lane leads uphill from Still Creek in Greenbelt, a forested park that city planners once ambitiously hoped would ring Washington, D.C.

half-dozen species of colorful stem-and-cap and polypore mushrooms. As the narrow trail crosses Still Creek, it comes within 25 yards of the Baltimore-Washington Parkway. Climb uphill to the right where a secondary trail comes in on the right. Continue to follow the yellow blazes to the left past the bench.

About 2.0 miles into the hike, cross the end of Park Central Road. To the left begins a paved bike trail, and straight across is a secondary road that leads to the ranger station and camping area. Take a quick side trip to read the kiosks at the ranger station that describe the unique origin of the town of Greenbelt (just to the north) and how the park is helping to remove pollutants from Still Creek. Return to Perimeter Trail, and follow the signs past large yellow poplars to the artificially developed wetland buffer area that slows water flow and filters pollution. Hike downhill through rugged terrain over exposed roots and past numerous holly trees. The trail becomes a boardwalk through the wooded low wetlands. Cross Deep Creek, and at the end of the boardwalk, turn right at the trail fork. Even though it is an intermittent stream, this creek is responsible for significant erosion through this area.

After passing the point where the trail comes very close to the southern boundary, begin to traverse a relatively isolated portion of the park, heavily wooded and with more oaks and poplars and fewer evergreens. For 0.5 mile, hike just to the left of the gullies cut by Deep Creek, and then turn sharply to the right over both the creek and a maintained gravel path. Remain on the dirt trail as it wanders slightly up-hill past oak, beech, and poplar trees. The mile markers that were scarce in the Deep Creek area again come into view, here plotted every 0.2 mile.

Perimeter Trail follows the course of Still Creek (which is 50 to 150 yards to the left), crosses a gravel road, and heads uphill along the side of a ridge. After passing two intersections that connect with the Blueberry Trail loop, cross Still Creek over an elevated wooden bridge. Continue uphill, past the intersection with the Dogwood Trail loop and then adjacent to apartments on the park boundary. Following the trail gets tricky as it passes between Park Central Road on the right and the apartment complex on the left. Look carefully for the yellow blazes after crossing the wooded bridge and turn left past the bench, then right up the hill past the parking garage. Cross two more wooden bridges over intermittent streams, hike past the park police station, surrounded by willow oaks, and arrive back at the Sweetgum parking lot.

MORE INFORMATION

Greenbelt is administered by the National Park Service. There are no fees for hiking, horseback riding, bike riding, and picnicking, but there are fees for overnight camping. The U.S. Park Service ranger station near the campground is opened on weekdays and weekends (but is sometimes not staffed when rangers are on patrol). Other facilities include bathrooms, picnic areas, a baseball field, and children's playgrounds. On the first Saturday of the month starting at 11:00 A.M., the University of Maryland partners with park authorities and volunteers to identify and remove invasive plants from the park.

Other trails include the 1.1-mile Azalea Trail loop around the Sweetgum Picnic Area, located near the park entrance; the 1.4-mile Dogwood Trail in the center of the park; and the 1.0-mile Blueberry Trail, located near the campgrounds.

TRIP 13
LAKE ARTEMESIA AND THE NORTHEAST BRANCH TRAIL

Location: College Park and Berwyn Heights, MD
Rating: Easy
Distance: 3.5 miles round-trip
Elevation Gain: 20 feet
Estimated Time: 2.0 to 2.5 hours
Maps: USGS Washington East; trail map available at the website for the Prince George's County Department of Parks and Recreation.

This peaceful, mostly level hike meanders through hardwood forests, wetlands, and the domains of birds both live and mechanical. A birding trail, fishing piers, and plenty of resting places at the lake make this an enjoyable trip of discovery for all ages.

DIRECTIONS

From I-95/I-495 (Capital Beltway), take Exit 23 for Kenilworth Avenue (MD 201) south. Drive 1.5 miles, then turn right onto Paint Branch Parkway. Free parking is available at the Ellen E. Linson Swimming Pool/Herbert W. Wells Ice Rink at 5211 Paint Branch Parkway on your left past the bridge over the Northeast Branch. *GPS coordinates*: 38° 58.583′ N, 76° 55.393′ W.

By Metrorail, take the Green Line to the College Park–U of MD station.

TRAIL DESCRIPTION

The full Northeast Branch Trail is a 3.0 mile-long leg of the Anacostia Tributary Trails network, reaching through northern Prince George's and eastern Montgomery counties in Maryland. On this hike, you'll travel a sampling of it, along Northeast Branch Creek and around the College Park Airport runway, to its junction with the loop trail around Lake Artemesia.

This hike is designed to be a Metro-friendly sojourn outside the boundaries of the city proper. If you're coming to College Park by car, start the hike from the Paint Branch Parkway crosswalk at 52nd Avenue.

From the top of the steps coming up from the College Park–U of MD Metro station, look slightly to your left for the intersection of River Road and Paint Branch Parkway. Walk to the southeast corner of that intersection,

Alongside the trail bearing its name, the northeast branch of the Anacostia runs with snowmelt on a spring-thaw day; its bank is a good vantage point for spotting small aircraft.

standing in front of the U.S. Food & Drug Administration building (5100 Paint Branch Parkway), then follow Paint Branch Parkway east for two blocks.

Cross Paint Branch Parkway at the 52nd Avenue crosswalk (begin your hike here if you parked at the pool/rink) and continue walking east along the sidewalk on this side of the road. Pass the 94th Aero Squadron Restaurant sign, then watch for the pointed brown wooden Northeast Branch trail marker, not much taller than the guardrail, and turn left down the trail entrance spur path, which is the steepest part of this hike.

At the bottom of the entrance path, continue straight ahead toward a chain-link fence in the distance. Along the trail here are a couple of large, lovely American holly trees. The trail and fence will bend around the end of the College Park Airport runway. This is a perfect spot from which to watch small craft landing on a pleasant day. (Bring a blanket if you plan to sit; no benches are provided.) Wilbur Wright trained the first military aviators at this airport, which celebrated its 100th anniversary in 2009 and was the site of the first controlled helicopter flight in 1924. You can also step up on the creek bank for a good glimpse of the Northeast Branch running south to join with the Anacostia, Washington, D.C.'s, "forgotten river."

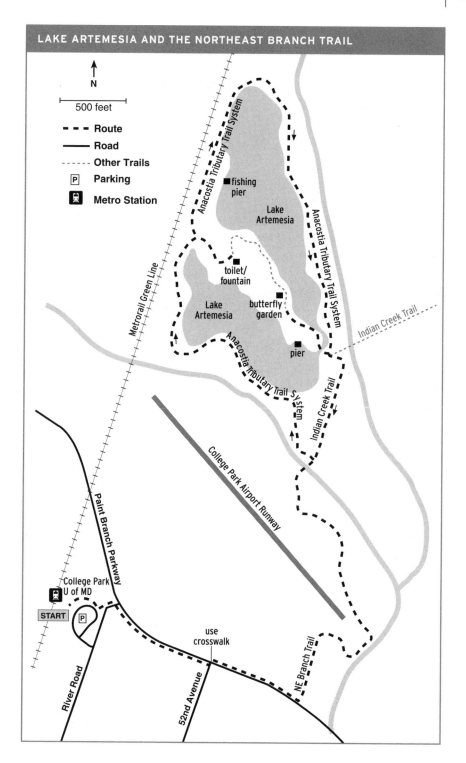

LAKE ARTEMESIA AND THE NORTHEAST BRANCH TRAIL

N

500 feet

- - - Route
—— Road
----- Other Trails
P Parking
Metro Station

Anacostia Tributary Trail System

fishing pier

Lake Artemesia

Anacostia Tributary Trail System

Metrorail Green Line

toilet/ fountain

Lake Artemesia

butterfly garden

Indian Creek Trail

pier

Anacostia Tributary Trail System

Indian Creek Trail

College Park Airport Runway

Paint Branch Parkway

College Park U of MD

START   P

use crosswalk

River Road

52nd Avenue

NE Branch Trail

Continue along the trail through the oak woods, past the Anacostia Herring Restoration Area sign and over the wooden-decked steel bridge. By the far foot of the bridge, near the Northeast Branch Trail's zero-mile marker, a sign will point to the left for Lake Artemesia. Look for deer tracks in this area. Pass the black-painted chain-link fence and gate to enter the Lake Artemesia Natural Area. Turn left on the lake loop trail, and follow it along the lake's southern shore. Start watching for green and great blue herons, loons, and various ducks in the water, and check out the nesting boxes along the fence, home to swallows and eastern bluebirds year-round. Wayside signs describe local natural and human history.

This 38-acre lake was constructed in the 1980s, when Metrorail needed sand and gravel to build up the nearby Green Line roadbed extension. In 1972, Mrs. Artemesia N. Drefs, whose family had owned land hereabouts since the 1890s, donated some acreage—where a smaller lake also named Artemesia, for her mother and grandmother, already existed—to the county. The family had raised bass and goldfish in these waters. Following Mrs. Drefs's wish for a lasting natural area on this spot, Metro struck a deal: It would use the fill soils it dredged out locally to build its Green Line, thereby saving $10 million in material and transportation costs, and, in return, it would spend $8 million turning the resulting excavation into a green haven for wildlife and humans.

Turn right onto the peninsula path if you're in need of a pit stop: Rest rooms and a water fountain are available at the blue-roofed building. Then retrace your steps back to the lake loop trail and turn right to continue following the western shore. A floating fishing pier will be on the right; local fishing fans say that good trout can be reeled in here. At the northern tip of the lake is a gazebo next to a copse of loblolly pines, a good vantage point for watching the gulls, ducks (ruddy and ring-necked), and grebes (pied-billed and horned) on the water and in the vegetation along the shoreline. Keep following the lake loop trail around to the eastern shore, watching for woodpeckers, cardinals, nuthatches, and other small birds in the forested area on the left.

Turn right to cross the steel bridge onto the peninsula again. You'll see the covered octagonal pier with plenty of benches on the left; the right-hand path leads to a butterfly and wildflower garden on the northern edge of the peninsula. Walk back across the bridge and take the right-center path, then take another right to follow Indian Creek Trail back toward the Northeast Branch. You might see deer or rabbit tracks here, or a black-crowned night heron along the creek. Continue for a short distance until Indian Creek Trail ends by the foot of the first steel bridge you crossed. Go straight back up over that bridge onto Northeast Branch Trail, and you're on your way back around the runway to the parking lot or Metro station where you began.

MORE INFORMATION

Northeast Branch Trail and Lake Artemesia are maintained by the Prince George's County Department of Parks and Recreation and the Maryland-National Capital Park and Planning Commission. Phone 301-699-2255; TTY 301-699-2544. In an emergency, call the park police at 301-459-3232; www.pgparks.com/Things_To_Do/Nature/Lake_Artemesia.htm. These are multiuse trails, so be aware of cyclists and other fast-moving users. Bicycles may be rented at the pool/rink facility. Lake Artemesia Park closes at dark. Leashed dogs are allowed. No alcoholic beverages are permitted. Fishing is allowed by permit: Visit www.dnr.state.md.us/fisheries/ for information. Birding information can be found at www.pgaudubon.org/LGBirdingTrail.html.

TRIP 14
CATOCTIN MOUNTAIN PARK AND
CUNNINGHAM FALLS STATE PARK

$

Location: Thurmont, MD
Rating: Difficult
Distance: 10.4 miles
Elevation Gain: 2,200 feet
Estimated Time: 5.5 to 6.0 hours
Maps: USGS Blue Ridge Summit and USGS Catoctin Furnace; free
NPS map of Catoctin Mountain Park; Cunningham Falls official state
trail guide

**Catoctin Mountain Park and Cunningham Falls State Park offer
true mountain trails only an hour from Washington, D.C., with a
pristine waterfall as the featured attraction.**

DIRECTIONS
From I-95/I-495 (Capital Beltway) inner loop, take Exit 38 (or from outer
loop, take Exit 35) onto I-270 north to Frederick and merge onto US 15 north.
Take US 15 approximately 18 miles north to Thurmont, and take the exit for
MD 77 west (east leads into town). Drive 2.5 miles and turn right onto Park
Central Road in Catoctin Mountain Park, and then turn immediately right
into the visitor center parking lot. *GPS coordinates*: 39° 38.03′ N, 77° 26.98′ W.

TRAIL DESCRIPTION
Catoctin Mountain, the easternmost ridge of the Blue Ridge Mountains, offers
serious mountain hiking only an hour from Washington, D.C. Two parks, each
comprising roughly 5,000 acres, border each other on the range's northern
stretch, near Frederick—Catoctin Mountain National Park to the north and
Cunningham Falls State Park to the south. Highlights of the parks include
44-acre Hunting Creek Lake, 78-foot Cunningham Falls, trout-rich Big Hunting Creek, several overlooks, an old whiskey still, a nineteenth-century iron
furnace, a historical arch bridge, and an aviary. The trail system is extensive,
though the hike outlined here is the only way to complete a circuit between
the two parks.

From the trailhead at the visitor center, begin a steep ascent toward Hog
Rock and Thurmont Vista through chestnut oak and hickory and spring-

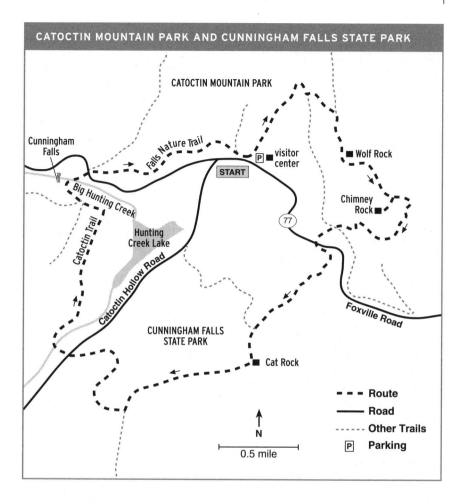

blooming dogwood, spicebush, mountain laurel, and rhododendron. At 0.6 mile, turn right (east), following the sign to Wolf Rock. Ascend by switchback to a second junction, at 0.8 mile, and turn left toward Wolf Rock. Begin a short, steep descent amid a field of huge boulders, and at 1.1 miles, turn right at a T intersection, again toward Wolf Rock. Go downhill on log steps and continue on the rocky spine of the ridge. At 1.4 miles, reach 1,400-foot Wolf Rock—a large shelf of quartzite rocks, part of the Weverton Formation deposited 550 million years ago. The fissured rocks resemble giant fists punching into the sky. Climb atop them and head to the left for a great view … in winter. Leaves mask the vantage in spring and summer. Watch for poison oak and poison sumac growing between rocks.

Return to the trail and head south toward Chimney Rock, 0.5 mile away, accessible via a steep access trail that cuts right. Chimney Rock offers an

Cunningham Falls in Cunningham Falls State Park cascades 78 feet down the east slope of the Catoctin Mountains. Early homesteaders used the falls for baptisms.

awe-inspiring view, year-round, of the mountains and valleys to the west, including the 1,500-foot Cat Rock peak to the southwest (the next major goal of this hike). There are several flat, exposed quartzite pedestals. After a strong dose of Catoctin Mountain beauty, return to the main trail and begin a steady downhill under old-growth hickory and chestnut oaks. Turn right at 2.2 miles, away from a sign that points to the Crow's Nest Campground (a 500-foot drop), and onto a westward trail that travels downhill over switch-backs, dropping 400 feet over a short 0.7 mile. At 2.7 miles, reach an intersection under a stand of young pines and go straight to descend to MD 77 and Big Hunting Creek (at 2.9 miles). Turn left along the road a short distance, passing the entrance road to the National Park Service administration office, then cross the road (carefully) to a parking area at the trailhead to Cunningham Falls State Park.

Head into the woods on the yellow-blazed Cat Rock/Bob's Hill Trail and begin an uphill climb that is among the most strenuous in this book—more than 700 feet in 1.3 miles to reach Cat Rock. Begin the ascent on a rocky path through pines, and at 3.7 miles, cross over Bear Branch, a rocky streambed tumbling down the mountainside. At 3.9 miles, the orange-blazed Old Misery Trail leaves to the right, offering access to Hunting Creek Lake. Soon after, notice a sign that points right to Bob's Hill—go straight to Cat Rock, returning to this point after visiting the 1,500-foot, 360-degree overlook. Scrambling to the top of these rocks is more challenging (and fun) than Wolf Rock. Return to the main trail and turn left toward Bob's Hill, starting a well-deserved level stretch atop the ridge, where ferns, moss, and young saplings add diversity. At 5.9 miles (1.7 miles from Cat Rock), reach a T intersection and turn right onto the blue-blazed Catoctin Trail, a 27-mile trail that connects with the Appalachian Trail to the south at Gambrill State Park.

Proceed downhill—gradually at first, then more steeply—on a winding dirt path through thick old-growth forest. Clumps of deep-green ferns grow along the mountainside seepages. The trail becomes rocky in its final descent, crosses Catoctin Hollow Road, and reaches Hauver Branch (at 7.7 miles). Take care on the slick rock footholds across the branch. Proceed up a short, steep rock scramble and then hike parallel to the ridgeline, crossing two feeder streams before reaching a clearing at the campground entrance. Cross the road and head back uphill, negotiating several ups and downs on wooden steps before reaching a T intersection with the yellow-blazed Cliff Trail. Turn left on a short stretch where Catoctin Trail and Cliff Trail run together, then turn right at 8.8 miles where a sign reads Return to Falls and Cliff Trail turns to the right. Head down a dramatic cliff side with large granite boulders, following the sound of cascading water, and turn left again onto Lower Trail. It becomes a boardwalk and reaches the falls at the hike's 9-mile mark.

The largest cascading waterfall in Maryland, the 78-foot Cunningham Falls was named for a local photographer, whose scenic shots popularized the location. Though sometimes crowded, the falls are a fitting climax to the hike. After a thorough rest, carefully pick your way across the rocky Big Hunting Creek to the boardwalk on the other side, and follow it to cross MD 77 (carefully again—it's at a hairpin turn). Soon after reentering Catoctin Mountain Park, turn right onto Falls Nature Trail. Follow it 1.2 miles along the side of the ridge. A little wooden walkway over a small feeder stream is the last landmark before you return to the visitor center at 10.4 miles.

MORE INFORMATION

Catoctin Mountain Park is open year-round, dawn to dusk. Camping, picnicking, wildlife viewing, fly-fishing, and cross-country skiing are all available. Leashed pets are allowed on all trails. Visit www.nps.gov/ncr/cato/ or call 301-663-9330.

Cunningham Falls State Park: Swimming is permitted at Hunting Creek Lake between Memorial Day and Labor Day. Pets are allowed on all trails (except Lower Trail to the Cunningham Falls). A number of interpretive programs are offered. There is a fee, which changes depending on the season. Visit www.dnr.state.md.us/publiclands/western/cunningham.asp or call 301-271-7574.

NEARBY

At the south end of Cunningham Falls State Park—accessible by Catoctin Hollow Road—is a nineteenth-century furnace and the ruins of an ironmaster's house. The furnace, nicknamed "Isabella," was built in the 1850s, but an earlier version, built in 1774, produced pig iron for the cannons of George Washington's Continental Army. North of the furnace, directly off of Catoctin Furnace Road, is the Catoctin Wildlife Preserve Zoo, which has 450 animal species. South Mountain State Park, at a mountain pass important during the Civil War Battle of Antietam, is 10 miles west of Catoctin/Cunningham.

Also of note is Camp David in the northern portion of Catoctin Mountain Park. The presidential retreat hosted the Camp David Accords, a 1978 agreement between Egypt and Israel, and is the site of Evergreen Chapel.

TRIP 15
ANTIETAM NATIONAL BATTLEFIELD

Location: Sharpsburg, MD
Rating: Easy to Moderate
Distance: 3.5 miles
Elevation Gain: 400 feet
Estimated Time: 2.0 to 2.5 hours
Maps: USGS Keedysville; National Park Service map, available free at visitor center; Battlefield America topographical map, available for purchase at visitor center

Follow sleepy Antietam Creek at the quiet southern end of Antietam National Battlefield and a series of ridges in beautiful farm country that belies the bloody contest waged here.

DIRECTIONS

From I-495 (Capital Beltway) inner loop, take Exit 38 (or from outer loop, take Exit 35) onto I-270 north to Frederick. Take I-70 west. Take Exit 29 onto MD 65 south toward Sharpsburg. Travel 11 miles to downtown Sharpsburg and turn left onto MD 34 (Boonsboro Pike), pass Antietam National Cemetery, and turn right onto Rodman Avenue. At a T intersection turn left onto Branch Avenue and follow it to where it ends at a 25-spot parking lot above Burnside Bridge. *GPS coordinates: 39° 27.029' N, 77° 43.961' W.*

TRAIL DESCRIPTION

September 17, 1862, was the costliest day, in terms of human life lost, in American history. Two armies, 40,000 Confederate and 75,000 Union soldiers, met in a ferocious series of clashes on the rolling Piedmont terrain of western Maryland. Before the battle, General George McClellan, commander of the Army of the Potomac, pushed General Robert E. Lee's Army between the Potomac River and Antietam Creek, forcing the Confederates to trade blood for ground to survive.

Although McClellan had a large numerical superiority, he advanced his men piecemeal, first in the north, at the Miller Cornfield, West Woods, and Dunker Church; then in the center, at Bloody Lane; and finally in the south, at Burnside Bridge. The southern portion of the battlefield is the terrain covered in this hike, upon which Lee's army was saved, literally in the nick of time, by

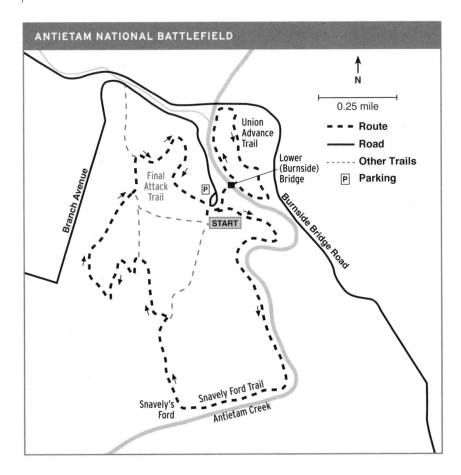

ANTIETAM NATIONAL BATTLEFIELD

N

0.25 mile

- - - Route
—— Road
----- Other Trails
P Parking

Union Advance Trail

Final Attack Trail

Lower (Burnside) Bridge

Branch Avenue

P

START

Burnside Bridge Road

Snavely Ford Trail

Snavely's Ford

Antietam Creek

Confederates arriving from Harpers Ferry. Today the area is much the same as it was before the 12-hour bloodletting—peaceful countryside with hills and farms and an unspoiled creek, now all protected by the National Park Service (NPS). The hike goes along Antietam Creek and then on the hills south of Sharpsburg and includes two interpretive trails, Union Advance Trail and Final Attack Trail.

From the parking circle on the west side of Antietam Creek, walk down the steps to Burnside Bridge and the beautiful two-trunked sycamore tree beside it—a sapling at the time of the battle. The Federals needed to cross the three-arched bridge, but they faced stiff resistance from Confederates entrenched on the opposite hillside, and it took three separate attacks and 500 casualties to carry what today looks like a small span across a languid creek. Walk north along the stone wall—where fallen men were temporarily buried after the battle—and begin a 1-mile circle hike on Union Advance Trail, which enters

Shielded by a split-rail fence and overhanging hickories, hikers walk along the ridge top at the south end of Antietam National Battlefield. Antietam Creek is a good place to spot rare, spiky-barked water locusts.

the woods and climbs 60 feet to an overlook before circling past a monument to the 11th Connecticut Infantry and returning to the bridge. Go back up the hill and turn left where a sign points to Snavely Ford Trail. Follow Antietam Creek south to the ford where Union troops finally crossed and relieved the pressure on Burnside Bridge. Not far down the path is Georgian's Overlook, the 20th Georgia Regiment's lethal perch. Proceed downhill, dropping 130 feet in elevation over 0.25 mile to the river and continue to the right. (Benches are provided along the route.) The walk becomes prettier, quieter, and more secluded. Pass riverside pawpaws, sycamores, hickories, yellow poplars, black walnuts, black birches, and curious, spiky-barked water locusts.

At 2.0 miles into the hike, turn west with the river where steep cliffs rise on the opposite banks. Near Snavely's Ford (another 0.3 mile), turn north with the trail along the edge of the park's property and climb 40 feet in elevation over the next 0.25 mile. Turn left at the sign for Final Attack Trail.

Climb 40 more feet in elevation to an open area, where the trail becomes grassy and is lined with cedars and black locusts. A cornfield emerges on the right. Turn left at a T intersection underneath three conspicuous walnut trees onto historic Otto Lane. Union infantry and artillery stood on this ridge in preparation for the final attack intended as the knockout blow against the Rebels. Wind downhill to a small stream and then uphill 70 feet to the top of a hill bedecked with a majestic hackberry tree, beneath which is a welcoming bench. The stone wall behind it marks the park's boundary. The final Confederate attack came over this hill, the men of General A. P. Hill's division marching from Harpers Ferry and crashing into the Union flank just in time to save the main force.

Follow the ridge off the hill and through high grass dotted with cotton thistle and Queen Anne's lace. Walk a straight stretch with cropland rising to the left and a row of trees on the right, passing the 16th Connecticut Infantry obelisk honoring the 43 men in that regiment killed in action. Next, go downhill among emerald-green cedars to the valley, then turn right and go uphill, returning to Otto Lane at an opening in the fence. Take a left. Follow the lane north between split-rail fences and more hackberry trees, with cannons amassed on the ridge to the left—the farthest point of advance for Union forces. At an intersection where the trail splits four ways, take either of the trails that heads right and then swing left (north) on a path through a field at the top of the ridge. To the left-front in the valley, note the Otto and the Sherrick farms, both witnesses to the battle, and beyond them on the high ground, Antietam National Cemetery. Make a U-turn back to the south and follow more cedars, with South Mountain close enough that you can see individual trees set against a blue sky. Walk down, up, and downhill again, and then through a field back to the parking lot.

MORE INFORMATION

Three-day passes can be purchased for $4 per person or $6 per family. Stop at the visitor center at the north end of the battlefield for interpretive maps on Union Advance Trail, Final Attack Trail, and other battlefield trails. Go to www.nps.gov/anti/planyourvisit/hiking.htm for information on the fighting at West Woods and Bloody Lane.

TRIP 16
SUGARLOAF MOUNTAIN

Location: Dickerson, MD
Rating: Moderate to Difficult
Distance: 5.3 miles
Elevation Gain: 1,375 feet
Estimated Time: 3.0 to 3.5 hours
Maps: USGS Buckeystown and USGS Urbana; free sketch map at trailhead

Sugarloaf Mountain offers a challenging mountain hike close to Washington, with dozens of wildflower-rich trails.

DIRECTIONS
From I-495 (Capital Beltway) inner loop, take Exit 38 (or from outer loop, take Exit 35) onto I-270. Take Exit 22 onto MD 109 south (Barnesville/Hyattstown exit) and drive 3.0 miles to the intersection of Comus Road. Turn right on Comus Road (west) and drive 2.5 miles to the base of Sugarloaf Mountain. Take the second right up the mountain road to West View parking. *GPS coordinates:* 39° 15.092′ N, 77° 23.611′ W.

TRAIL DESCRIPTION
Sugarloaf Mountain is a "monadnock," a mountain that stands alone after the bedrock surrounding it has eroded away. The mountain is capped by 200-foot-thick, erosion-resistant quartzite that formed deep within the earth's crust 300 million years ago, when the North American and African continental plates collided to form Pangaea. A dominant 150-foot-high quartzite cliff rises from Sugarloaf's western edge, with jumbles of talus—rock split from the cliff by water freezing in joints and fissures—scattered beneath it. The unique geologic history of the mountain is complemented by a unique ecosystem, where plants indigenous to the Mid-Atlantic coastal plain, Piedmont, and mountain region can all be found.

Trail maps can be obtained at the West View or East View parking lots, or at the wooden building just beyond the gated entrance at the base of the mountain. This hike starts from the West View lot. The recommended hike to the summit begins with a sharp ascent from the West View parking lot and

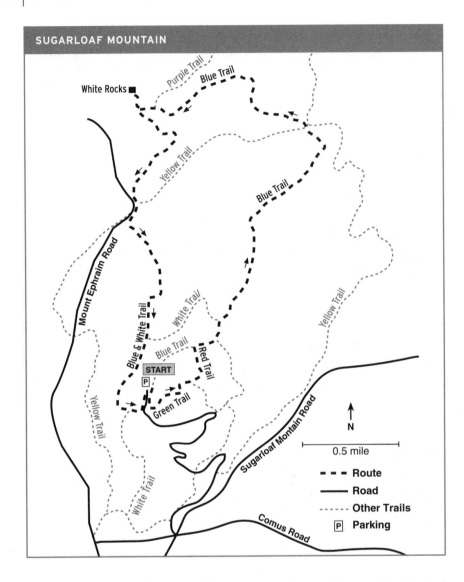

SUGARLOAF MOUNTAIN

White Rocks ■

Purple Trail

Blue Trail

Yellow Trail

Blue Trail

Mount Ephraim Road

White Trail/

Blue & White Trail

Blue Trail

Red Trail

START

P

Green Trail

Yellow Trail

Yellow Trail

White Trail

Sugarloaf Montain Road

Comus Road

N

0.5 mile

- - - Route
— Road
---- Other Trails
P Parking

descends down the other side of the mountain, finally following Blue Trail as it circles the northern ridge.

From the West View lot, start Green Trail just beyond the covered wooden shelter. The trail rises 325 vertical feet over a quarter-mile. Begin a gradual climb and then a sharper ascent over granite rocks that lead to a series of steep stone steps to the 1,282-foot summit affording a must-see view of the Frederick Valley and the bluish Catoctin Mountains on the horizon. The point where the Catoctin range abruptly ends to the south is Point of Rocks, where the Potomac River rolls through and where the circa-1833 Monocacy Aqueduct

This view from the 1,300-foot summit of Sugarloaf Mountain looks west over forest and farmland to the Catoctin Mountains in the distance. Rare table mountain pine thrives on the summit.

can be seen. Start down the quarter-mile Red Trail opposite the overlook. At the trailhead is a mini forest of *Chionanthus*, or fringe trees, which are usually found in tropical or subtropical climates. Pass Orange Trail on the right, and then begin a steep descent. In spring showy jack-in-the-pulpit, yellow corydalis, black cohosh, and wild geranium bloom on the forest floor. The high elevation also nurtures a unique canopy of black birch, red maple, tupelo, chestnut oak, and hickories. At 0.5 mile is a T intersection with Blue Trail and a northwesterly view on Bill Lambert overlook.

Blue Trail (also called Northern Peaks Trail) is a challenging 5-mile circuit that loops back to West View. Continue downhill and turn left where White Trail merges briefly. Turn right when Blue Trail leaves White Trail and passes a sign that indicates it is 2 miles to White Rocks overlook. After a brief level stretch, climb steeply to the left and onto the crest of the northern ridge. Hike the narrow summit. In the summer, watch for blueberry and huckleberry bushes (with edible berries) and deerberry bushes (with hard, inedible berries). Violets, cut-leafed toothwort, yellow corydalis, and the rare early saxifrage bloom in spring, followed by black cohosh in June. Continue downhill and onto level ground before climbing over moss-tinged granite rocks. This section is especially beautiful in early spring, when shadbushes unfurl creamy-white blossoms against the gray-pink rock.

At the peak of this small rise, climb the large pile of rocks for a view of the western wooded slopes. Then the trail plunges downward 100 feet to a five-way intersection with the Blue, Yellow and Purple trails. Continue ahead on Blue Trail bearing left and meandering uphill before navigating a challenging set of switchbacks to a 1,015-foot-high summit—the highest point on the northern ridge and the approximate halfway mark. This is the most isolated portion of the trail. An ancient-looking cairn sits on the summit. Then track downhill in the direction of White Rocks overlook, following the spine of the ridge. In spring, look for jack-in-the-pulpit and bulbous, beautiful pink lady's slipper.

Pass Purple Trail as it comes in on the right and turn on a spur trail to White Rocks, where two overlooks offer views to the west of Lilypons Water Gardens; Adamstown, Buckeystown, and Frederick; and Catoctin and South mountains. When leaving White Rocks, ignore an incorrect sign that indicates West View parking is back toward the overlooks, and instead go right on a trail that forms a U-turn with the one you came in on. The trail descends, ascends, and winds around to the left before reaching partially open meadows.

Reach Mount Ephraim Road at a valley and wade through a small, shallow tributary of Bear Branch. Pass a parking area and another stream flowing underneath the road, and follow the road to the right. Turn left on Blue Trail and begin a gradual ascent adjacent to the Bear Branch tributary. The deep, rocky streambed carves its right of way below a steep mountainside, bringing color in the form of cinnamon ferns, skunk cabbage, spicebush, Indian cucumber root, and the rare and beautiful whorled pogonia. American beeches and dogwoods are common on this stretch, as are resident birds such as ovenbirds, wood thrushes, and red-eyed vireos. Turn abruptly to the right about 0.5 mile from the road and begin ascending. Turn right at a T intersection where White Trail again merges, and stay fairly level along the side of a boulder-strewn ridge before turning left uphill to the parking lot.

MORE INFORMATION

Sugarloaf Mountain is open to the public and there is no fee. The mountain also offers bicycling and rock-climbing opportunities. The mountain's Strong Mansion is open to visitors and can also be reserved for social events.

NEARBY

Visit Lilypons Water Gardens, which has 300 acres of seasonally colorful aquatic plants and holds public events. See www.lilypons.com for more information. Also nearby is Monocacy Natural Resources Management Area, which contains miles of wildflower-rich hiking trails.

TRIP 17
BLACK HILL REGIONAL PARK

Location: Clarksburg, MD
Rating: Moderate
Distance: 6.8 miles
Elevation Gain: 320 feet
Estimated Time: 2.0 to 2.5 hours
Maps: USGS Germantown

**Black Hill Regional Park, surrounding the 500-acre Little
Seneca Lake, is a butterfly hotspot with meadows that attract
hundreds of monarchs during their semiannual migrations in
April and September.**

DIRECTIONS
From I-495 (Capital Beltway) inner loop, take Exit 38 (or from outer loop, take
Exit 35) onto I-270. At Exit 16, go right on Father Hurley Boulevard (which becomes MD 27/Ridge Road). Turn left onto MD 355 (Frederick Road) and go 1.0
mile, turn left onto West Old Baltimore Road and go 1.5 miles, and turn left onto
Lake Ridge Drive into the park. Follow Lake Ridge Drive 1.5 miles to the visitor
center near Little Seneca Lake. *GPS coordinates:* 39° 12.025′ N, 77° 17.301′ W.

TRAIL DESCRIPTION
The park's 500-acre Little Seneca Lake was built—by damming Little Seneca
Creek—to provide an emergency water supply for residents of the metro area.
In the nineteenth century, the creek was used to power several lumber and
grist mills; the ruins of one are visible near where the creek enters the lake. The
trails here traverse rolling terrain with lots of elevation change but little that
is precipitous. Expect to encounter meadows, fields giving way to forest, thick
deciduous forest, and stands of conifers. A dizzying number of monarch butterflies visit the park in late summer and early autumn during their migrations
to and from Mexico.

Upon exiting the visitor center, turn left and go through a wildflower
meadow, then turn right on the asphalt Black Hill Trail. The meadow is planted
with milkweed, the larval host plant for monarch butterflies. Black Hill Trail
skirts Little Seneca Lake past wide-crowned Chinese elms, with picnic pavilions on the right. Where the trail reaches Lake Ridge Drive at 0.6 mile, stop

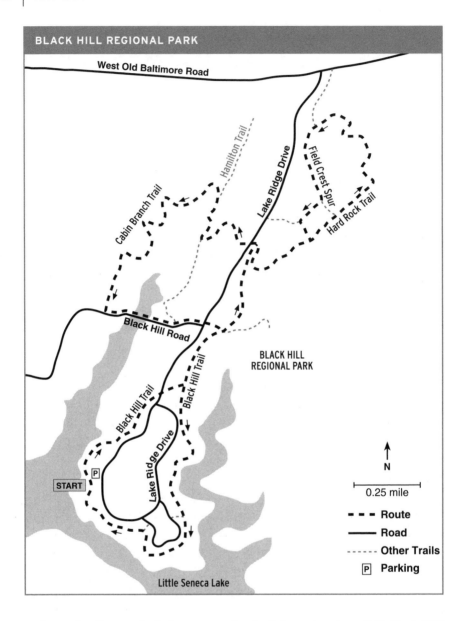

BLACK HILL REGIONAL PARK

West Old Baltimore Road

Hamilton Trail

Lake Ridge Drive

Cabin Branch Trail

Field Crest Spur

Hard Rock Trail

Black Hill Road

BLACK HILL
REGIONAL PARK

Black Hill Trail

Black Hill Trail

Lake Ridge Drive

START

P

N

0.25 mile

– – – Route
——— Road
······· Other Trails
P Parking

Little Seneca Lake

at the park office on the left to see a mineshaft from the circa-1850 Black Hill Gold Mine. Local resident George Chadwick transformed the mine into a bomb shelter during the Cold War, and used fieldstone from the mine to build the current park office.

Cross Lake Ridge Drive and follow a grassy clearing, visible between two thin strips of trees, passing a greenhouse and reaching the natural-surface Black Hill Trail where Black Hill Trail splits in two to loop south around the tip of the peninsula. Turn left on the rocky trail through sycamores and yellow poplars and hike to a four-way intersection, then turn right for a quick side trip down a steep gravel road to a bridge over Little Seneca Creek. On a small side trail to the right, just beyond the bridge, are the remains of Water's Mill, built by Zachariah Water in 1810. It became one of the few in the area to press flax seed in the production of linseed oil before closing in 1895. The river power in this area was vital to the local farm economy until the railroad made it possible to bring cheaper flour and cornmeal from the Midwest.

Return across the bridge and take the first right before the gravel trail, and then a second right to return to Black Hill Trail heading north. Cut across a pipeline clearing and then walk parallel to a streambed to the right, almost reaching Lake Ridge Drive before making a U-turn and crossing the stream. Follow the stream south on the opposite slope and come back to the pipeline clearing before turning left and heading gradually uphill on a bed of loose, sprawling rocks. Pass two grass connector trails on the left and reenter the forest. Begin the loop on Hard Rock Trail. Go between stone ruins, and, curving to the left, exit the forest at a meadow, at the center of which is a bluebird nest. Stay straight on what is now the Field Crest Spur (though a sign indicates the Field Crest Spur branches right) and enter another large meadow serving as a "monarch way station." Pass a maintenance yard on the left and then take the second left onto a connector trail, which leads back to Hard Rock Trail.

Turn right and as the trail rises from the streambed at 3.3 miles, turn right across Lake Ridge Drive, and start on Cabin Branch Trail. At the T intersection, turn right onto the combined Cabin Branch and Hamilton trails, followed by a left to cross a stream where Cabin Branch Trail goes its own way. Travel south parallel to the main stream and over a series of hills carved by small feeder streams. At 4.5 miles, reach a pipeline clearing and turn left, over a third tributary stream, and then immediately turn right (pay attention—the trail is unmarked). Leave the forest as the trail cuts through a claustrophobic tunnel of shrubs, before reaching a mowed swath near Black Hill Road.

Turn left on Black Hill Road and cross a dammed causeway over the lake. Continue past the start of Hamilton Trail on the left and cross Lake Ridge Drive again, turning right on Black Hill Trail. Pass the grass connector trail previously taken from the park office and tramp south, passing several side trails that lead to playgrounds and parking areas. Stay with the forested high ground above the lake. At 6.1 miles, the trail becomes asphalt and passes various exercise stands. Turn left at a T intersection just before the roadway, continuing past a grove of tall yellow poplars. Go by the boat rental office and return uphill to the visitor center.

MORE INFORMATION

The park is open year-round, sunrise to sunset. On the first Saturday of September, the park holds Monarch Fiesta Day, which includes guided exhibits and butterfly tagging by park naturalists. The boat rental facility near the visitor center offers pontoon boat tours Saturday and Sunday from May to September. Rowboats, canoes, and kayaks can be rented over the same period for $8 an hour, or $27.50 for the day. Visit www.montgomeryparks.org/facilities/regional_parks/blackhill/index.shtm or call 301-972-9396.

NEARBY

For more hiking options, continue on Black Hill Trail past the mill site, where it becomes asphalt and turns south for 2 miles along the eastern shore of Little Seneca Lake. End at Wisteria Drive and return to the park. Another good option is Hoyle's Mill Trail, which travels through South Germantown Recreational Park to Seneca Creek State Park (Trip 6).

TRIP 18
MATTHEW HENSON TRAIL

Location: Viers Mill and Colesville, MD
Rating: Moderate
Distance: 4.5 miles (one way)
Elevation Gain: 235 feet
Estimated Time: 2.5 to 3.0 hours
Maps: USGS Kensington; online at park website

This attractive and very peaceful paved trail, meandering along Turkey Branch through a state park, provides flora and fauna sighting opportunities surprising in such a populated area.

DIRECTIONS

From I-495 (Capital Beltway), take Exit 33 for MD 185 (Connecticut Avenue). Drive about 3.0 miles and bear left onto Veirs Mill Road. Go about half a mile and turn left at the light onto Randolph Road. Then take the third right (at a traffic light) onto Dewey Road. Drive approximately four blocks until you see Winding Creek Local Park on the left (before Dewey Road makes a sharp curve right), and park here. *GPS coordinates*: 39° 03.467′ N, 77° 05.523′ W.

Pre-positioning a vehicle at the trail's end is highly recommended (see last paragraph of Trail Description). Park on Alderton Road. *GPS coordinates*: 39° 05.169′ N, 77° 02.053′ W.

TRAIL DESCRIPTION

Well-maintained, peaceful, wonderfully silent, and pleasantly hidden away, this trail, which opened in 2009, is as yet a largely undiscovered gem, particularly along its northern reaches. Deer, cottontail rabbits, mallard ducks, songbirds such as cardinals and finches, and butterflies are plentiful along the path to keep you company and provide enjoyment on your walk. The trail and the state park surrounding it are named in honor of Maryland native Matthew Henson, the African-American arctic explorer who was the first human being to reach the North Pole (see page 81).

Begin at the Winding Creek Local Park parking lot by looking for the white signs with green lettering pointing toward the trail. Start by heading northeast along the paved trail, following the extension of Dewey Road, and catch your first glimpse of babbling Turkey Branch. You'll soon see signs for

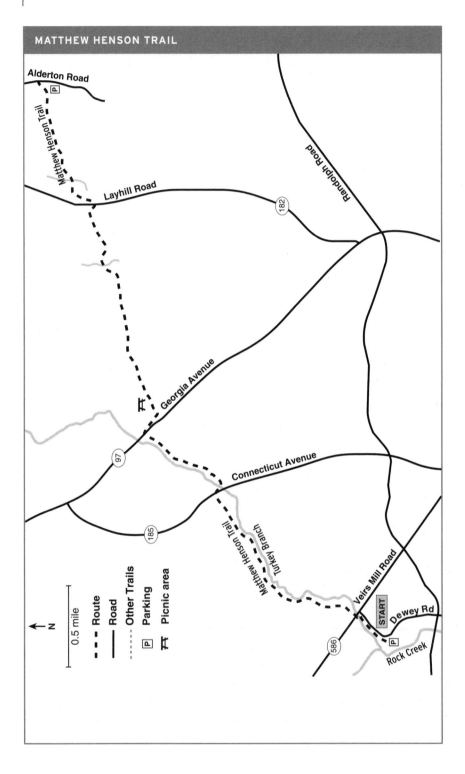

MATTHEW HENSON TRAIL

MATTHEW HENSON AND THE RACE TO THE NORTH POLE

Looking at an old photo of explorer Matthew Henson swathed in Arctic furs, with his dark skin and large, kind eyes, you wonder: What led this African-American man to the North Pole, of all places?

Henson was born in 1866 on a southern Maryland farm to sharecropper parents, who soon moved to Washington, D.C., in hopes of better opportunities. Orphaned by age 12, he sought adventure as a merchant-ship cabin boy, sailing the world, learning about mathematics, navigation, and cultures around the globe. When his captain died, Henson returned to Washington, finding work in an outfitter shop. There he met Navy officer Robert Peary, who was determined to attain the North Pole but had military orders to lead a surveying expedition to Nicaragua. Peary hired Henson as his manservant, and, impressed by the young man's abilities, took him on an 1891 Greenland expedition seeking paths to the Pole. When Peary warned him of Arctic hardships, Henson retorted, "I'll go north with you, sir, and I think I'll stand it as well as any man."

And he did. Henson became keen to represent *his* race in the race to the Pole. Peary insisted that Henson join every attempt to reach the Pole; it would take eight brutal and deadly treks across the crevasses of the Arctic icepack. The explorers learned from the Inuit natives, whom they rewarded with blankets and tools; they fathered children with Inuit women. But only Henson learned the Inuit language.

Peary chose Henson as the one non-Inuit to accompany him on the final push to the Pole in April 1909. A weakened Peary rode in a dogsled while Henson, nearly losing his life in a crevasse, forged ahead to plant the U.S. flag at the top of the world. By then, Henson no longer felt like anyone's servant. But Peary saw things differently.

Upon their return to the U.S., Peary seriously downplayed Henson's achievement as the first to set foot at 90 degrees north latitude, and Henson received only an obscure federal clerk's job in New York. Meanwhile, Peary and a pretender, Frederick Cook (a physician on the 1891 Greenland expedition who falsely claimed to have reached the Pole a year earlier than Peary), were showered with glory, medals, and cash. Not until age 70 was Henson accepted into the exclusive Explorers Club. Today, however, his remains rest adjacent to Peary's in Arlington National Cemetery, and his Inuit descendants still speak of him as *Maripahluk*: "Matthew, the Kind One."

the Veirs Mill Road crossing: the trail will jog left to cross an access road, then make a quick right turn to cross the six-lane Veirs Mill Road itself. Watch for the black barred fences, and note that this crossing has neither a marked crosswalk nor a walk signal. There is a button to push, but it seems merely to set off flashers to warn oncoming traffic, which can be traveling at high speeds; use caution.

Honeysuckle spills over the fence just across Veirs Mill Road, and the easy-to-follow paved trail continues parallel to residential Turkey Branch Parkway on the left and alongside a forest renewal area to the right. The parks commission is working to remove invasive plant species and to restore a natural habitat for plants and animals. Wild grapevines and bamboo can be seen along this segment of the hike. Just as you pass Grenoble Drive on the left, notice a grove of sycamores on the slope. You'll come now to the "10 mile" post. Note that these markers encompass mileage for the connecting Rock Creek Trail as well, so subtract 9 miles from each for an accurate guideline; you're now at the 1-mile point on Henson Trail.

Near the rows of planted American hollies is the first of several benches along the trail, and just past is a large hemlock tree with honeysuckle vines entwined in its branches, sprawling 20 feet in the air. At mile 1.3 is an emergency call box (these are also located at mile 1.8 and mile 3.1). Now you're approaching the Connecticut Avenue overpass; connector trails lead up to this main road. Follow the main trail under the bridge and around to a curving boardwalk, then over a steel bridge. As the path meanders, look for a big, old, leaning willow tree to the right. Another steel bridge leads to the Georgia Avenue crossing—this one has no button to push, but does provide a painted crosswalk.

The trail turns to the right, winds around a church, and begins to climb: The crossing is at mile 2.1, and the trail will incline until about mile 2.8, when it descends to the long wooden boardwalk through wetlands. But first, pause for a break or picnic at the benches behind the church. And just a little farther on, there's a shade pavilion and some picnic tables for public use. Moving on, come to a downslope and the start of the 0.6-mile boardwalk, which passes through a cattail marsh and crosses a couple of small streams. A horse farm is off to the right. At mile 3.7, cross Layhill Road, near another church. A crosswalk, push button, and walk signal make this one easier.

Now the last leg of the trail bears left into an open meadow area, where deer can often be seen. Flowering crabapple trees make a pretty picture in early spring. Cross the steel bridge and walk up a slope into a wide meadow, also frequented by whitetails, and see the final crosswalk of this hike, taking you over the countrylike two-lane Sullivan Road and past Layhill Village Local

Lush ferns border the longest of Matthew Henson Trail's boardwalks as it runs downhill into a cool, shady marsh.

Park with its ball fields. A last downslope leads to one more boardwalk, and soon you'll find the trail ending at a T intersection with Alderton Road.

Note: This is a one-way trail ending in a rather rural area, so you'll do well to pre-position a vehicle on Alderton Road, where street parking should not be a problem, or at Layhill Village Local Park if you're up for backtracking a bit. Taxis are not likely to be found in the quiet Alderton Road neighborhood, or even a mile back along Layhill Road, to take you back to Winding Creek Local Park. If you can't manage to place a vehicle at trail's end, take at least two phone numbers for local cab companies before starting out.

MORE INFORMATION

Matthew Henson Trail is maintained by the Montgomery Parks division of the Maryland-National Capital Park and Planning Commission. Contact: Montgomery County Department of Parks, 9500 Brunett Ave., Silver Spring, MD 20901. To report trail problems or suggest repairs, call 301-670-8080. Park Police (nonemergency) can be reached at 301-949-8010. Website and trail map: www.montgomeryparks.org/PPSD/ParkTrails/trails_MAPS/matthew_henson_trail.shtm. The only rest room available along this trail is the portable toilet at the starting point in Winding Creek Local Park. No trash receptacles are provided on the trail.

TRIP 19
CAPITAL CRESCENT TRAIL

Location: Bethesda, MD and Georgetown, Washington, D.C.
Rating: Moderate
Distance: 8.0 miles (one way)
Elevation Gain: −310 feet (downslope)
Estimated Time: 4.0 to 4.5 hours
Map: USGS Washington West

Very popular with local commuters, this shady, gently descending paved rail-trail travels through historic areas in Maryland and Washington, D.C., offering views of the Chesapeake & Ohio Canal, the Potomac River, and several attractive old railway crossings.

DIRECTIONS
From I-495 (Capital Beltway), take Exit 34 (Wisconsin Avenue/Bethesda/Rockville) and follow MD 355 (Rockville Pike/Wisconsin Avenue) south 2.8 miles. Turn left on Willow Lane. Elm Street Park is one block ahead on your left. Paid public parking is available in several garages and metered lots nearby. *GPS coordinates:* 38° 58.948′ N, 77° 05.522′ W.

By train, take Metrorail's Red Line to the Bethesda station. Exit the station near a yellow abstract sculpture along Wisconsin Avenue at the intersection with East-West Highway. Cross to the eastern side of Wisconsin Avenue, and walk south three blocks to Elm Street (not signed for southbound traffic), just past the Air Rights Building. Turn left on Elm and walk one block straight into Elm Street Park, the address for which is technically 4601 Willow Lane.

TRAIL DESCRIPTION
Capital Crescent Trail is a local rails-to-trails creation that follows the roadbed of the Baltimore & Ohio's (B&O) old Georgetown Branch line. This line began in the 1880s when B&O's competitor, the Pennsylvania Railroad, refused to allow other rail companies access to its Potomac River bridges in and around Washington, D.C. The B&O planned instead to build a new river crossing near present-day Chain Bridge, connecting Baltimore and Washington with the South via this route. By the early 1900s, rail companies were working more cooperatively, and that trans-Potomac connection north of Washington, D.C., was never built. The branch line did operate from Georgetown to Silver

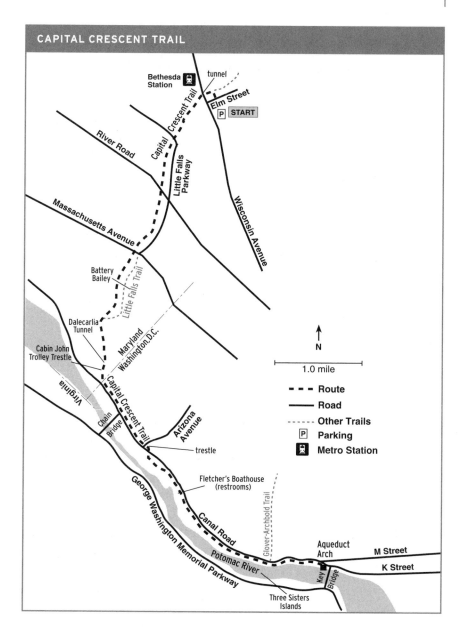

Spring, mainly as a freight route, until 1985. Local efforts created the present trail, popular with commuters, athletes, and leisure seekers.

From Elm Street Park, look north between two jungle gyms for the path leading into the Wisconsin Avenue tunnel. Turn left into the tunnel to begin the hike. At first, the trail signs will read Georgetown Branch Trail in honor of the old rail line now recreated as a hiker-biker trail. Note that you're beginning the hike at approximately the 3.0 mile marker (trail mile count begins at the Lyttonsville–Silver Spring end), so subtract 3.0 miles from the figures on trail mileposts to get a rough idea of your progress. Travel through the 855-foot tunnel beneath Wisconsin Avenue and two office buildings constructed to use the "air rights" over the old roadbed. When you emerge, follow the yellow markers to the corner of Bethesda and Woodmont avenues. Turn right on the sidewalk to the Bethesda Avenue crosswalk (a sign will point toward Capital Crescent Trail), then cross Woodmont and bear right to reach the brown trail-head sign. Turn onto the paved trail—a water fountain and benches are available just down the path by the wayside sign explaining trail history.

You might not realize as you walk that the trail slopes gently downhill. Be advised, however, that it's posted Montgomery County Parks Department policy not to clear snow or ice from the trail after winter storms, so use caution if warranted by the weather. The first road crossing comes just before the 1-mile point: a crosswalk at Little Falls Parkway, which is a major artery. A quarter of a mile farther, past a small park on the right with lovely white pines, comes the crossing at Dorset Avenue, a more residential road. At milepost 4.5 (our 1.6-mile point) is another rest and water stop by the inclined bridge over busy River Road.

You'll soon come to the marker for Loughborough Mill, built around 1830 by local businessman and federal office seeker Nathan Loughborough. The mill was closed in the early 1860s when the Loughborough family—Virginians by birth and inclination—moved south to support the Confederacy.

At milepost 5.5 (our 2.6) is a brief reference to and glimpse of Battery Bailey, a nearby Civil War fortification built to protect Washington's water reservoir from Confederate attack. At mile 3.0, look for a majestic old oak tree on the right.

Moving along, cross the "bridge over nothing" at Little Falls Trail that protected the water conduits below from the railway's weight and vibrations. Those conduits allow water to flow from the Potomac River into the Dalecarlia Reservoir now visible on the left. Just ahead is the 341-foot-long brick Dalecarlia Tunnel, built in 1910—one of the trail's jewels. Walking through its cool, dim passage, note the arched "step-backs" or "duck-ins" intended to protect track workers from passing trains.

At milepost 6.5 (our 3.7) is another rest and water stop, just before the Cabin John Trolley Trestle, which passes over an old streetcar route popular with summer visitors traveling to the historical Glen Echo amusement park. Look right and see crabapple trees blooming in early spring; look left to the Washington Aqueduct water tower, "established 1853." You'll now cross the

Capital Crescent Trail's Arizona Avenue trestle was built in 1910, of pieces salvaged from three older bridges, and decked for bicycles in the 1990s.

boundary into the District of Columbia at our mile 3.9. (Be advised: Except at Fletcher's Cove and Boathouse, there are no resting places along the Washington, D.C., leg of the trail.)

The Chesapeake & Ohio Canal is just below the trail at this point, and the Potomac River and many elegant cliffside homes are visible. Look above you as well, to get a sense of the Potomac's erosive power over time. The landscape is wilder now, and invasive kudzu spills over the branches of large trees. Wild strawberries and blackberries appear at trail's edge in late spring and summer. At milepost 7.2 (our 4.4), if things aren't too overgrown, you might glimpse historical Chain Bridge at river level. Vines also grow up and over the Arizona Avenue Trestle, another trail showpiece you'll cross half a mile ahead, built around 1910 from pieces salvaged from other structures.

From here, the trail parallels the C&O Canal and its towpath. Half a mile more brings you to Fletcher's Cove and Boathouse at our mile 5.6. Portable toilets, a seasonal snack bar and boathouse, picnic tables, and water fountains are found here in a shady riverside park. Pale-yellow columbines grow here, and at mile 6.7 the stone wall of the canal berm is exposed, near some rough steps leading up to the towpath.

This leg of the trail has some spectacular vistas over the Potomac River; one in particular looks out on Three Sisters Islands, which mark the northernmost navigable point on the river for large craft. This is why the water often smells brackish—the Potomac is a tidal river all the way up to Great Falls. At our mile 7.5 is a stone and concrete bridge in the woods, which connects the trail to Foxhall Road and Glover Archbold Hiking Trail. Next, pass the green-painted Washington Canoe Club before reaching the stone Aqueduct Arch. The arch is actually an old abutment from a highly advanced canal bridge, built in 1843, that carried canal barges and mules across the Potomac River to connect with the Alexandria Canal. After the Civil War, the Aqueduct Bridge was revamped with two decks to carry both water and road traffic.

At this point, you can climb the wooden steps on the left up to the towpath, then turn right and cross under one overpass to the steps leading up to M Street. To find a Metrorail station, walk across Key Bridge into Virginia and proceed about four blocks to the Rosslyn station (Blue/Orange Lines), or hail a cab on M Street to the Dupont Circle station (Red Line) near 20th and P streets NW or to Foggy Bottom station (Blue/Orange Lines) at 23rd and Eye (I) streets NW.

MORE INFORMATION
Write ahead for a free full-color trail brochure with a map and historical points of interest: Coalition for the Capital Crescent Trail, P.O. Box 30703, Bethesda, MD 20824; include a self-addressed stamped envelope. Recorded information line: 202-234-4874. A trail map is also available online at www.cctrail.org. An all-volunteer network supports and promotes the trail; maintenance is managed by a public-private partnership between Montgomery County Parks and the National Park Service. For information on Metrorail schedules, routes, and fares, call 202-637-7000 or visit www.wmata.com. Parking is free on weekends and holidays at Montgomery County's Waverly Garage, about three blocks from this hike's starting point in Bethesda, on Montgomery Avenue between Waverly and Pearl (*GPS coordinates:* 38° 59.038′ N, 77° 05.487′ W).

NEARBY
Restaurants and taxis are plentiful along M Street. The famous iron stairs from the film *The Exorcist*, leading up toward the Georgetown University campus (the film's screenplay was written by a Georgetown alumnus), are visible on the western side of the brick, clock-towered Car Barn, an old trolley storage and repair facility. Just east of the Key Bridge is a park dedicated to Francis Scott Key, the Georgetown resident and lawyer best known for penning "The Star-Spangled Banner."

TRIP 20
BILLY GOAT TRAIL AT GREAT FALLS $

Location: Great Falls, MD
Rating: Difficult
Distance: 8.2 miles
Elevation Gain: 650 feet
Estimated Time: 4.0 to 4.5 hours
Maps: USGS Falls Church; Potomac Appalachian Trail Club Map D
Potomac Gorge Area; free sketch map at visitor center; free NPS map
of C&O Canal at visitor center

**Billy Goat Trail at Great Falls, Maryland, is one of the metro
region's most popular—and most spectacular—hikes, tracing the
top of the 50-foot Mather Gorge above the Potomac River.**

DIRECTIONS

From I-495 (Capital Beltway) near American Legion Bridge, take Exit 41 (Card-
erock/Glen Echo) onto Clara Barton Parkway and drive west to a T intersection.
Turn left onto MacArthur Boulevard. Go 2.5 miles to the intersection with Falls
Road. Turn left into park. *GPS coordinates*: 39° 0.15′ N, 77° 14.81′ W.

TRAIL DESCRIPTION

Billy Goat Trail is actually three separate trails, all linked by the Chesapeake &
Ohio (C&O) Canal towpath. This hike proceeds downriver on sections A and
B—the first a difficult rock scramble, the second somewhat easier—and returns via less-used forest trails. The C&O Canal towpath offers flat ground between the challenging sections. The land here falls within the Potomac Gorge,
a biologically diverse 15-mile stretch located at the fall line. Surprisingly for a
metropolitan region, this is one of the continent's most intact fall lines, unaf-
fected by dams and riverfront development. At Great Falls, the river drops 60
feet in less than 1.0 mile. Rare plant species such as Indian grass, rough rush
grass, and bluestem—more common to Midwest prairies—survive here, deposited during periods of intense flood scouring. Threatening these species
are human footfalls—stay on the blazed trails—and nonnative species such as
Japanese honeysuckle, kudzu, and garlic mustard.

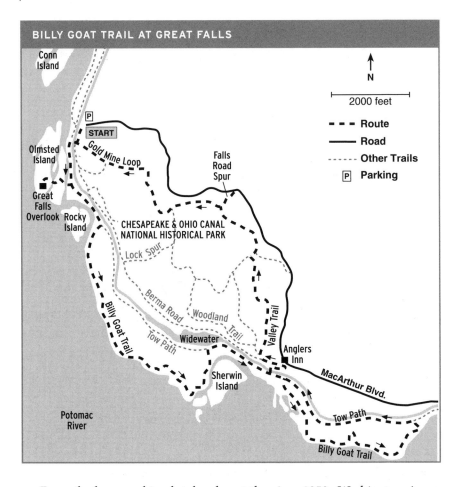

BILLY GOAT TRAIL AT GREAT FALLS

From the large parking lot, head past the circa-1850s Washington Aqueduct gatehouse to the Great Falls Tavern Visitor Center, which has in-depth exhibits on the ill-fated C&O Canal. (The canal took decades to build and was quickly usurped as a transportation corridor by the B&O Railroad.) The building was constructed in 1828 as a lock house, and the lock tender added a three-story north wing as a hotel/tavern for weary barge workers in 1831. From the tavern, cross the canal on the footbridge at lock 20 and turn left downstream on the towpath past locks 19 and 18. Turn right (just before lock 17) for a 0.1-mile side trip over the pedestrian bridge to Great Falls Overlook on Olmsted Island. The overlook offers a tremendous view of Great Falls. The island landscape here—a jumble of flat boulders crisscrossed by deep crevices—was once the Potomac riverbed. Swirling, sediment-filled river eddies carved out the crevices and potholes over geologic time. An ecologically unique bedrock terrace forest—with white oak, northern red oak, hickory, Virginia pine, and federally endangered wildflower species such as wispy yellow nailwort and hardy rock skullcap—thrives here and on Bear Island to the south.

Return to the towpath and continue past lock 17. At 0.8 mile, 30 yards before a footbridge and stop lock—the point where the canal enters Widewater, a natural channel left dry when the river shifted course—turn right onto the blue-blazed Billy Goat Trail A. The 1.7-mile Trail A follows the eastern edge of Bear Island—another ancient riverbed—atop the Mather Gorge. Overuse is threatening the more than 50 rare plant and animal species on the island, so do not stray off the path. American hornbeam has been replanted in several damaged areas.

Start on a rocky trail through the woods, then reach a shelf of boulders over the gorge, where, to the right, level rocks at cliff's edge make a nice picnic spot. Carefully scramble atop the narrow-edged boulders, following the blazes forward, before swinging behind an escarpment at the edge of the gorge and gradually descending toward the river. Next, call on reserve energy for a challenging 50-foot climb along a sloping cliff face (the most difficult portion).

Continue as the trail snakes along the edge of the gorge, passing several ponds and rocky hills. Descend to a point of rocks above a large channel of the Potomac River. A seashell-filled landing, shaded by sycamores, can be accessed at low water. The hill just to the left is Sherwin Island; beyond it on the opposite heights is the conspicuous brick auditorium of the Madeira School, an all-girls private boarding school. Continue as the trail curves back toward the canal at the end of Bear Island, following a large channel on the right. Traverse several rocky hills cut by streams, then head left away from the channel to the C&O Canal towpath at the end of Widewater, at 2.5 miles.

Turn right on the towpath and head past the entrance to a bridge over the canal that leads back to Old Angler's Inn and connections to other trails (to which this hike returns). Continue 160 yards to the start of Billy Goat Trail B. This area, another bulge of land in the Potomac's watercourse, is a floodplain forest dominated by sycamore, ash, and elm trees. Follow the narrow path 80 yards into the woods, then swing left with the blue blazes and follow the crest of the bluff before descending to the river. Proceed downstream, at one point veering sharply inland around a gully and then returning to river's edge. Opposite a large island, turn left away from the river and climb back to the C&O towpath, at 4.5 miles.

Turn left, keeping the canal on the right, for a 0.9-mile return trip to the bridge that leads to Old Angler's Inn (an interpretive sign marks the intersec-

From Olmsted Island, just north of Billy Goat Trail, hikers can take in the roiling waters of Great Falls ... and marvel at experienced kayakers battling class 5 rapids.

tion). Cross the bridge and head uphill. At the Cropley parking lot, make a hairpin turn up and to the left onto a wide path—Berma Road—that runs atop the Washington Aqueduct on the east side of Widewater. Near a small power station, turn right onto the yellow-blazed Valley Trail.

Follow the valley for 0.6 mile to a T intersection at 6.3 miles with the blue-blazed Gold Mine Loop. Turn right and head uphill on an old woods road, passing a yellow-blazed spur to Rockwood School. At a point where the main trail veers 90 degrees to the left, take the spur trail to the ruins of the Maryland Mine.

Gold fever began at Great Falls when a Union soldier discovered specks of gold while washing skillets in a stream. Following the war, investors swarmed the area and built several 100-foot-deep mineshafts. Profits were minimal, however, and pits, shafts, trenches, and tunnels came and went. The rusty ruins here were part of the Maryland Mine, which even in its heyday was a rickety contraption of sheds and shanties stuck together on stilts at different levels.

Turn right back onto the loop and ascend a draw, where the path follows an old prospecting trench. Reach a Y intersection at 7.2 miles where the loop closes, and turn slightly right to descend to an old roadbed—what was once the Washington and Great Falls Railroad, which ran trolleys to the area. Turn right on the roadbed and ascend slightly, passing through dense hardwood forest. After 200 yards, turn left off the raised roadbed and continue downhill 300 yards to the trailhead near Great Falls Tavern, at 8.2 miles.

MORE INFORMATION

The park entrance fee is $4. Mule-drawn canal boat rides are offered three times daily, Thursday to Sunday, April to October. Tickets can be purchased at the Great Falls Tavern Visitor Center. The National Park Service also offers ranger-guided hiking tours of Great Falls, biking tours on the C&O Canal, and overnight stays (by advance reservation) at Riley's Lockhouse.

Dogs are prohibited on Olmsted Island and Billy Goat Trail A. Swimming at Great Falls is prohibited because of dangerous underwater currents. To learn more about human pressures on the Potomac Gorge and what can be done to lessen them, consult the Nature Conservancy's *Good Neighbor Handbook: A Guide to River Friendly Living in the Middle Potomac Region* (2005).

NEARBY

Glen Echo Park—site of a restored amusement park that once attracted crowds of Washingtonians—the Clara Barton House, and Cabin John Trail are all worthwhile visits on the Maryland side of the Potomac Gorge.

CENTURIES OF PERSEVERANCE: THE CHESAPEAKE & OHIO CANAL

The dream of a trade route to the Ohio River began back in Colonial days and contributed to the nightmare of the French and Indian (Seven Years') War. Then came the founders: Thomas Jefferson advocated development of waterways to the West; George Washington, thinking of future trade and transport possibilities, selected sites for the new capital and a federal armory along the Potomac. The Patowmack Company, organized by Washington in 1785, prepared the way for a vast canal project by dredging river shallows near the District and blasting locks around Great Falls. But progress seemed elusive. Skilled canal labor, for instance, was nonexistent in the new nation; untrained slaves and indentured laborers did much of the work.

A new organization, the Chesapeake & Ohio Company—with the Erie Canal's former chief engineer on board—pushed westward from D.C. in 1828 through the Potomac Valley's rugged terrain. But by the time the canal reached Cumberland, Maryland, in 1850, the speedy, up-and-coming Baltimore & Ohio Railroad had beaten it there (and beyond) by 8 years. This limited the canal mainly to local traffic—coal for the foundries and breweries of Georgetown, produce for the city's markets. By 1860, decades of legal battles and loan interest had left the company facing massive deficits; the C&O would never come within 100 miles of the Ohio River.

Post-Civil War growth put investors into the black at last. But in 1889, with railroads enjoying ever greater transportation dominance, a terrible hurricane caused flooding that sent barges and lock houses into the nearby Potomac. Repairs were prohibitively expensive for the canal company, so the prosperous B&O Railroad took over the beleaguered waterway in 1890 and kept it going. In 1924, though, when another major flood hit, canal operations were halted. Nature's bad moods likewise stumped New Deal efforts to reinvent the canal as a recreation area.

Following World War II, plans were introduced for a scenic parkway along the C&O. But avid outdoorsman and Supreme Court Justice William O. Douglas insisted that people couldn't truly enjoy the canal from inside an automobile. He invited *Washington Post* editors, who advocated the parkway plan, to hike the entire C&O towpath with him. Douglas easily completed the 8-day trek (it seems the editors made it only partway), raising strong public —and editorial—support for a towpath recreation area. In 1971, the C&O was designated a National Historical Park at last.

TRIP 21
WOODSTOCK EQUESTRIAN PARK

Location: Beallsville, MD
Rating: Moderate
Distance: 2.2 miles
Elevation Gain: 100 feet
Estimated Time: 1.5 hours
Maps: USGS Poolesville; online at park website

Deeply rolling farmland, rich fields, and forest in the Maryland countryside make for a unique hike over rustic trails, with butterflies, deer, and—if you're lucky—horses as companions.

DIRECTIONS

From I-495 (Capital Beltway) inner loop, take Exit 38 (or from outer loop, take Exit 35) onto I-270 north. Take Exit 6 for MD 28 (West Montgomery Avenue). Continue on MD 28, past the intersection with Beallsville Road, to the stone walls on the right marked "Dr. William Rickman Equestrian Center." Turn right between these walls into the avenue of sycamores, and proceed to the gravel parking lot. *GPS coordinates:* 39° 11.444′ N, 077° 25.143′ W.

TRAIL DESCRIPTION

The drive to Woodstock Equestrian Park passes rolling meadows, apple and peach orchards, roadside produce stands, and abundant trees. Historical farmhouses, cemeteries, and barns dot the landscape. Upon entering the park, you'll pass several farm buildings dating to 1861. The park gets its name from nearby Woodstock Farm, owned in the 1790s by George Washington. If it has rained recently, be sure to wear stout boots with plenty of traction. Woodstock's trails are mostly stubble and plowed soil, sometimes uneven and muddy. Yet this recently opened horse haven—still expanding to provide all manner of equestrian facilities to Montgomery County residents, including for jousting and carriage driving—offers a wonderful country hiking experience. The 825-acre park has about 16 miles of hiking and riding trails.

Please note that there are no facilities of any kind at the Dr. William Rickman Equestrian Center entrance, where this hike begins. Stop on your way north along Darnestown Road, at the Moritz Greenberg Equestrian Center parking lot, for a portable toilet if needed, and possibly a look at riders on the

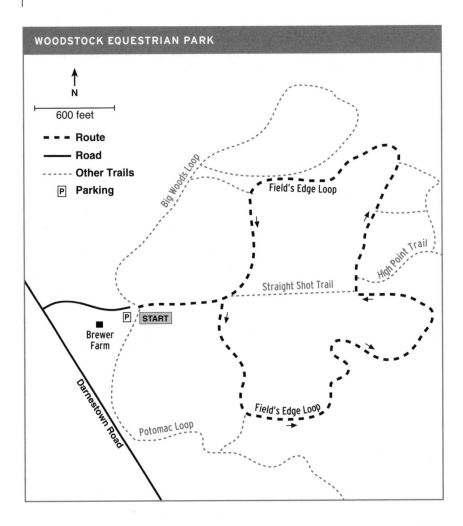

WOODSTOCK EQUESTRIAN PARK

N

600 feet

- - - Route
——— Road
······ Other Trails
P Parking

Big Woods Loop

Field's Edge Loop

High Point Trail

Straight Shot Trail

P START

Brewer
Farm

Darnestown Road

Field's Edge Loop

Potomac Loop

jumping course. Be sure to bring water and snacks from home. Because of the rugged terrain and multiple steep inclines on this hike (although none is more than 100 feet), it is rated as moderate despite the short distance.

From the Rickman parking lot, look away from Darnestown Road and follow the sign to the Straight Shot Trail gravel path, heading eastbound. The trail leads up a small slope, then down over packed cobblestone into a shady glade. At 0.2 mile, look for the marker pointing right onto the Field's Edge Loop and follow it into the mowed stubble grass. From here, the trail will travel up a hill along the rim of the three-lobed farm field for which it's named, likely planted in a multi-annual rotation of wheat, soybeans, or corn. Down in the woods to your right is a small stream, which seems to attract white-tailed deer and cottontail rabbits—move quietly and you're likely to surprise one or two.

Wide panoramas of dramatic skies, rolling farmland, and blue-green foothills are seen from Woodstock Equestrian Park's Field's Edge Loop trail.

When large trees abut a field's edge, with no buffer zone of brushy plants and seedlings for wildlife cover, the resulting shade can prevent crops near that edge from growing to full size; this is one aspect of what's been termed the "edge effect." Researchers also point out that the creation of too many edge habitats close together—"habitat fragmentation," as can happen in areas experiencing exurban development—tends to deprive local flora and fauna of the benefits of deep forest cover: more humidity; protection from wind and sun; reduced vulnerability to predation; less likelihood of isolation in an area insufficient for the overall population of the species. Stubble and high grass also provide some of these benefits for wildlife.

Continue following the trail down the initial slope and around a curve to a rolling up-and-down section, then cross an open area. At this point is a steep slope down to the right that's not part of the trail proper, so walk straight across toward the next copse of trees. Around this copse, the trail turns right and downhill into the second lobe of the field. Red and white clovers, bees, and butterflies of several species and colors are abundant here in spring and summer.

The next up slope will be a steepish climb to the eastern intersection of Straight Shot Trail with the Field's Edge Loop. From this vantage point (roughly the halfway point of the hike), you have a lovely panorama of fields and blue hills in the distance. Now bear right toward the wooded area to continue the hike; the loop will meander into the forest's edge for a brief time. You've now started on the third, longest, and most irregularly-shaped lobe of the trail.

Come out of this wooded section to cross a bit of open field, then go around a bend. You might hear running water in the woods because you're again close to a local brook. Continue along the field's rolling edge and on to the climb up the last big slope. Then descend this hill across a utility right of way and down to rejoin Straight Shot Trail, turning right and walking the last 0.2 mile to return to the parking area.

MORE INFORMATION

Woodstock Equestrian Park is an ongoing joint effort by the Woodstock Equestrian Park Foundation and Maryland-National Capital Park and Planning Commission. The park's Dr. William Rickman area is located at 20207 Darnestown Road, Beallsville, MD 20839; phone 301-444-3121. A trail map and further information are online at www.equestrianpark.org/home.htm. The park closes occasionally for a day or two at a time in fall and winter for deer hunting; call first. Maryland-National Capital Park and Planning Commission's equine resources coordinator can be reached at 301-495-2478.

TRIP 22
LITTLE BENNETT REGIONAL PARK

Location: Clarksburg, MD
Rating: Moderate
Distance: 6.6 miles
Elevation Gain: 300 feet
Estimated Time: 3.0 to 3.5 hours
Maps: USGS Urbana; free maps at parking lot information stands

Little Bennett Creek carves this underused 3,700-acre park into a series of rolling hills that, when combined with historic mills, barns, and schoolhouses, makes for a diverse and stimulating hike.

DIRECTIONS

From I-495 (Capital Beltway) inner loop, take Exit 38 (or from outer loop, take Exit 35) onto I-270 north. At Exit 18, go right on MD 121 (Clarksburg Road). Continue on Clarksburg Road across MD 355 (Frederick Road). Enter Little Bennett Regional Park and turn right into the third lot off Clarksburg Road— the Kinglsey parking area. *GPS coordinates:* 39° 14.590′ N, 77° 17.140′ W.

TRAIL DESCRIPTION

Little Bennett Regional Park preserves a link to the nineteenth-century world when industrialization was just getting underway and local economies were vital to a community's survival. Montgomery County recognizes eleven historical sites within the park including a one-room schoolhouse; lumber, grist, and bone mills; a chapel cemetery; a tobacco barn; and several residences. The park is large, and hiking to these relics of the past on shady country lanes gives the impression of a sustainable, self-sufficient, almost idyllic world.

The park also has the largest Allegheny mound builder ant colony in the mid-Atlantic region The 6.6-mile hike passes the ant colony and several of the historical sites with terrain consisting of choppy hills and low, rounded ridges carved by Little Bennett Creek and its several tributaries. The trail fords streambeds, scales steep hills, and spans open meadows, most of it north of Little Bennett Creek. Maps can be found at the information stands located at all trailhead parking lots.

From the parking lot, enter the forest on Kingsley Trail, where a sign points toward the schoolhouse. Flat and wide, the trail follows Little Bennett Creek

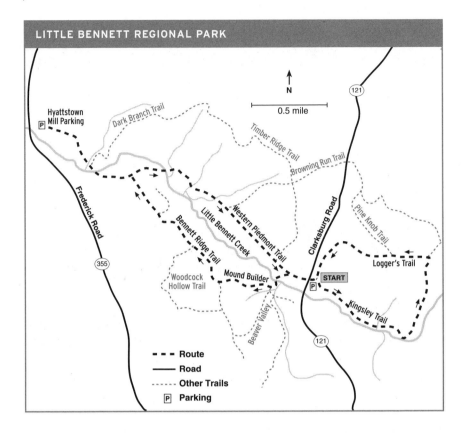

LITTLE BENNETT REGIONAL PARK

under leafy black walnut trees to a T intersection, where the schoolhouse is visible on the right. Turn right and cross a wooden suspension bridge to see the structure, which housed pupils between 1893 and 1935 and was named for Luther G. King, who operated a whiskey distillery at the opposite end of the valley that also bears his name.

Recross the bridge and start north on the wide Purdum Trail. The first stretch is the steepest in the park, climbing 120 feet in just a few hundred yards before leveling off, crossing an old campground and narrowing to a dirt trail in the woods. After 1.3 miles, turn left onto Logger's Trail and travel a low ridge until it descends to the Kingsley parking area and completes a 2.3-mile loop.

After crossing Clarksburg Road, begin on the wide, gravel Western Piedmont Trail. About 200 yards past the road, turn left onto Beaver Valley Trail, slosh through a wet area (flooded by beaver activity upstream), and cross a bridge on Little Bennett Creek. Turn left immediately after the bridge and proceed into the forest, turning onto Mound Builder Trail. Follow this 0.4-

Kudzu blankets trees and grasses in the Little Bennett River valley. An invasive species, kudzu thrives in the mid-Atlantic as winters become more temperate.

mile, rock-and-gravel trail gradually uphill to where a sign indicates the start of a 450-foot-long stretch of Allegheny mound builder colonies reputed to be the largest in eastern North America. The colonies are built vertically to catch sunlight, which aids larvae incubation. Tread quickly and lightly, especially on hot days when thousands of ants swarm among the nests and across the trail. Although not poisonous, they are defensive and will crawl in boots and up pant legs to deliver painful bites. After the nests, turn right at a T intersection onto the gravel Bennett Ridge Trail.

Emerge into a meadow where Woodcock Hollow Trail intersects from the left, and continue north on Bennett Ridge. In a ghostly pine grove, go straight where Owl Ridge Trail departs to the right. Continue over a muddy, low-lying area, and then along the banks of Sopers Branch on the left and large shale-like boulders protruding from the right.

Come to a T intersection with an unmarked gravel trail. In the woods to the right are the stone ruins of David A. Zeigler's water-driven saw and bone mill, where animal bones were ground for fertilizer in the late 1800s. Straight ahead past a yellow gate is Prescott Road. Turn left on Hyattstown Mill Road and cross a bridge spanning Sopers Branch where the road becomes wider and

Prescott Road again intersects from the left. The site of Zeigler's Sumac Mill is a few strides past Prescott Road on the left. In the swampy woods to the north was once a 5-acre millpond, formed by damming Little Bennett Creek. A walk south on Prescott Road leads to Zeigler's intact log house and the Montgomery Chapel Cemetery where an Episcopal Church once stood.

Continue north on Hyattstown Mill Road to the still-standing Hyattstown Mill and nearby miller's residence. This is one of the oldest mills in the Washington, D.C., area, constructed between 1783 and 1794 and operated as both a "merchant mill," selling high-quality flour on the local market, and a "country mill," grinding corn for local farmers. By the 1920s, it could no longer compete with mills in Germantown and Rockville that sat astride the Baltimore & Ohio Railroad and ground wheat and corn from the Midwest more cheaply. Montgomery County purchased the mill in 1966.

Return on the same trail and, after the intersection with Bennett Ridge Trail, parallel the headrace to Zeigler's saw and bone mill. Upon arriving at the fast-moving Little Bennett Creek, ford it and a tiny feeder stream as well. Continue past the intersection with Pine Grove Trail.

Forge ahead under a power line and past a picnic area on the right, then cross Browning Run, yet another tributary of Little Bennett Creek. The trail becomes paved and wide here, and intersects twice with Browning Run Trail before returning to gravel. Follow a wide, straight, and level portion of the trail. At 6.4 miles, Tobacco Barn Trail comes in from the left. Go straight to return to Clarksburg Road and the Kingsley parking area.

MORE INFORMATION

There is no fee for the park, and it is open year-round, sunrise to sunset. More than 20 miles of trails can be explored, as well as historical sites and the Little Bennett Golf Course. Dogs are allowed, but must be leashed. Visit www.montgomeryparks.org/facilities/regional_parks/little_bennett or call 301-528-3450.

NEARBY

Hawk's Reach Nature Center organizes daily hikes as well as summer activities such as hayrides, dog shows, and reptile displays. Below Hawk's Reach are 91 campsites, the only camping area in Montgomery County. The campground is open April 1 to November 31.

TRIP 23
PATAPSCO VALLEY STATE PARK

Location: Elkridge, MD
Rating: Difficult
Distance: 6.9 miles
Elevation Gain: 1,300 feet
Estimated Time: 3.0 hours
Maps: Waterproof Maryland Park Service trail maps available at Avalon Visitor Center; USGS Relay

Cascade Falls on the ridge east of the Patapsco River is the highlight of this hike.

DIRECTIONS

From I-95/I-495 (Capital Beltway), go north on I-95 to Exit 47 (BWI Airport) and go east on I-195. Take Exit 3 to Elkridge and turn right at the stoplight onto US 1 south. Take the next right on South Street, then an immediate left into Patapsco Valley Park. Pass through the contact station ($2 fee for state residents; $3 for nonresidents). Travel under the Thomas Viaduct and turn left at the T intersection with Gun Road. Park at the far end of the first lot. *GPS coordinates: 39° 13.70′ N, 76° 43.60′ W.*

TRAIL DESCRIPTION

The park extends along nearly 35 miles of the Patapsco River in Maryland, from Elkridge in the east to Woodbine in the west. The river valley encompasses more than 14,500 acres and is divided into multiple recreation areas. This hike is in the eastern section, known as the Avalon, Hilton, Glen Artney, and Orange Grove areas, all named for long-gone mill towns.

Though the mills are no longer here, the river valley remains a transportation corridor. Maryland Area Regional Commuter (MARC) trains rumble across the breathtaking 704-foot Thomas Viaduct, which was the largest bridge in the nation at the time of its completion in 1835 and remains the oldest stone arch railroad bridge still in use.

This hike starts from the Avalon area parking lot on the southern side of the Patapsco River and encompasses five major south-side trails. Leave the lot and hike north on River Road, turning left onto the orange-blazed Ridge Trail. After a bracing climb up 180 feet, turn slightly left at the intersection at the

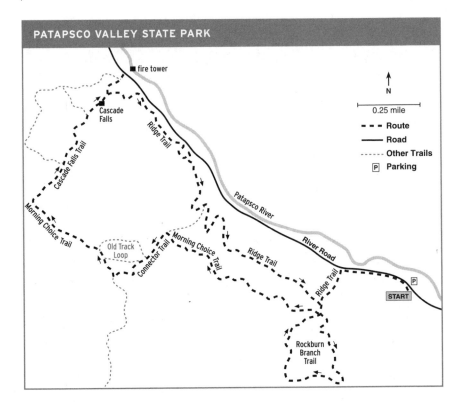

PATAPSCO VALLEY STATE PARK

■ fire tower

Cascade Falls

Ridge Trail

Cascade Falls Trail

Morning Choice Trail

Old Track Loop

Connector Trail

Morning Choice Trail

Patapsco River

Ridge Trail

River Road

Morning Choice Trail

Ridge Trail

Ridge Trail

P Parking

START

Rockburn Branch Trail

N

0.25 mile

- - - Route
—— Road
- - - - Other Trails
P Parking

top, where the Rockburn Branch loop and the Morning Choice trails diverge. Turn left and hike the 1.2-mile, purple-blazed loop, enjoying the mature open forest and pleasant views into stream valleys. Return to the start of the loop and begin a leisurely stroll uphill on the yellow-blazed Morning Choice Trail, heading north. Pass through big-leafed pawpaw thickets, reach a large open field, and travel along the edge of the woods. Come back into tree coverage beneath a large shagbark hickory. Just ahead are the remains of two old two-story houses and a connector trail to Ridge Trail.

Go on to another open field that marks the edge of the Belmont Conference Center lands (center just visible uphill to the left). Reenter the woods, and, after a slight uphill, plunge down across the source of a creek, then up a second draw to a series of wide curves. On the left is an open area with a large climbing wall. Turn sharply left and pass the Old Track Loop on the right. Continue underneath a massive grove of tulip trees, and come to a T intersection (both branches are Morning Choice Trail) and turn right to pass a bamboo thicket, a short link-up with the edge of the Old Track Loop and Norris Lane. Take time to admire the old, squat, burly maple tree, then go downhill to a Y intersection, bearing right onto the blue-blazed Cascade Falls Trail.

Cascade Falls, which must have once attracted the valley's mill workers just as surely as it attracts sightseers today, is the perfect place to stop for lunch. Along with the Thomas Viaduct, Bloedes Dam, and the old suspension bridge, it is one of the best-known sites in the park.

At the T intersection, turn right again and look for the Cascade Falls stream on the left. During the Great Depression of the 1930s, families were allowed to camp out for the entire summer in this park, and many of the campsites were along Cascade Falls and its tributaries. Follow the stream, crossing it twice on small bridges. Then cross a tributary and the main stream two more times. Notice the dramatic cliffs on the opposite bank. Climb a rocky ridge above the water to reach the falls themselves, where the stream course is strewn with large boulders and the water drops 15 feet into a pool. Follow a spur of Cascades Trail as it crosses the stream just below the waterfall and makes its way to River Road and the site of Swinging Bridge, a metal-and-wire structure that shortened the distance workers had to travel to get between the mill towns. (It was destroyed by Hurricane Agnes in 1972.)

Go south on River Road and take the first left heading back uphill onto Ridge Trail for a challenging 1.3-mile ridge run that undulates down and up the sides of steep draws, and turns back on itself in tight switchbacks. Mountain laurel, dogwood, and pawpaw crowd the trail. After passing the connector trail on the right, take the second left past twin dogwood gatekeepers to con-

Pawpaw trees, which are found all over this region, bloom in late spring and bear fruit in early fall.

tinue on Ridge Trail. Wind down along the side of two draws and then crest a hill before running along the side of a very steep ridge to the left. Finally, drop to the right via a series of switchbacks, through patches of pawpaw, and return to River Road. Turn right back to the parking lot.

MORE INFORMATION

Besides hiking, Patapsco Valley State Park is perfect for road biking (paved trails extend down either side of the river), mountain biking (especially on Rockburn Branch Trail), swimming and fishing (at numerous points on the Patapsco River), and photography (Ilchester Rocks Trail and the Thomas Viaduct provide excellent vantages for photographing trains). Dogs are welcome on all the trails. There is a fee of $2 per person. Visit www.dnr.state.md.us/publiclands/central/patapsco.asp.

TRIP 24
GREENWELL STATE PARK

Location: Hollywood, MD
Rating: Moderate
Distance: 4.5 miles
Elevation Gain: 290 feet
Estimated Time: 2.5 to 3.0 hours
Maps: USGS Hollywood; Maryland Department of Natural Resources
Trail Guide (www.dnr.maryland.gov/publiclands); sketch map online
at www.greenwellfoundation.org/

**Hike diverse terrain including pine forests, agricultural fields, tidal
creeks, and sandy beaches at this idyllic state park on the banks of
the Patuxent River.**

DIRECTIONS
From I-95/I-495 (Capital Beltway), take Exit 11 onto MD 4 east (Pennsylvania
Avenue) in the direction of Upper Marlboro. MD 4 becomes MD 4/MD 2.
Drive approximately 50 miles, then cross the Patuxent River Bridge. At the
traffic light after the bridge, turn right onto MD 235 north. At the third traffic light, turn right onto MD 245 (Slotterley Road). Travel approximately 3.0
miles and turn right onto Steer Horn Neck Road. Travel 0.8 mile and turn left
into the park, which is open year-round. *GPS coordinates:* 38° 21.933′ N, 76°
31.502′ W.

TRAIL DESCRIPTION
In 1971, the Greenwell family donated 600 acres on the Patuxent River in St.
Mary's County to the state of Maryland to provide public recreational facilities, especially for people with disabilities. The ten color-coded dirt trails—including two shoreline trails—loop through the park for a total of 10 miles and
are fairly level, wide, and well marked. The hike offers spectacular views of the
broad Patuxent River with a bonus—historical tobacco barns.

From the parking lot near the circa-1880 Rosedale Manor, cross the access
road and follow River Trail to the right side of white rail fences surrounding
the horse pastures. Turn right at the revetment—piled rocks that prevent erosion—along the small cove, and follow the trail around the point to the right.
Continue along River Trail past the fishing pier and the ranger station on the

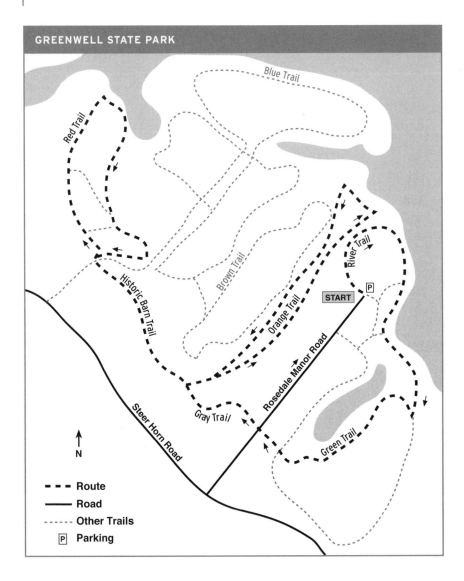

GREENWELL STATE PARK

right to the sandy swimming beach. Pick up the trail on the other side of the beach and follow it for 1,000 yards between the shoreline and the trees until reaching a path on the right that leads away from the water. Follow the path uphill through the woods where it intersects Green Trail along the edge of a large field. Turn right and follow Green Trail as it curves left and skirts the edge of the field. Follow the tree line and the contours of the terrain through the middle of the field to a tidal pond. Leave the edge of the field and enter the woods for about 150 yards. Upon reemerging from the woods, turn right, but instead of following the trail as it reenters the woods, continue left along

Hikers have commanding views of tranquil coves at Greenwell Sate Park, located near the mouth of the Patuxent River on Maryland's Western Shore.

the tree line for 100 yards to the first of four historical tobacco barns. These are some of the oldest barns in tidewater Maryland. Go back to where the trail enters the woods to the left, hike 200 yards to the edge of a new field, and then to the gravel access road for the park.

Cross the road and turn left down the gravel Gray Trail, following it between the fields to a small parking lot with a kiosk. Walk past it and turn left on the other side of the line of barrier trees. Follow marker posts to the edge of the field around to the right, then turn left on Barn Trail through a break in the trees. Travel 150 yards straight along the tree line to the second historical barn and then, farther on, a third, which is the oldest of its type in Tidewater Maryland. Continue to the gravel road and follow it to the left. Where the road turns 90 degrees left, Yellow Trail starts to the left and Red Trail to the right.

Walk straight ahead along Red Trail to the fourth historical barn. Then enter the woods and travel through a mostly deciduous forest with occasional tall pines. Hike up a slight incline, follow the wide trail along the top of a ridge past locust, white oak, holly, and red maple trees, and then go down the left side of the ridge. A creek runs at the bottom of a deep ravine to the left. Continue downhill over a log into a wide field. Turn left and follow the path along the edge of the field. Leave the path and walk through the trees past large oaks and beeches to the point of land above the river; with luck, one can spot beavers, otters, or muskrats in Hog Neck Creek below. Continue along Red Trail as it follows the irregular boundaries of the field. Below to the left, through the trees, the river cove gives way to a marshy tidal area.

At the end of the field, the marker post leads to the left back to Gray Trail. Move through the trees for 200 yards, then cross the gravel road. Follow Gray Trail straight ahead past the sign for the Blue Trail on the right. At the end of the field, turn left, walk through the break in the trees, then go right along the tree line. Follow the tree line as it curves left, and turn right back to the small parking lot with a kiosk at the head for Orange Trail.

Orange Trail is a challenging loop around a deep wooded ravine. Enter the woods on the right path of Orange Trail and hike past the large wild cherry tree. Coming out of the woods, head along a short beach, cross a small wooden bridge, and head uphill back into the ravine. At the large beech tree near the lip of the ravine, turn left off Orange Trail, and walk to the immense oak tree on the bluff for another spectacular view of the Patuxent River. Follow Gray Trail and turn left on the access gravel road, past the fenced horse pastures to the parking lot.

MORE INFORMATION

There is a $3 service fee per vehicle. Other activities at the park include fishing and crabbing from the pier, swimming at two beaches, kayaking and canoeing, horseback riding, bicycling, picnicking, and hunting. On weekends, model aircraft are flown from a landing strip inside the Yellow Trail loop. The nonprofit Greenwell Foundation provides children's nature programs, recreational and therapeutic horseback riding, guided kayak trips and lessons, and weekend vacations for service members recovering from post-traumatic stress disorder.

2

WASHINGTON, D.C.

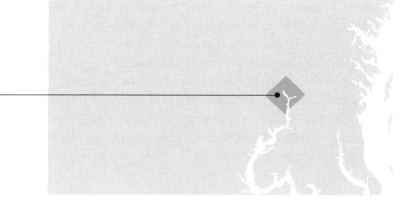

SURPRISINGLY, THE DISTRICT OF COLUMBIA OFFERS MANY NATURAL TRACTS where hikers can escape the stress of the nation's power corridors, and enjoy the solace of wood and stream. These respites include large forested areas such as the 1,750-acre Rock Creek Park (twice the size of New York's Central Park), Kenilworth Aquatic Gardens, and Roosevelt Island, and thinner strips of land tucked between neighborhood streets and the city's embassies, monuments, museums, bridges, and historic structures. Washington's longstanding moratorium on building any structure higher than the 555-foot Washington Monument creates a low-to-the-ground, sprawling skyline that encourages distinctive enclaves: the National Mall; the unique neighborhoods of Georgetown, Adams Morgan, Dupont Circle, Columbia Heights, Anacostia, and Brookline; and the green spaces that draw hikers, bikers, and inline skaters.

Rock Creek Park comprises a significant portion of northwest Washington, D.C., and contains Civil War–era fortifications, historical structures, a planetarium, and horse stables. The Rock Creek Trail follows Rock Creek through the park and beyond, from the Potomac River in the south to Lake Needmore, above Rockville, Maryland, in the north. East-west trails etch their way through the park's river valleys and rolling hills, offering creative hiking combinations. Two smaller subsections of Rock Creek Park are included in Trip 30, Around Georgetown—Dumbarton Oaks Park and Montrose Park.

These green corridors link to the Chesapeake & Ohio Canal Trail, which skirts the Potomac on the Georgetown waterfront, as it begins its journey to Cumberland, Maryland, 185 miles away.

Complementing the relative wilds of Rock Creek are the meticulously planned and engineered green spaces of the National Arboretum and Kenilworth Aquatic Gardens. The arboretum is an oasis for tree lovers, with rare dwarf conifers, ancient bonsais, and once-thought-extinct dawn redwoods. Kenilworth Aquatic Gardens is filled with brilliant-flowered lotuses and water lilies sustained within a marsh habitat. Both of these nature reservations straddle the Anacostia River and attract ospreys, great blue herons, egrets, and bald eagles, along with a host of migratory songbirds.

Two islands—the natural Roosevelt Island and the human-made East Potomac Park—offer quiet, secluded walks in Washington, D.C. Also included is the ever popular walking tour of the National Mall, the nation's backyard and, with the monuments and Smithsonian museums, an area for nearly limitless exploration and investigation.

TRIP 25
THEODORE ROOSEVELT ISLAND
AND THE POTOMAC HERITAGE TRAIL

Location: Arlington, VA, and Washington, D.C.
Rating: Easy
Distance: 4.7 miles
Elevation Gain: 160 feet
Estimated Time: 2.0 to 2.5 hours
Maps: USGS Washington West; downloadable NPS map at www.nps.gov/this

Theodore Roosevelt Island offers a secluded, woodsy landmass to explore between the skyscrapers of Arlington and the National Mall in Washington, D.C.

DIRECTIONS

From downtown Washington, D.C., take US 50 (Constitution Avenue) west. Continuing as it becomes I-66, go across the Theodore Roosevelt Memorial Bridge, staying in the right lane. Take the first right exit and then another right onto the George Washington Memorial Parkway going north (the island is accessible only from the northbound lanes of the GW Parkway). Take the first right turn (after 300 yards) into the Theodore Roosevelt Island parking lot. To return south back to Washington, drive 0.8 mile north and take the first left exit onto Sprout Run Parkway, then take the first left exit onto the southbound GW Parkway. *GPS coordinates*: 38° 53.745′ N, 77° 4.010′ W.

By Metrorail, take the Blue or Orange Line to Rosslyn station and walk 0.8 mile to the trailhead. Hike north downhill on North Moore Street, cross Nineteenth Street, turn right along Lee Highway, cross North Lynn Street, and turn left down it. At the far corner, turn right onto Mount Vernon Trail, following it south to the trailhead.

TRAIL DESCRIPTION

In the early 1800s, Teddy Roosevelt Island was the summer home of John Mason, son of Virginia statesman George Mason. John erected an elegant brick mansion on the highest point of land, providing views across the Potomac River to the White House and Capitol Building. Georgetown's wealthy elite would gather for dinners and dances on the Masons' manicured lawn beneath

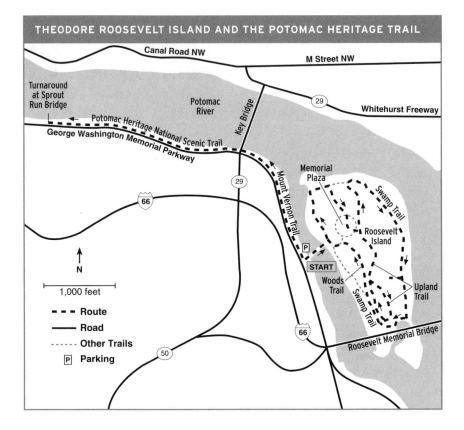

THEODORE ROOSEVELT ISLAND AND THE POTOMAC HERITAGE TRAIL

Canal Road NW

M Street NW

Turnaround at Sprout Run Bridge

Potomac River

29

Whitehurst Freeway

Potomac Heritage National Scenic Trail

George Washington Memorial Parkway

Key Bridge

Memorial Plaza

29

Mount Vernon Trail

66

Swamp Trail

Roosevelt Island

N

1,000 feet

P

START

Woods Trail

Upland Trail

Swamp Trail

- - - Route
——— Road
----- Other Trails
P Parking

66

50

Roosevelt Memorial Bridge

stately oak and linden trees. But in 1833 John was forced to relinquish his island as collateral for unpaid loans. The official family story held that the mosquitoes had gotten too bad. In 1931, the Theodore Roosevelt Memorial Association purchased the 88.5-acre island and donated it to the federal government as a tribute to the former president. The Roosevelt Memorial was officially dedicated in 1967.

This hike includes a circuit around Theodore Roosevelt Island and a straight out-and-back on the rugged Potomac Heritage National Scenic Trail to the Three Sisters (three rocks in the Potomac). From the parking lot on the west bank of the Potomac River, head a short distance south to the long, wide footbridge that crosses the Potomac—called Little River in this section. While crossing, look north to the Key Bridge and Georgetown and south to the Arlington Memorial Bridge. At the island end of the footbridge, a kiosk board shows a map of the island's well-maintained trails. Turn left on Swamp Trail and follow the broad path along the west shore. Tree diversity here en-

The memorial on Theodore Roosevelt Island remains much less visited than those of fellow presidents on the National Mall—and perhaps the 26th president would have wanted it that way.

riches the hike: Expect to see sycamore, yellow poplar, beech, elm, holly, ash, hophornbeam, black walnut, young maples, and large pin oak trees.

A historical sign along the trail describes the causeway built in 1805 between the northern end of the island and Virginia. The causeway was built for foot traffic and to serve as a dam to flush out the accumulated settlement on the north end of the island, allowing ships to continue to reach Georgetown. The causeway was not completely removed until 1979. At the intersection near the sign, go straight ahead a few dozen steps to discover a small deciduous tree peculiar for this area, the Osage orange, which flowers in June and bears distinctive fruit in the fall—softball-sized and yellow-green with a bumpy surface and milky juice that smells faintly of oranges.

Retrace the few dozen steps and take the trail now to the left, climbing up the gentle ridge that runs the length of the island. At the second intersection, marked with post 5, turn right near the water fountain and walk down the broad Woods Trail to the Theodore Roosevelt Memorial. It is startling to find such an elaborate memorial in the middle of the woods. A moat flanked by large willow oaks encircles four 21-foot-tall granite tablets and a 17-foot-tall bronze statue. At the center of the structure, turn left and exit across one of the stone "bridges."

This view toward Georgetown and the Francis Scott Key Bridge is from the walkway that leads to Theodore Roosevelt Island.

At the T intersection with marker post 7, turn right on Upland Trail. Hike along the low ridge of the island and turn left at the fork marked with post 8. In winter, look through the trees to the left to see marshland below and the Watergate Hotel and Kennedy Center across the water. Hike around the trail loop, past a sign about the Mason estate near marker post 9, to an intersection with a short trail on the right that connects with Swamp Trail below. Take the right fork to the second sign that marks the spot of the Mason mansion. All that remains are a few bricks.

The trail continues back to intersection number 8. Head back down Upland Trail past intersection 7 near the Roosevelt Memorial to the T intersection at marker post 6. Turn right on Swamp Trail, which becomes a wide elevated boardwalk that runs 800 yards through the swampy portion of the island. Extending to the right side off the main trail is a short section of boardwalk with views of a tidal marsh that fills and drains on a cycle.

Turn right along the end of the island near the Theodore Roosevelt Bridge. Under the bridge is Little Island. The boardwalk ends and the trail continues on dry land up a short hill, then continues to curve to the right past a large oak tree with a trunk 5 feet in diameter. Most of the trees on the island are younger than 100 years—much of the land was cleared for farming and gardens in the late 1800s—but in this area, trees are older and larger.

Hike past the connector trail to Upland Trail on the right and past public rest rooms in a small brown building, also on the right. About 200 beyond the rest rooms, the trail splits; the narrow Swamp Trail heads downhill to the left, and the wide Woods Trail heads to the right. Take Woods Trail to the right and walk 300 yards to the next intersection. Stay to the left and head toward the water to the T intersection marked with post 2. Turn right on Swamp Trail, then turn left back over the foot bridge to the parking lot.

Follow Mount Vernon Trail north past the two parking lots, and go to the right along the river at the Potomac Heritage Trail sign near the bottom of the ramp. The narrow, light-green–blazed trail squeezes between the George Washington Memorial Parkway on the left and the Potomac River on the right. Head through a small meadow, past ivy-covered trees and then under the arches of the Key Bridge—along the way are great views of the Georgetown waterfront, Key Bridge, and Georgetown University. The sound of parkway traffic is steady, but seems to fade with steady hiking—except where the trail actually follows the shoulder of the road for about 150 yards.

Near the area of the Three Sisters—stone formations jutting out of the Potomac River—the trail narrows as it is pressed between the parkway retaining wall and a post-and-rail fence at the top of the steep riverbank. One hundred fifty yards farther, reach the point where Sprout Run joins the Potomac River. Turn around here, and head east back along the same Potomac Heritage Trail to the Theodore Roosevelt Island parking lots.

MORE INFORMATION

The park is open daily from 6 A.M. to 10 P.M. There are no fees, but parking is limited and tends to fill on weekends. During spring and summer, park rangers lead guided tours. See www.nps.gov/this.

NEARBY

An alternate circle around the island is available via boat—rent one at Thompson's or Jack's Boats underneath the Key Bridge. Also visit nearby Franklin Roosevelt Memorial, the Tidal Basin, and East Potomac Park.

TRIP 26
POTOMAC RIVER:
GEORGETOWN TO LINCOLN MEMORIAL

Location: Arlington, VA, and Washington, D.C.
Rating: Easy
Distance: 5.7 miles
Elevation Gain: 130 feet
Estimated Time: 2.5 hours
Map: USGS Washington West

This mostly urban hike combines the charm of the Georgetown riverfront with several iconic Washington, D.C., buildings and monuments.

DIRECTIONS

From downtown Washington, D.C., take US 50 (Constitution Avenue) west. Turn left at 23rd Street NW and head to the Potomac River behind the Lincoln Memorial. From the Arlington Memorial Bridge, cross into Virginia, go straight 180 degrees through the traffic circle, and proceed on Memorial Drive. With the Women in Military Service for America Memorial ahead, take the first left into the long parking area. The George Washington Parkway in Virginia also services Memorial Drive from both the north- and southbound lanes. *GPS coordinates*: 38° 52.90′ N, 77° 03.80′ W.

By Metrorail, take the Blue Line to the Arlington Cemetery stop.

TRAIL DESCRIPTION

Georgetown was built as the farthest navigable port on the Potomac River. Established in 1751, it began as a hub for the tobacco trade, and the first building constructed was a tobacco inspection house. Later, the wharf and its environs profited from the Chesapeake and Ohio (C&O) Canal, which operated from 1836 to 1924 between Georgetown and Cumberland, Maryland, 185 miles upriver. Today, Georgetown is a trendy and expensive area of the city, but a hike along the canal's towpath hearkens to its river-centric industrial heyday. The hike detailed here is a composite, combining the C&O Canal towpath in Georgetown and the Rock Creek and Mount Vernon trails as they follow the shores of the Potomac River. Follow this map closely, and supplement it with any Washington city map.

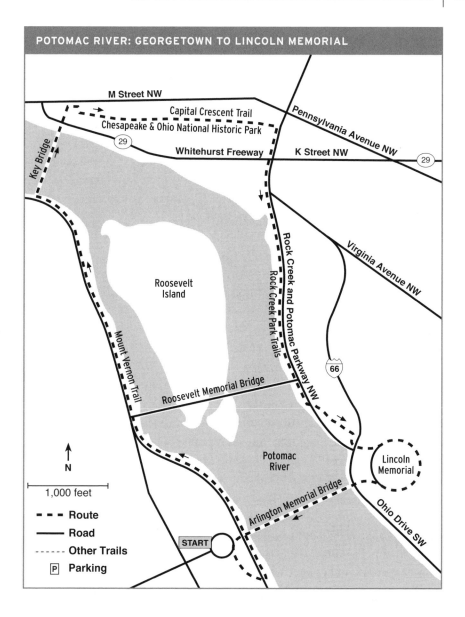

POTOMAC RIVER: GEORGETOWN TO LINCOLN MEMORIAL

Start at the Arlington National Cemetery visitors' parking lot if driving or the Arlington Cemetery Metro stop on the Blue Line if arriving via Metro. Walk east on the south sidewalk along Memorial Drive, away from the cemetery and toward the Potomac River. Follow the sidewalk to the right side of the traffic circle, cross Washington Boulevard at the crosswalk, and turn right at the T intersection. Cross the freeway off-ramp at the crosswalk where the trail becomes an asphalt path, and follow the path into a grove of oak trees. At the split in the path, take the left fork toward the river, cross the George Washington Memorial Parkway to Mount Vernon Trail, and turn left.

Head past large weeping willows at river's edge and oaks on the left. Go underneath the Arlington Memorial Bridge and across a foot bridge over the northern end of the Boundary Channel that marks the border between Washington, D.C., and Virginia. Continue underneath the Theodore Roosevelt Bridge where the trail becomes a wide plank path and walk past the two parking lots opposite Theodore Roosevelt Island. Head up a concrete ramp, turn 90 degrees to the left, and cross the bridge over the George Washington Parkway. Turn right and then left following an asphalt path up the hill to the intersection of North Lynn Street and North Lee Highway.

Turn right on the sidewalk and follow North Lynn Street on to the Francis Scott Key Bridge, which was built by the U.S. Army Corps of Engineers and completed in 1923. The views from the Virginia end of the bridge are spectacular and include Georgetown University and the top of the National Cathedral. Watch carefully for traffic when crossing the exit ramp for the Whitehurst Freeway. At the Georgetown shore, look down to the right to see the C&O Canal and towpath, on which construction began in 1828.

Leave the bridge and turn right into the circa-1993 Francis Scott Key Memorial Park, near the site of Key's home (now torn down). Walk down the stairs to the C&O Canal towpath. Stay on the near side of the canal and turn left down the narrow towpath with the high, gray stone wall on the left. Follow the path about 700 yards under four foot bridges and then under Wisconsin Avenue and 31st Street. Head up the ramp, cross Thomas Jefferson Street, then pass the C&O Canal Visitor Center—one of six along the entire 184.5-mile canal and definitely worth a visit. The trail continues past lock number 1 to the beginning of the canal where it joins Rock Creek. Step off the brick C&O Canal towpath, turn right onto asphalt Rock Creek Trail, and cross Rock Creek.

Head under a bridge, across the crosswalk, past the brown sign for the Kennedy Center, and under a second bridge (Whitehurst Freeway). Be attentive to speeding bicycles. Continue parallel to the Rock Creek and Potomac Parkway, then follow the trail across the road, under a third bridge, and across another road. Walk 150 more yards, and on the right, Rock Creek empties into the Potomac. Follow the trail along the Potomac River past two famous buildings opened in 1971—the Watergate complex, where a 1972 break-in at the Democratic National Committee headquarters inaugurated the Watergate scandal that would end Richard Nixon's presidency, and the John F. Kennedy Center for the Performing Arts. Pass underneath the Theodore Roosevelt Bridge and

A hiker enjoys a view of old canal-front factories on the C&O towpath in Georgetown. The once industrial and now fashionable town formed at the highest navigable point of the Potomac—and then thrived on canal traffic from points upriver.

reach, uphill past the Watergate steps, an overlook area with scenic views of the Potomac River.

Continue to the Arts of Peace statues that flank the end of Rock Creek Parkway—Music and Harvest on the right and Aspiration and Literature, on the left. To safely cross to the south side of the busy Arlington Memorial Bridge, walk around the Lincoln Memorial. (Turn left at the base of the statues, and stay on the outer sidewalk around the Lincoln Memorial Circle.) The Lincoln Memorial was constructed in the style of a Greek Doric Temple with limestone and marble from Indiana, Colorado, and Georgia, and was dedicated in 1922. After viewing the iconic 20-foot-tall statue of Lincoln, turn east for a splendid view of the National Mall, including the Reflecting Pool, World War II Memorial, Washington Monument, and U.S. Capitol in the distance.

Continue around the circle on the outer sidewalk, always using the crosswalks to get safely to the south sidewalk of the Arlington Bridge. Step onto the bridge and pass between the Arts of War statues—with Valor above you on the left and Sacrifice across the road on the right. Ahead, atop Arlington National

Cemetery, sits the Arlington House, Robert E. Lee's ancestral home. Arlington Cemetery is the final resting place for more than 300,000 military veterans and the site of the perpetually guarded Tomb of the Unknowns and the graves of John, Robert, and Edward Kennedy. Next, reach Columbia Island—a part of the District of Columbia. Follow the trail as it curves to the left, then in 100 yards turn right across Washington Boulevard, over Boundary Channel, and along Memorial Drive back to the Metro Station or the Arlington Cemetery parking lot.

MORE INFORMATION

The Georgetown C&O Canal visitor center organizes mule-drawn canal rides and walking tours of the historical warehouse district; visit www.nps.gov/choh/planyourvisit/georgetownvisitorcenter.htm or call 202-653-5190.

NEARBY

Visit Georgetown's Old Stone House, the gold-domed Farmers and Mechanics' Bank, and beautiful Dumbarton Oaks. Also see Theodore Roosevelt Island (Trip 25) and Around Georgetown (Trip 30) hikes, and nearby memorials such as the Vietnam Veterans Memorial and the Korean War Veterans Memorial.

TRIP 27
NATIONAL ARBORETUM

Location: Northeast Washington, D.C.
Rating: Easy to Moderate
Distance: 8.2 miles
Elevation Gain: 800 feet
Estimated Time: 4.5 to 5.0 hours
Maps: USGS Washington East; color map in free arboretum brochure

The National Arboretum offers an ever changing hike of constant discovery because its fifteen special collections contain flora and fauna from around the world.

DIRECTIONS

From downtown Washington, D.C., take US 50 (New York Avenue NW, becomes NE at North Capitol Street) heading east. Drive 3.5 miles and turn right onto Bladensburg Road. After 0.4 mile, go left onto R Street and drive 0.2 mile to reach the arboretum's main entrance. To get back onto New York Avenue for the return trip, return via R Street, turn right on Bladensburg Road, and turn left onto Montana Avenue, which intersects New York Avenue. *GPS coordinates:* 38° 54.47′ N, 76° 58.14′ W.

Via public transportation, take the Orange or Blue line to Stadium Armory Metrorail and transfer to the northbound Metrobus B2. Exit the bus at Bladensburg Road and R Street and walk the 0.2 mile on R Street to the arboretum.

TRAIL DESCRIPTION

Founded in 1927, the National Arboretum in northeast Washington, D.C., is a 446-acre living museum dedicated to plant research and education. The goal of this hike is to see the entire grounds while stopping to study or admire the various collections. Driving and biking are speedier ways to view the arboretum, but traversing its wonders on foot helps put each new collection into perspective and offers an intimate look at the diverse plant life.

From the parking lot, walk past the tram kiosk and proceed past the koi pond to the National Bonsai & Penjing Museum, a complex of structures accessed through a Japanese stroll garden. The museum houses trees maintained in miniature, and the Japanese Pavilion has a must-see white pine that survived the Hiroshima atomic blast in 1945 (see page 126) and was one of

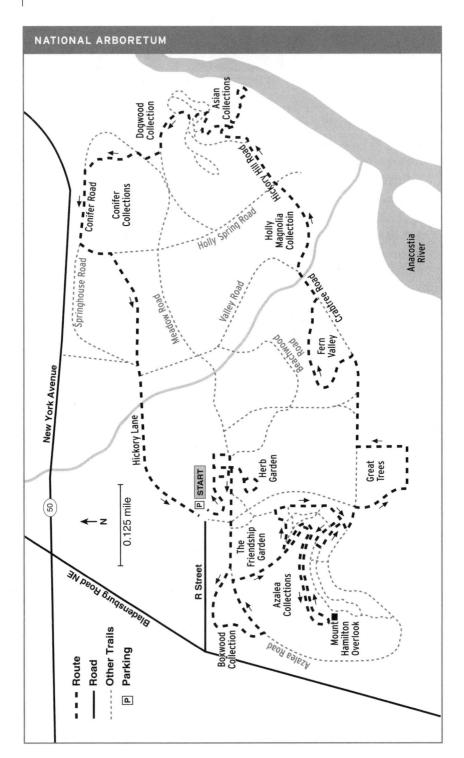

NATIONAL ARBORETUM

These Corinthian columns at the National Arboretum originally supported the old East Portico of the U.S. Capitol–the backstop to countless famous speeches, including Abraham Lincoln's inaugural addresses. They were moved here in 1984.

53 bonsai given to the United States by the Japanese government for the 1976 bicentennial. The American Pavilion contains *Goshin*, a famous bonsai work by John Naka.

Exit the museum to the south onto Meadow Road, where a right turn leads immediately to the 2.5-acre National Herb Garden. Enter beneath a hanging garden to a cul-de-sac path along which are 800 types of herbs, and proceed to a rose garden with historical varieties once widely cultivated across Europe. Return to Meadow Road and turn left, passing a display called "Power Plants" that highlights promising bioenergy sources. Continue past the intersection with Eagle Nest Road and turn right down a path that leads past the National Boxwood Collection and beds of perennials that bloom from late February through July.

Return to Azalea Road and turn left, then take the first right just before the entrance to the Boxwood Collection. Head past a parking area to a mulch path that ascends Mount Hamilton. This 40-acre high ground is adorned with the arboretum's stunning Azalea Collection. Proceed to the overlook by turning right at the first fork and traveling 0.25 mile to where the path ends in a cul-de-sac, affording fine views of the U.S. Capitol 2.0 miles west. Returning from the overlook, turn right at the fork and stay to the left past a second fork before turning left at a third fork to loop around Lee Garden. As you go around the north side of the pond, turn right at a T intersection to head south, and turn

PEACE AND LONG LIFE: SPIRIT WITHIN A TREE

They live quiet, highly restricted, sometimes *very* long lives—often outlasting their caretakers—in cramped quarters. Grown usually from standard-size stock or seed, they are artificially kept small, their appendages bound by fired clay, rope, and wire. They undergo countless prunings and root reductions, performed with reverence and patience by masters using the tools of an ancient art.

In the Japanese tradition they are known as *bonsai* ("tree in pot") and grown in shallow, plain, ceramic trays to showcase the beauty of the plants. Chinese growers call them *penjing* ("scene in pot") and cultivate them in deeper, more decorative containers, sometimes adding whimsical animal and human figurines. For centuries, both cultures have honored these miniature giants of the inner forest.

Perhaps surprisingly, under such constant attention, they thrive and tend to live longer than their wild counterparts. Maintained as a symbol of spiritual simplicity, tranquility, and depth—allowed to grow and flower according to their natures, yet deliberately refined to a standard of minimal-

A gift to the United States from Japan, this 400-year-old white pine bonsai tree survived the atomic blast at Hiroshima. A symbol of perpetuity and survival, it is the jewel in the National Arboretum's crown.

PEACE AND LONG LIFE: SPIRIT WITHIN A TREE (continued)

istic, truth-enhancing beauty—they are a sort of Buddhist "middle path" in high horticultural art.

Western interest in bonsai blossomed in the 1950s and 1960s, when the Allies occupied Japan and Asian thought came into vogue. Sadly, by that time, many centuries-old bonsai, in the ancient and renowned Japanese Imperial collection and elsewhere, had become casualties of World War II bombings.

"Further limitations release deeper powers," wrote the poet May Sarton. She could have been speaking of one bonsai in particular in the National Arboretum's National Bonsai & Penjing Museum: a prized Japanese white pine standing about 3 1/2 feet tall and 4 feet wide. On Aug. 6, 1945, this bonsai was living at the Yamaki Bonsai Nursery, within 2 miles of where the first atomic bomb was dropped on Hiroshima. Concrete walls surrounding the nursery saved this bonsai and others nearby from devastation.

The tiny tree was presented to the United States in 1976 as a Bicentennial peace-and-reconciliation gift by bonsai master Masaru Yamaki, a descendant of the grower who began training the little evergreen nearly four hundred years ago, in 1625. Generations of the Yamaki family had cared for it ever since; they too survived the 1945 blast. This lush, healthy, venerable old tree's branches form successively rising green, soft steps—as if the plant itself is happily beckoning visitors to keep growing, to flourish, to overcome. And to seek peace in simplicity.

left at the four-way intersection to arrive at a tended avenue known as Henry Mitchell Walk. At its end is the Morrison Garden, a squared-off structure of bricks that encases 15,000 Glen Dale hybrid azaleas.

Exit the garden at the south end and turn right onto the circle, take another right, then an immediate left to join a steep mulch path on the south side of Mount Hamilton. Travel this path for a short distance and take the first right followed by another right. This area on the south side has 15,000 of the Glen Dale hybrids arranged in overlapping colors and bloom times. When you return to the circle, turn right to link up with the paved Azalea Road.

Turn left on Azalea Road. Walk 100 yards and turn right onto Eagle Nest Road along the left side of the National Grove of State Trees. Turn left into the parking lot area and take another left at a marble half-circle display etched with the leaf of each state's tree. Upon leaving the grove, gravitate toward its eastern side, turn left onto a roadway lined with scarlet oaks (D.C.'s tree), and then take a right back onto Crabtree Road.

Follow Crabtree Road to a left turn onto Ellipse Road, which leads to the National Capitol Columns. After viewing them, return south on Ellipse Road, and turn right back onto Crabtree Road, passing the arboretum's Youth Garden on the right and then two small side trails on the left before taking a left into the main entrance to Fern Valley. This area is planted with ferns, wildflowers, shrubs, and trees native to the eastern United States and is a prime spot for bird-watching. At a central intersection near a shed, turn left and circle around to the north. Proceed through a microcosm of the natural ecology of the eastern forests. Just after the path crosses the stream, it arrives back at Crabtree Road.

Turn left and then quickly right on Hickey Hill Road, passing the Holly and Magnolia Collection on the left. Continue past the intersection with Holly Spring Road and trek uphill to the arboretum's Asian Collection. Take the first right and follow a sharp descent that wraps around China Valley. Return on the path and turn right up steep stone steps to the pagoda, turning left, and then making the first right to skirt the edge of Asian Valley. Turn right at the T intersection and travel around a circle, taking another right at its opposite end to dip down into the Japanese Woodland. Turn left at an alcove at the southern end, go straight past a three-way fork, and continue north to a parking area on Hickey Hill Road.

Hickey Hill Road makes a U-turn back to the west, passing the Dogwood Collection on the right. Take the first right past a stand of dawn redwoods onto Conifer Road. Beyond them, turn left into the maze of the 15-acre Gotelli Dwarf and Slow-Growing Conifer Collection, making your way generally north through 1,500 firs, cedars, pines, yews, and spruces. After navigating the trees, return to Conifer Road at the northern edge of the arboretum, near New York Avenue. From here, return to the administration building parking lot via a 1.25-mile walk, first turning left onto Holly Spring Road and then quickly right onto Hickey Lane, which drops onto the parking lot from the north.

MORE INFORMATION

National Arboretum trams run from 10:30 A.M. to 4 P.M., and tickets can be purchased at the kiosk near the parking lot. Tram rides last 45 minutes and cost $4 for adults and $2 for children. They depart from the Arbor House gift shop near the Friendship Garden.

For more information, visit www.usna.usda.gov.

TRIP 28
KENILWORTH AQUATIC GARDENS

Location: Kenilworth, Washington, D.C.
Rating: Easy
Distance: 2.5 miles
Elevation Gain: Minimal
Estimated Time: 1.5 to 2.0 hours
Maps: USGS Washington East; free sketch map of the aquatic gardens
(but not River Trail) in the visitor center

**This easygoing hike visits ponds teeming with summer-blooming
water lilies and lotuses and the last remaining wetlands on the
Anacostia River.**

DIRECTIONS

From downtown Washington, D.C., take US 50 (New York Avenue NW, becomes NE at North Capitol Street) and take I-295 (Kenilworth Avenue) south
to the Quarles Street/Eastern Avenue exit. Go straight through the light at
the top of the ramp and then turn right onto Douglas Street. Turn right onto
Anacostia Avenue. The park is on the left. *GPS coordinates*: 38° 54.743′ N, 77°
56.413′ W.

By Metrorail, take the Green Line to Deanwood Station, then walk across
the pedestrian overpass to Douglas Street. Walk north on Douglas to Anacostia Avenue and turn right into the park entrance (0.4-mile walk). You can also
take the V7 Bureau of Engraving bus to the corner of Kenilworth Avenue and
Douglas Street.

TRAIL DESCRIPTION

Kenilworth Aquatic Gardens—at the northern end of 11-mile-long Anacostia
Park—protects the last remaining tidal marshland in the District of Columbia.
Located on the east side of the Anacostia River 8.0 miles north of its confluence with the Potomac, it has a unique history rooted in the commercial
production of water lilies and lotuses. In the 1920s, L. Helen Fowler, owner of
W. B. Shaw Lily Pond, imported lilies and lotuses from Asia, Egypt, and South
America and built a greenhouse and sales office (today's visitor center). The
spot was a favorite with outdoorsy Washingtonians, including President Cal-
vin Coolidge. In the 1930s, when a misguided U.S. Army Corps of Engineers

KENILWORTH AQUATIC GARDENS

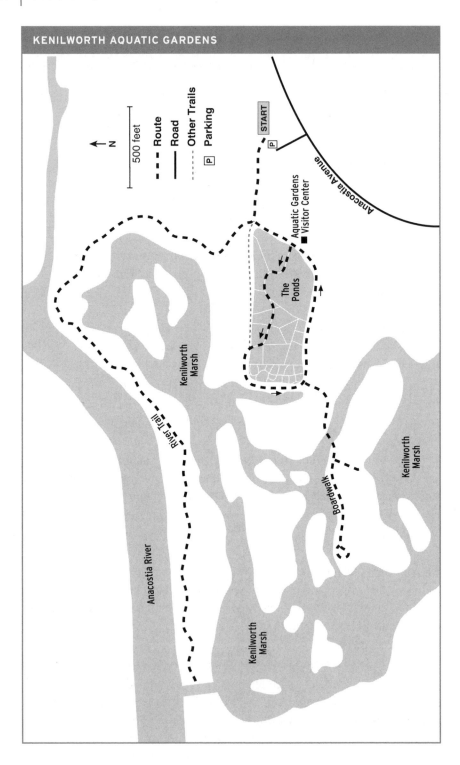

A great blue heron stalks its prey in the lily ponds at Kenilworth Aquatic Gardens, which come alive in the summer months with brilliant lily and lotus flowers.

project to fill in the wetlands threatened the aquatic gardens, the National Park Service stepped in and purchased them for $15,000, renaming them Kenilworth for the nearby farm community.

Today, the site has 75 acres of freshwater tidal marsh and 45 ponds filled with tropical and hardy water lilies, lotuses, and other aquatic species. The best time of year to see these blooming water plants begins in late May, peaks in July, and ends in mid-September. The best time of day is the early morning, to view the surreal spectacle of night bloomers closing and day bloomers opening. Afternoon heat and sun will cause the day bloomers to close. In general, the hardy lilies are located in the central ponds, the tropical lilies—including the giant, platter-like *Victoria amazonica*—in the western ponds farthest from the visitor center, and the lotuses in the large pond in front of the visitor center and the southern ponds.

To begin the hike from the parking lot on the gravel path, walk past the greenhouses to the left, go through a gate, and reach a sign marking points of interest. Take the second right to begin the 1.5-mile out-and-back on Marsh Land and River Trail. This trail runs along an artificial spit and borders a marsh on the left that the NPS constructed in 1992. At 0.2 mile, at the concrete ruins of an old tower on the left, reach the Anacostia River and follow it to the left. Wintertime affords views of the river and the stone Corps of Engineers sea wall on the opposite shore. In spring and summer, blackjack and northern red oak, red and silver maple, willow, tupelo, sycamore, black locust, black birch, holly, black walnut, sweetgum, and yellow poplar comprise the view to the right.

Go 100 yards farther to reach a bench on the left with wide-open views of wetlands—vibrant and almost tropical in summer and silent and peaceful in winter. At 0.75 mile, reach the end of River Trail, where on the right is a bench underneath a dual-trunked sycamore tree. Take the path leading down to the riverbank and the inlet where tidal waters reach the marsh. A stone wall to the left ends abruptly in broken shards—in another misguided engineering effort, it once blocked the very water that now feeds this natural ecosystem. Return to River Trail and head back to the aquatic gardens via the same route.

Back at the entrance sign, continue along the front of the ponds. Pass several distinctive trees—an American bald cypress, a large magnolia, and a few hollies—and a wooden greenhouse built in 1913 before reaching the visitor center. Stop in to pick up a hand-drawn map of the ponds and to see interesting relics such as Helen Fowler's 1936 book on growing water lilies, complete with her pastel drawings. See also the information about particular plant species found at the gardens, including the pink-flowered East India lotus. This lotus thrives in the pond behind the visitor center, the offspring of 600-year-old seeds discovered in Manchuria and planted in 1951.

From the visitor center, step around back (if it is summer) to see the East India lotuses, then head straight onto the dike between a giant pond of lotuses on the left and one of yellow-flowered spatterdock on the right. Come to another pond and turn left, then take the next right and stay left at the fork, heading through the heart of the winter hardy water lily collection. Head toward the tropical lilies by crossing a wooden walkway and turning right at the next T intersection, then going left around the outside edge of the *Victoria amazonica*. This tropical lily is the most dramatic in the park. Discovered in the deep, wide lagoons of South America, its leaves can grow 7 feet wide and have edges turned up to form a platter-like rim. The flowers open at dusk and remain open all night in August and September.

Continue south on a gravel road between the tropical lilies and the marsh and turn right onto the boardwalk at the "Boardwalk Closed at 4 P.M." sign. Walk out onto the zigzagging walkway past a few unique paperbark maple trees, and stay straight to the far platform to take in the ecological bounty of this mid marsh zone, including native cattails, buttonbush, wild rice, arrow arum and pickerelweed—and two wild varieties of flowering aquatic plant, the spatterdock and the American lotus. Also look for great blue herons, great egrets, belted kingfishers, and raptors.

On the way back, detour to the right to visit a second platform, then return to the gardens and turn right, walking along the southern rim past more East India lotuses. Walk back across the front of the visitor center and turn right back to the parking lot.

MORE INFORMATION

Kenilworth Park is open 8 A.M. to dusk. Kenilworth Aquatic Gardens is open daily 7 A.M. to 4 P.M. Dogs are allowed in the gardens but must be on a leash; www.nps.gov/keaq/.

NEARBY

Directly across the Anacostia River from Kenilworth is the National Arboretum (Trip 27). Also visit the Frederick Douglass National Historic Site, the Center For African-American History and Culture, and the Anacostia Historic District, all in southern Anacostia. Finally, the 10-mile Fort Circle Trail is another excellent Anacostia hiking option—it follows a chain of forested parks on heights that were fortified during the Civil War.

TRIP 29
ROCK CREEK PARK

Location: Washington, D.C.
Rating: Moderate
Distance: 6.0 miles
Elevation Gain: 840 feet
Estimated Time: 2.5 to 3.0 hours
Maps: USGS Washington West; Potomac Appalachian Trail Club Map
N; NPS map at the nature center

Rock Creek Park is a natural oasis in the heart of the nation's capital—1,700 hilly, wooded acres that contain the surprisingly turbulent Rock Creek, historic sites, and miles of challenging trails.

DIRECTIONS

From downtown Washington, D.C., take Connecticut Avenue NW north to Nebraska Avenue NW. Turn right on Nebraska Avenue for 0.4 mile. Turn right onto Military Road and drive east 0.7 mile. Then turn right onto Glover Road to enter Rock Creek Park, driving 0.4 mile and taking the first left to the parking lot for the Rock Creek Park Nature Center and Planetarium. *GPS coordinates:* 38° 57.54′ N, 77° 03.08′ W.

Or use the Metrorail and Metrobus. From either the Friendship Heights Metro station (Red Line) or the Fort Totten station (Read, Yellow and Green lines), take Metrobus E2 or E3 down Military Road. Exit at Oregon Avenue opposite Glover Road. From the southeast side of the intersection, walk uphill a short distance to reach the nature center.

TRAIL DESCRIPTION

Rock Creek Park is a national park that covers 1,754 acres—more than twice the area of Central Park in New York City. Rock Creek Park was established by an act of Congress and signed into law by President Benjamin Harrison on September 27, 1890, the same year that Yosemite became a national park. The two major trails are the blue-blazed Valley Trail that follows the east side of the creek and the green-blazed Western Rim Trail that follows the park's western ridge. This hike follows Western Rim Trail north, cuts east across the wooded hills, and returns south on Valley Trail.

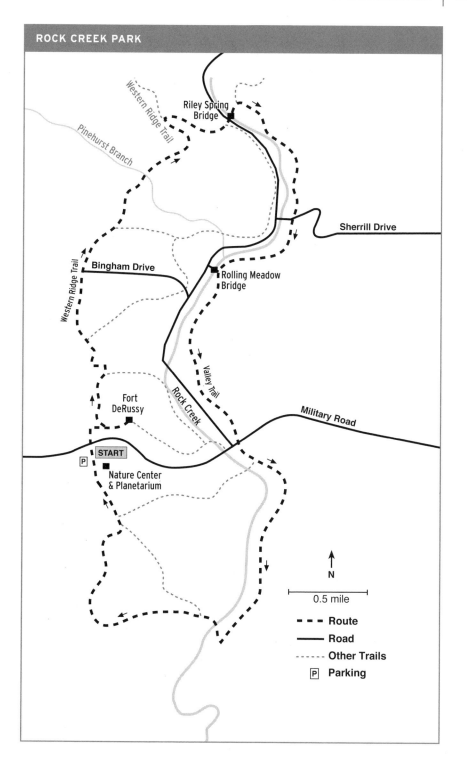

ROCK CREEK PARK

Western Ridge Trail

Pinehurst Branch

Riley Spring Bridge

Sherrill Drive

Western Ridge Trail

Bingham Drive

Rolling Meadow Bridge

Valley Trail

Rock Creek

Fort DeRussy

Military Road

START

P

Nature Center & Planetarium

N

0.5 mile

- - - **Route**
───── **Road**
- - - **Other Trails**
P **Parking**

From the nature center, walk straight out the front door to the blacktop Western Rim Trail that parallels Glover Road. Follow signs to Fort DeRussy, crossing Military Road and proceeding uphill. When you reach the NPS sign about the history of Fort DeRussy, turn right and follow the green blazes. Stay straight on the dirt trail and continue past where the green-blazed Western Rim Trail goes north. After a short distance, there is a sign, a plaque, and a spur trail on the left that leads over the fort's 150-year-old, dirt-covered fortifications.

After visiting the fort, return to the intersection with the green-blazed Western Rim Trail and turn right. Head downhill on a series of gradual, easygoing switchbacks. At 0.7 mile into the hike, where a sign points straight ahead for Milkhouse Ford, turn left and stay on Western Rim Trail. Next, cross a small creek and make a right, traveling between the Park Police horse stables and garden plots. Turn left at the T intersection with the service road and then follow the green-blazed blacktop trail to the right. Cross Bingham Drive and turn right into the woods on a dirt trail. Head uphill through thickets of viburnum bushes—rich with red berries all the way through autumn—and cut to the left at the Y intersection. Go downhill; bend to the right at the valley and then turn immediately left to cross Pinehurst Branch Trail. Ford the stream and head uphill through beeches and oaks. At the top of the hill, the trail passes through a narrow section and then takes a right turn (unmarked) in the direction of the Riley Spring Bridge. Head downhill to the Y intersection, and go left toward Beach Road and the bridge.

At 2.7 miles, cross the bridge over Rock Creek and turn right onto the blue-blazed Valley Trail, where a sign indicates it is 1.6 miles to Military Road. Here Rock Creek is gentle and meandering, but farther south it gets rocky and turbulent. Start through an area of gnarled black birches, and pass under the Sherrill Drive Bridge before fording a small feeder stream. Pass Rolling Meadow Bridge on the right and cross a wooden walkway over another stream. Just after crossing the stream, make sure to cut left at the Y intersection. Go uphill to the edge of the public golf course, descend to Beach Drive, and edge back uphill at a blue-blazed black birch tree. After scaling the precipitous ridge, drop back down again to the road and cross under Military Road.

Here the trail follows Beach Drive south to the Park Police station. Just after, at a blue-blazed oak tree at the foot of a steep ridge, cut left up the ridge and away from Rock Creek. Cross several large boulders and proceed uphill again to a wooden bridge spanning a small ravine. Turn right immediately after the bridge to stay on the blue-blazed Valley Trail.

Go back downhill over more rocky terrain, following Rock Creek on the right. At the Rapids Bridges, cut down off Valley Trail to make a crossing.

After descending from the ridge-running Valley Trail, pause at Rapids Bridge for a view of Rock Creek at its rockiest and most tempestuous.

This bridge offers perhaps the best view of Rock Creek in the entire park, with water slamming over, under, and around large boulders to both the north and south. Turn left at the T intersection at the end of the bridge; walk approximately 75 yards and turn right onto an unmarked trail. Go steeply uphill, staying to the left at the Y intersection over Ross Drive. Cross Glover Road at 5.7 miles and go straight ahead to the green-blazed Western Rim Trail; then turn right. Go around a hill to the right, cutting sharply left to stay on the trail just before reaching Grant Road. Cross and return to the nature center.

MORE INFORMATION

Rock Creek Park's amenities include 29 picnic areas, a large recreation field, 25 tennis courts, a public golf course, a 1.5-mile exercise course, bicycle routes, 13 miles of bridle trails, an equestrian field, and a horse center. More information can be found at www.nps.gov/rocr/.

TRIP 30
AROUND GEORGETOWN

Location: Georgetown, Washington, D.C.
Rating: Moderate
Distance: 6.9 miles
Elevation Gain: 800 feet
Estimated Time: 3.5 hours
Maps: USGS Washington West

Follow woodsy avenues on each side of Georgetown for a secluded circuit hike around the heart of Northwest Washington.

DIRECTIONS
Take Metrorail's Red Line to the Woodley Park-Zoo/Adams Morgan station on Connecticut Avenue. (Public parking is very limited in availability and duration, so driving is discouraged for this hike.) *GPS coordinates:* 38° 55.50′ N, 77° 03.14′ W.

TRAIL DESCRIPTION
Rock Creek Park includes not just the wide swath of forest along the Rock Creek valley in Northwest Washington, but also several narrow strips of parkland circling Georgetown—Montrose, Dumbarton Oaks, Whitehaven, and Glover-Archbold. This circuit hike takes advantage of these green avenues in the midst of an urban landscape. Sights include the Connecticut Avenue Bridge, Holy Rood Cemetery, an abandoned railway to Glen Echo Amusement Park, canal locks, Key Bridge, and Mount Zion Cemetery.

From the Woodley Park/Adams Morgan Metro, head downhill on 24th Street. Cross Calvert Street and at the bottom of the hill, south of the Connecticut Avenue Bridge and its famed Roland Hinton Perry lion sculptures, turn right onto the paved Rock Creek Trail. Continue on, and just before the bridge across Rock Creek, turn right on the gravel Parkway Trail (unmarked) that follows the west bank downstream. Take this leafy route past Normanstone Trail on the right. Just before going under the ivory-covered Massachusetts Avenue Bridge, notice the remains of a quarry visible on the right. Workers at this quarry mined norite stone—a type of sea-bottom basalt that underlies much of Georgetown—used to construct the buildings at Dumbarton Oaks.

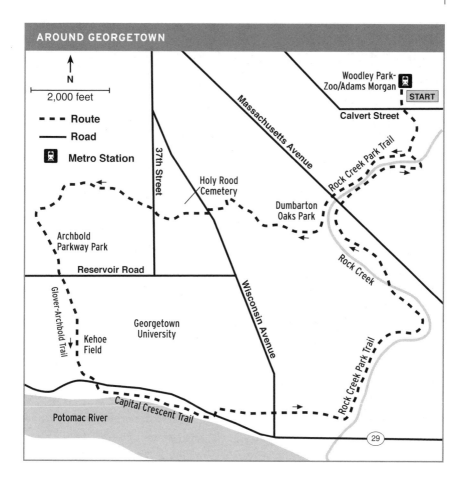

At 0.7 mile, leave Rock Creek and follow the dirt trail uphill along a rocky tributary, skirting the north end of Montrose Park and eventually reaching a T intersection with "Lovers Lane" and the entrance to Dumbarton Oaks Park. Cross the lane, enter the park, and proceed on a dirt trail along the left side of the creek. This "in-between" landscape—rich in sugar maples, American beech, tulip trees, flowering dogwoods, oaks, and hickories—was originally part of the private Dumbarton Oaks estate, serving as a buffer between the formal gardens and the wilds of Rock Creek Park.

Hike past a stone bridge and crumbling stone chimney to cross the creek below conspicuous hornbeams and dogwoods, and head uphill. Enter a small bowl-shaped field with wildflowers, and then pass through wild shrubbery and a swampy section before climbing a dirt switchback on the far side of the bowl. Upon reaching Whitehaven Road, turn left.

A busy thoroughfare from a quiet spot: the Francis Scott Key Bridge and Rosslyn, VA, as seen from the C&O Canal towpath in Washington, D.C.

At Wisconsin Avenue, cross and go right for a short detour to Holy Rood Cemetery—one of the highest points in the District of Columbia. Established by the Holy Trinity Church in 1832, the cemetery has a tree-framed view of the Washington Monument, gravestones in various states of disrepair, and proximity to the arterial bustle of Wisconsin Avenue that create a uniquely Washington, D.C., atmosphere. After strolling around the cemetery, return south down Wisconsin Avenue.

Take the next right onto 35th Street, and just before Whitehaven Parkway, make a right onto a yellow-blazed trail, and ascend wooden steps up the ridge. Level off and descend the steps to 37th Street. Cross the street and enter Whitehaven Park, following a line of maple trees and passing a dog park. Return to the brush and follow the yellow blazes past a community garden on the left and a rope climb on the right to reach a T intersection at a row of town homes. Turn right; go left at a Y intersection through hornbeams and beeches; and upon reaching the T intersection, go left onto Glover-Archbold Trail.

Heading south toward the water, cross Foundry Branch and hike uphill through maple-rich forest. Cross Reservoir Road, turn left past a bus stop, and turn right downhill on a barely discernible dirt trail. Go beneath several large tulip trees and past black walnuts to the right. Return to the woods and stay straight past a trail coming in from the right. Go under an abandoned, rusted railroad bridge (the remains of a trolley that once took Washingtonians to Glen Echo amusement park) and come to Foxhall Road. Turn left and then take another left downhill to reach a pedestrian tunnel beneath the Chesapeake & Ohio (C&O) Canal. Go through the tunnel and come out onto Capital Crescent Trail. Take a small side trail to the left to immediately connect with the gravel/clay C&O Canal National Historic Park towpath.

Continue on the towpath, and just after the Key Bridge cross over to the north side of the canal. Continue east through Georgetown. The path becomes brick, passing a series of lift locks, the National Park Service visitor center and a bust of Supreme Court Justice William O. Douglas, before reaching Rock Creek Trail. Bend left and follow the trail as it parallels busy Rock Creek Parkway. Eventually the trail turns left into the woods and then crosses Rock Creek on a bridge, with Mount Zion Cemetery on the left and a clearing where old Lyons Mill once stood on the right.

Proceed beneath the Massachusetts Avenue Bridge on the opposite bank from the first section of the hike. Eventually, the trail crosses Rock Creek again and returns to the exercise area just before the Connecticut Avenue Bridge. Turn left uphill along Shoreham Drive, cross Calvert Street, and return to the Woodley Park-Zoo/Adams Morgan Metro station.

MORE INFORMATION

There is no fee for this hike, and dogs are permitted.

NEARBY

Well worth a visit, Dumbarton Oaks estate and gardens are open to the public 2 to 6 P.M., Tuesday to Sunday. Visit www.doaks.org for details.

Also of interest, the C&O Canal Visitor Center (1057 Thomas Jefferson Street) in Georgetown is open from 9:30 A.M. to 4:30 P.M., Wednesday to Sunday. From April to October, the visitor center offers hour-long canal rides through the lift locks on a replica of an 1800s canal boat as well as guided walks of Georgetown every day at noon. For more information about this national park, visit www.nps.gov/choh/.

TRIP 31
EAST POTOMAC PARK
AND HAINS POINT

Location: Southwest Washington, D.C.
Rating: Easy to Moderate
Distance: 4.5 miles (loop)
Elevation Gain: 30 feet
Estimated Time: 3.0 to 3.5 hours
Map: USGS Alexandria

Mostly level, and filled with architectural and natural beauty, this scenic loop route takes in two founders' memorials, four bodies of water, and dozens of cherry trees.

DIRECTIONS

From downtown Washington, D.C., take US 50 (Constitution Avenue) west. Turn left at 15th Street SW (becomes Raoul Wallenburg Place at Independence Avenue SW). Turn left at Maine Avenue SW and immediately turn right onto East Basin Drive SW. Turn left on Ohio Drive SW. Continue past the U.S. Park Police headquarters to the stop sign at Buckeye Drive, and turn right. Go to the next stop sign, at Ohio Drive, and make another right. Drive under the railroad bridge; you'll then see three free parking lots on your right—C, B, and A—for the founders' memorials. *GPS coordinates* (Parking Lot C): 38° 52.645′ N, 77° 02.198′ W.

By Metrorail, take the Blue/Orange Lines to the Smithsonian station and use the Independence Avenue exit. Turn left (west) on Independence Avenue and walk two blocks to 15th Street (Raoul Wallenberg Place) SW. Turn left here, around the red-brick U.S. Forest Service headquarters, and walk downhill to Maine Avenue. Cross the avenue and follow the walkway leading to your left along the Tidal Basin. Begin your hike at the Jefferson Memorial (see the final three paragraphs of the Trail Description). The walk to and from the Metro station will add about 1.3 miles to your hike.

TRAIL DESCRIPTION

East Potomac Park is one of Washington's larger and better-known green spaces, but even in the busy spring tourist season, there is room here to stretch

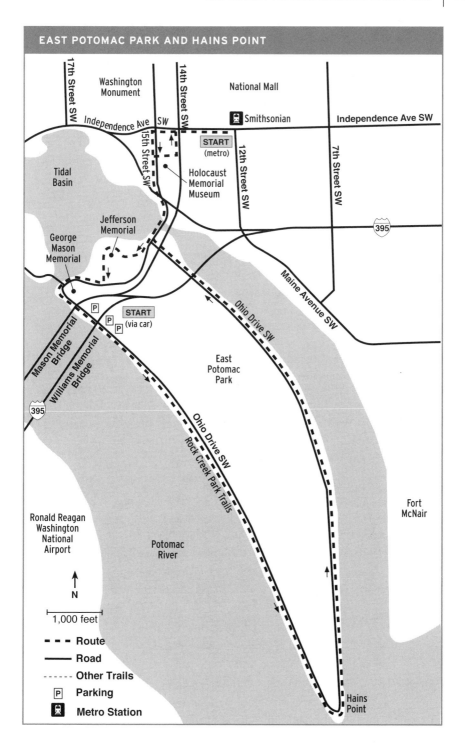

EAST POTOMAC PARK AND HAINS POINT

17th Street SW

Washington Monument

14th Street SW

National Mall

Independence Ave SW

Smithsonian

Independence Ave SW

15th Street SW

START
(metro)

12th Street SW

7th Street SW

Tidal Basin

Holocaust Memorial Museum

Jefferson Memorial

395

George Mason Memorial

Maine Avenue SW

Mason Memorial Bridge

Ohio Drive SW

P
P
P

START
(via car)

East Potomac Park

Williams Memorial Bridge

395

Ohio Drive SW

Rock Creek Park Trails

Fort McNair

Ronald Reagan Washington National Airport

Potomac River

Hains Point

N

1,000 feet

- - - Route
——— Road
------ Other Trails
P Parking
Metro Station

WASHINGTON'S SAKURA—AND THOSE WHO'VE LOVED THEM

Eliza Scidmore, an American travel writer and photographer and the National Geographic Society's first female trustee, made her initial tour of Japan in 1885 with her brother George, a diplomat who served in the Far East for many years. She was enchanted by the beauty of the flowering cherry trees (*sakura*) she saw there —a poignant, centuries-old symbol of ephemeral life, love, and springtime in Japanese culture. Upon returning to Washington, she approached the superintendent of public buildings and grounds to propose that such trees be planted along the Potomac riverbanks then being reclaimed from swampland. That superintendent, and his successors for the next twenty-plus years, refused or ignored her requests.

Meanwhile, another local world traveler, Department of Agriculture botanist David Fairchild, had also taken a fancy to the fragile, delicately rosy, fleeting *sakura*. He made a test planting of 100 trees on his suburban Maryland estate and found them well suited to the local climate. For Arbor Day 1908, he presented cherry saplings to children from each of the District's schools, to be planted in their schoolyards as is commonly done in Japan. He also suggested transforming the Speedway (along modern-day Independence Avenue SW) into a "Field of Cherries," and publicly lauded Eliza Scidmore as a great authority on Japan.

Scidmore then decided to plant *sakura* in the District, even if she had to raise the funds for them herself. Additionally, in early 1909, she elected to bypass the parks superintendent and go straight to the top: She wrote to new First Lady Helen "Nellie" Taft. Mrs. Taft had also toured Japan—en route to Manila in 1899 when her husband had been appointed commissioner of the Philippines. Later, as U.S. Secretary of War in 1905, William Howard Taft had helped to negotiate the treaty that ended the Russo-Japanese War, and had been warmly welcomed in Japan. The First Lady was strongly interested in beautifying Washington, and embraced the cherry tree idea.

Suddenly, *sakura* were all the rage. Japanese chemist Jokichi Takamine (the discoverer of adrenaline), visiting Washington that April, heard of the plan, and asked his friend, Japanese diplomat Kokichi Midzuno, if the First Lady would accept a donation of 2,000 cherry trees. Midzuno encouraged the gift, and suggested making it in the name of the city of Tokyo. Mrs. Taft gladly accepted. A few days later, Superintendent of Public Buildings and Grounds Colonel Spencer Cosby ordered the purchase of 90 Fugenzo cherries, which were planted south of today's Lincoln Memorial. (They have since disappeared.)

In January 1910, Tokyo's gift of 2,000 trees landed in Washington—infested with invasive insects. At the order of President Taft, they were burned, with the exception of a dozen or so that were planted experimentally in East Potomac Park. The destruction of the trees nearly set off an international incident; letters of explanation and deep regret flew east and west among Secretary of State Philander Knox, Japanese ambassador Viscount Chinda, Superintendent Cosby, and Yukio Ozaki, the mayor of Tokyo.

Diplomacy saved the situation; Mayor Ozaki, wishing to show his gratitude to President Taft for the 1905 treaty, was gracious and undaunted. With Takamine's financial help, Tokyo generously gifted a second shipment of 3,020 trees—comprising twelve varieties, including 1,800 Yoshinos with their famous single white-pink blossoms—which arrived in February 1912. On March 27, Mrs. Taft and Viscountess Chinda (the Japanese ambassador's wife) planted Washington's first two Yoshino cherries along the Tidal Basin's northern bank, near today's Franklin D. Roosevelt Memorial. Cherry blossoms quickly became a powerful tourist attraction.

But it wasn't only tourists they drew. The small, bitter fruits of these trees serve as important food for birds. And in 1982, beavers were first spotted cruising the Tidal Basin for a potential home. Over time, they have managed to cut down more cherry trees than George Washington. When three beavers were humanely trapped in 1999, after having got their teeth into at least eight trees, their release location was kept top-secret due to heated controversy and local desire for revenge against the vandals.

The National Park Service continues to propagate and plant cherry-tree grafts along the Tidal Basin, preserving the genetic line and incomparable loveliness. Postwar Japan asked for help in replacing trees damaged by World War II bombings; Washington repaid Tokyo's gift with 55 cuttings from the Tidal Basin Yoshinos in 1951, and another 2,000 in 1980. And so the wheel of life continues to turn.

The expected life span of a Yoshino cherry is 45 years. Yet, a century later, some 60 of the original 1912 trees, and possibly a handful of the diseased 1910 shipment, live on as a blooming testament to life and springtime—perhaps even to love.

Lunchtime strollers enjoy East Potomac Park's path alongside the Washington Channel, with D.C.'s Southwest Waterfront in the background.

out and recreate. The park offers multiple leisure facilities, as well as impressive groves of ornamental cherry trees, which put their energy into flowering rather than fruiting. East Potomac Park is a perennial favorite spot for enjoying the beauty of several varieties of cherry blossoms in season, usually late March to late April.

From the memorials parking lots, cross Ohio Drive, then turn left and begin your walk along the riverside path, passing the intersection at Buckeye Drive. You might notice some flowering cherry trees that resemble willows with their flexible branches; these are the Weeping Higan variety and bear small pink-purple flowers usually in early to mid-April. Soon you'll see the first of the park's several rest room buildings across the road, among a grove of Kwanzan cherries, with ruffly, double-pink blossoms that appear around mid-April. Continue walking on a long straightaway, where locals like to fish along the riverbank. Look across the river to catch a glimpse of the beige-limestone Pentagon, headquarters of the U.S. Department of Defense, and the three curving, soaring spires of the Air Force Memorial. Farther downriver are the towers of Crystal City, behind architect Cesar Pelli's yellow-arched terminal at Ronald Reagan Washington National Airport. The curving northern approach to the airport over the Potomac, known as the "River Visual," is one of the more interesting and challenging for pilots nationwide.

Walk past the playground and picnic area and, as you approach Hains Point, the park's southern tip, you'll see Old Town Alexandria and the Woodrow Wilson Bridge several miles to the south. Major General Peter Conover Hains (of the Army Corps of Engineers, and a veteran of wars from the Civil War to World War I) designed the Tidal Basin you'll see later in this hike, and the island underfoot was built largely from soils dredged to create that artificial lake. Here at Hains Point is the confluence of the Anacostia and Potomac rivers. Named for the native peoples living along its banks when European colonists first settled here, the once-pristine Anacostia has long been pollution's victim, and cleanup efforts progress slowly.

As you round the point, watch for dark-green-and-white helicopters: Anacostia Naval Air Station, the Washington, D.C., home to presidential flight group Marine Helicopter Squadron One (HMX-1 "Nighthawks"), isn't far away. And on the point across the channel from you is Fort Lesley J. McNair, with its ornate red-and-beige National War College building and neat brick Generals' Row. The water you see now is the Washington Channel, which provides a safe harbor for private watercraft, rescue squads, and fishing vessels.

To your left, past a stop sign, are the park's golf course, miniature golf range, and swimming pool. Continue past the tennis complex, then cross under the highway and train bridges on this leg of Ohio Drive. At the T intersection, walk straight across the road (this is still Ohio Drive), turn right on the sidewalk, then quickly turn left onto a narrow path leading down to the water's edge. (Metro riders, follow the Tidal Basin sidewalk to your right to return to the Smithsonian station.)

If you're here in early spring, it might look as though huge pale-pink snowballs—the famed Yoshino cherry trees in bloom—are ringing the lake. This is the Tidal Basin, constructed in the early 1900s to help drain the lowlands roundabout by taking in the overflow when the Potomac's water levels rise because of Chesapeake Bay tides. Despite this effort, most of the large structures near here are "floating" to some degree upon mucky soil. They include the basin's seawall, portions of which have been sinking over the years—hence, the repairs in progress at this writing.

Look left toward the round-topped Jefferson Memorial. Make your way along any open path to the water side of this beautiful neoclassical structure—reminiscent of the third president's own designs for Monticello and the University of Virginia rotunda. Notice the frieze above the columns: young Jefferson, aged 33, stands before the other members of the committee assigned to draft the Declaration of Independence—John Adams and Benjamin Franklin most notably. The memorial's interior is both inspiring and cool on a warm day; you might also enjoy the exhibit in the lower level about Jefferson's many accomplishments, juxtaposed with world events during his era.

Walk back out to Ohio Drive along the large square lawn, turning right just past the hexagonal snack bar. Cross to your left at the stop sign and proceed into the George Mason Memorial's circular garden. You might not have heard much of Mason—sometimes called the "forgotten founder"—yet you're probably familiar with many of his principles, which strongly influenced Jefferson's Declaration, as well as the Bill of Rights that was added to the Constitution to spell out clear limits on the new national government's power over individuals and states. The garden in spring blooms with daffodils and flowering shrubs.

Turn left when leaving this memorial park, and proceed around a curve, then under the bridges back to the memorial parking lots.

MORE INFORMATION

East Potomac Park and the memorials along the Tidal Basin are maintained and administered by the National Park Service; www.nps.gov/nama/index. htm; 202-485-9880. Rest rooms and water are available at the Jefferson Memorial and at several locations in East Potomac Park. Park roads are sometimes closed because of flooding, and parking anywhere nearby can be hard to find in spring during cherry blossom time. Taking Metro is suggested; note, however, that doing so will add about 1.3 miles to your total round-trip walk.

TRIP 32
THE NATIONAL MALL

Location: Washington, D.C.
Rating: Easy to Moderate
Distance: 3.7 miles
Elevation Gain: –70 feet (downslope)
Estimated Time: 3.0 hours
Maps: USGS Washington East, Washington West

This hike explores the beauties of nature to be found in many lesser-known, peaceful urban nooks and landscaped gardens along the National Mall.

DIRECTIONS

By train, take Metrorail's Blue or Orange Line to the Capitol South station. Exit at 355 First Street SE, just south of the southwest corner of First and C streets SE. (Public parking in the city's tourist areas is very limited in availability and duration, so driving is discouraged for this hike.) *GPS coordinates:* 38° 53.143′ N, 77° 00.360′ W.

TRAIL DESCRIPTION

Exit the Capitol South Metro station and walk left to the corner of First and C streets SE. Continue uphill one block along First Street SE, cross Independence Avenue, then follow the path leading diagonally left toward the Capitol's dome. These grounds are considered a jewel of landscape architecture by Frederick Law Olmsted, who also designed New York's Central Park. Along this path, note how Olmsted's ironwork viewing shelter is placed perfectly for apprecia-tion of the dome. Also look for the dozens of memorial trees planted over the Capitol grounds. Many are official trees of various states; others are dedicated to historical figures and events. Unfortunately, some of these special trees have succumbed over time to storms or to construction of the Capitol's visitor cen-ter beneath your feet.

Cross the plaza lengthwise (watching out for official vehicles) and walk around the Capitol's north wing—be sure to enjoy the view westward down the Mall from here. Proceed down Capitol Hill on the curving path to a hex-agonal red-brick structure, Olmsted's Summerhouse (often called the Grotto), built over a natural spring—a cool, pleasant resting place where you can fill

THE NATIONAL MALL

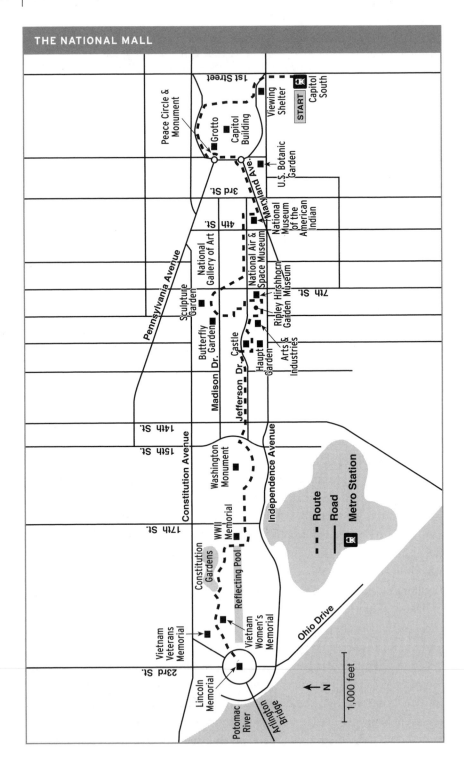

1st Street

Peace Circle & Monument

Grotto

Capitol Building

Viewing Shelter

START

Capitol South

Maryland Ave.

U.S. Botanic Garden

3rd St.

National Museum of the American Indian

4th St.

National Gallery of Art

National Air & Space Museum

Pennsylvania Avenue

Sculpture Garden

Ripley Hirshhorn Garden Museum

7th St.

Butterfly Garden

Castle

Madison Dr.

Haupt Garden

Arts & Industries

Jefferson Dr.

14th St.

15th St.

Washington Monument

Constitution Avenue

Independence Avenue

Metro Station

- - - Route
—— Road
Metro Station

17th St.

WWII Memorial

Constitution Gardens

Reflecting Pool

Ohio Drive

Vietnam Veterans Memorial

Vietnam Women's Memorial

23rd St.

Lincoln Memorial

Potomac River

Arlington Bridge

N

1,000 feet

your water bottle (although the fountains now flow with municipally treated water). Continue downhill into Peace Circle, named for Franklin Simmons's *Peace Monument* showing Grief sobbing on the shoulder of History for sailors lost during the Civil War. The monument's Carrara marble has suffered serious degradation from acid rain and weathering; restoration efforts are being made to prolong the statue's life. Cross the circle toward the Capitol Reflecting Pool, and turn back to see the West Front, where presidential swearing-in ceremonies have taken place since Ronald Reagan's first one in 1981.

Walk south toward the conservatory of the U.S. Botanic Garden, and enjoy its rooms of cacti, orchids, and desert and tropical plants. Outside, you'll find inviting open-air plots, including the quilt-inspired First Ladies water garden and a pesticide-free butterfly garden. Follow Maryland Avenue SW now away from the Capitol, toward the yellow-beige National Museum of the American Indian, whose flowing forms, designed in part by native people, represent natural elements such as clouds and earth. Cross Third Street into the museum's entrance courtyard—look along Maryland Avenue to see Nora Naranjo-Morse's organic sculpture *Always Becoming*—then walk around the building to enjoy the water feature, fire pit, and landscaping.

Continue along Fourth Street's southern sidewalk, noticing the sun and the first planets of the solar system in a to-scale representation stretching for blocks past the National Air and Space Museum. Cross Jefferson Drive, and walk diagonally across the grassy Mall toward the corner of Seventh Street and Madison Drive NW. Just across Seventh Street is the southeast gate of the National Gallery of Art's whimsical Sculpture Garden—enjoy splashing fountains in a large pool that becomes an outdoor ice-skating rink in winter. Many trees thrive here, such as magnolias, cedars of Lebanon, and Kentucky coffees. Walk out to Madison Drive again through the garden's southwest gate. Turn quickly right into the Butterfly Habitat Garden, where four different landscapes attract many of the 80 or so butterfly species known in Washington, D.C. Return to Madison Drive, and cross the grass back to the southern side of the Mall.

Head toward the doughnut-shaped, concrete building, the Hirshhorn Museum and Sculpture Garden, and pause in its sunken sculpture garden on the north side of Jefferson Drive—here you'll find among 60 other works a piece by Auguste Rodin titled *Crouching Woman*. Cross Jefferson Drive and the Hirshhorn's fountain courtyard, turn right on Independence Avenue SW, and turn quickly right into the Mary Livingston Ripley Garden. Ripley, an avid gardener and wife of a former Smithsonian Institution secretary, planned a Victorian-style "fragrant garden" on this spot—which had been slated to

WHAT'S IN A NAME: MR. SMITHSON'S LEGACY

Inside the ornate red-stone castle on the National Mall stands the crypt of James Smithson (1764?–1829), the English gentleman scientist whose large fortune was used to found the Smithsonian Institution. Smithson never visited the United States, and his moldering bones, resting here now, can't tell us what manner of man bestowed such an amazing gift.

Recent scholarship, however, delves into the Enlightenment world of this previously shadowy historical figure. Born James (or Jacques) Louis Macie, he was the offspring of an illicit romance between widowed aristocrat Elizabeth Macie and Hugh Smithson, first Duke of Northumberland. Unacknowledged and unsupported by his father, James in his thirties (after his parents' deaths) boldly took the family name Smithson, surname of the duke.

Inside the Smithsonian Castle's north portico is the crypt of James Smithson (a.k.a. Macie), the English gentleman-scientist and benefactor of the vast museum complex bearing his chosen name.

As Macie, however, he'd already gained renown for his work in the exciting new fields of chemistry and mineralogy. Following a student prodigy's career at Oxford, 22-year-old James was inducted into the exclusive, influential Royal Society, and soon published the first of his many papers in its journal. On the strength of these accomplishments, plus his personal charm and exuberance, he embarked upon a Grand Tour of the European continent, seeking scientific insights, kindred minds, and mineralogical specimens for his growing collection. He carried a portable laboratory, experimented with the properties of minerals (even tasting and sniffing them), and made strides toward systems of classification. He became friends with many of the era's brightest scientists. He witnessed events of the French Revolution and became a prisoner of war during Europe's lengthy Napoleonic Wars. He knew aeronauts, aristocrats, politicians, and inventors. But he had neither a wife nor children, and his one surviving blood relative, a nephew, died childless.

So Smithson, a savvy investor, bequeathed in gold all his wealth—about £105,000, or $508,000 at the time—"to the United States of America, to found at Washington, an establishment for the increase and diffusion of knowledge." It was to bear his chosen name. Astonished U.S. leaders wondered: Who was he, what did he intend, and why? Some say he admired the young America's Enlightenment-inspired ideals—a united country and open society, free from standing armies and the scourge of constant war. Others insist that Smithson bore a grudge against the aristocratic privilege ingrained in England. "My name," he once vowed, "will live on in the memory of men when the titles of [my ancestors] are extinct or forgotten."

His bequest certainly made his name well known, creating what is today the world's largest museum and research complex.

Furnished with pieces from the Smithsonian's historical garden collections, the National Mall's curvilinear, Victorian-inspired Ripley Garden welcomes visitors with its fountain and fragrant blossoms.

become a parking lot. The garden path leads back to Jefferson Drive. Turn left, pass the Arts and Industries Building, and enjoy the Kathrine Dulin Folger Rose Garden's scented splendor.

Follow the path to the left (south side) of the red Maryland sandstone Smithsonian Castle into the Enid A. Haupt Garden, with its old-fashioned, formal, clipped-shrubbery parterre beds. Notice the entrances to two underground museums, the African Art Museum and the Sackler Gallery, and the Asian-inspired, compass-pointed, granite-and-water Moongate Garden. Walk around the Castle's west end and follow Jefferson Drive west across Fourteenth and Fifteenth streets SW, then climb toward the Washington Monument's base.

When you arrive on top of the slope, try looking straight up at the monument—an odd effect of perspective makes it appear that the entire obelisk is tipping over on you! Enjoy the 360-degree vista—north to the White House, south toward the Jefferson Memorial, west to the Lincoln Memorial and Reflecting Pool—then walk west downhill toward Seventeenth Street. Cross that street and proceed down the wide entrance avenue of the World War II Memorial, whose green wall bears 4,048 golden stars, one for every 100 Americans lost in the war. Walk up the curving ramp to the left (past the Delaware column), through the Pacific arch, and around to the back of the green wall; you'll see a gate, inside which is one of two "Kilroy Was Here" inscriptions included in the memorial. The long-nosed, mischievous Kilroy boosted morale during the war years, as soldiers cheerfully vied to see who could doodle him in the most unexpected and inaccessible places.

Proceed across the eastern end of the Lincoln Memorial Reflecting Pool, turning left onto the second path, which emerges at the edge of the Constitution Gardens pond, opened in 1976 for the national bicentennial. Its central island, dedicated to the signers of the Declaration of Independence and reached by a pedestrian bridge, is a haven for ducks and geese. Algae overgrowth caused serious fish die-off here recently; the National Park Service has been working to prevent future losses. When the path splits near a hexagonal snack bar, keep left, proceeding toward the Vietnam Veterans Memorial. This path leads you past the three nurses and wounded soldier of the Vietnam Women's Memorial statue, by Glenna Goodacre. To your right you'll have a full view of Maya Lin's polished black memorial wall itself. Continue west along this walkway toward our hike's terminus, the massive marble Lincoln Memorial.

Myths regarding the memorial to Lincoln, and fascinating "coincidences" about his life, abound. Despite stories to the contrary, there is not one step here for each year of his life (although there is at his Kentucky birthplace). Nor has he turned his back on the South (although Robert E. Lee lived for many years just across the Potomac at Arlington Plantation, now Arlington National Cemetery); Lincoln's statue actually faces east. Look down on one of the step landings for the plaque marking where Dr. Martin Luther King Jr. stood as he delivered his 1963 "I Have a Dream" speech.

You can hail a taxi on Constitution Avenue NW, a block to the north, or in the parking area just south of the Lincoln Memorial. Or hike a bit farther to a Metro station—Arlington Cemetery station (Blue Line) across Memorial Bridge in Virginia, or Foggy Bottom station (Blue/Orange lines) about eight blocks north, at 23rd and Eye (letter I) Streets NW.

MORE INFORMATION

For information about riding Metrorail, call 202-637-7000 or visit www.wmata.com. Rest rooms and water fountains are available in the U.S. Capitol Visitor Center (strict security screening is in effect), the U.S. Botanic Garden, the National Gallery Sculpture Garden, and the memorials. For current information and updates on tourism and special events in the nation's capital and on the Mall, check out www.washington.org.

3

VIRGINIA

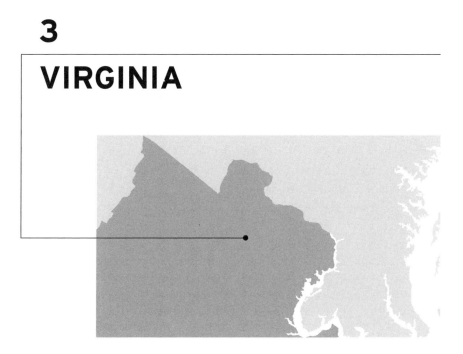

DESPITE ITS SUBURBAN DEVELOPMENT, northern Virginia is geologically and ecologically diverse, containing from west to east the Blue Ridge Mountains, the hills and stream valleys of the Piedmont, and the tidal marshlands of the Atlantic coastal plain. An obvious choice for nature lovers is to go west, away from the development to the farmlands and horse fields of western Loudoun and Fauquier counties. Here hikers can enjoy the rugged spine of the Bull Run Mountains (at Bull Run Mountains Natural Area and Wildcat Mountain Natural Area) and the Blue Ridge Mountains (at Sky Meadows State Park and G. Richard Thompson Wildlife Management Area). Farther west is Old Rag Mountain in Shenandoah National Park, one of the best day hikes—in terms of overlooks and challenging terrain—in the Mid-Atlantic states.

Closer to Washington, D.C., in busy Fairfax and Prince William counties, hikers can meander through the creased and folded landscape of the Virginia Piedmont, following stream valleys where old mills and mines reflect the way people once lived. Many of these hikes combine hilly climbs with walks along the Potomac River. Along the southward-flowing portion of the Potomac, facing east toward Maryland's Western Shore, are Leesylvania and Mason Neck state parks. In the tidal marshland and delicate sandy cliffs are bald eagles, osprey, and great blue herons. The Potomac River runs east, across from Washington, D.C., where close by are the roiling waters of Great Falls National

Park, Theodore Roosevelt's favorite spot to clear his head of the rigors of the presidency. In this same area are three lesser-known but still challenging and worthwhile hikes: Scott's Run Nature Preserve, Fraser Preserve, and Riverbend Park.

Inland hikers will find the larger, forested areas of Huntley Meadows Park, Prince William Forest Park, and Manassas National Battlefield, where centuries-old hardwoods have survived the axes of settlers and the bulldozers of developers. Northern Virginia also has its fair share of long out-and-back trails, frequented by bicyclists as well as hikers, including the Washington & Old Dominion Trail, the Cross County Trail, the Mountain Vernon Trail, the Potomac Heritage National Scenic Trail, and the Bull Run–Occoquan Trail.

TRIP 33
PRINCE WILLIAM FOREST PARK

Location: Quantico, VA
Rating: Moderate to Difficult
Distance: 7.9 miles
Elevation Gain: 600 feet
Estimated Time: 4.5 to 5.0 hours
Maps: USGS Quantico and USGS Joplin; free NPS map at visitor's
center

**Prince William Forest Park is the largest forested region in the D.C.
area. Its trails run along the north and south forks of the Quantico
Creek and span the hilly terrain in between.**

DIRECTIONS

On the Capital Beltway, from Exit 170 on the inner loop of I-95/I-495 (or from
Exit 57 of the outer loop of I-495), go south on I-95 and take Exit 150B onto
VA 619/Joplin Road. Go 0.4 mile and take the second right into the park on
Park Entrance Road. Go straight to the visitor center (a 150-million-year-old
piece of petrified wood is out front), then go back and take the first right into
the Pine Grove parking lot. *GPS coordinates:* 38° 33.66′ N, 77° 20.99′ W.

TRAIL DESCRIPTION

Prince William Forest Park protects more than 15,000 acres in the middle of
the busy I-95 corridor in Quantico, Virginia. The north and south forks of
Quantico Creek flow through the park, and a large percentage of the 37 miles
of hiking trails is along them.

This 7.9-mile hike traces the natural and human history of the park. The
hike starts northwest along South Fork Quantico Creek, travels east over forested hills—once farmland—and returns southeast via North Fork Quantico
Creek. From the west end of the Pine Grove parking lot, cross an open field and
start downhill on the western edge of the yellow-blazed Laurel Trail Loop. The
trees here are typical of the park's uplands—flowering dogwoods and hollies
below, beech limbs spreading horizontally and yellow poplars towering above.
At 0.4 mile, just over the suspension bridge, turn left onto the white-blazed
North Orenda Road. At 0.6 mile, at a double white blaze on a beech tree, turn
left onto the narrow South Valley Trail, and turn back toward the creek.

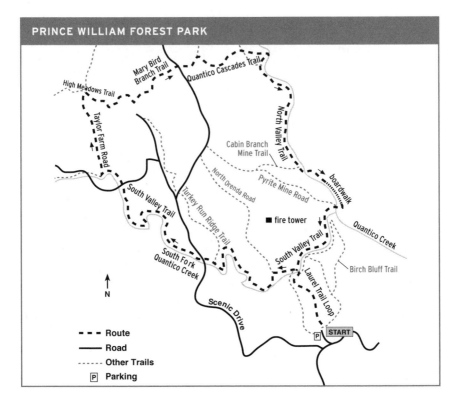

PRINCE WILLIAM FOREST PARK

Mary Bird Branch Trail
Quantico Cascades Trail
High Meadows Trail
Taylor Farm Road
North Valley Trail
Cabin Branch Mine Trail
North Orenda Road
Pyrite Mine Road
boardwalk
Quantico Creek
South Valley Trail
Turkey Run Ridge Trail
fire tower
South Valley Trail
South Fork Quantico Creek
Birch Bluff Trail
N
Laurel Trail Loop
Scenic Drive
START
P

- - - Route
——— Road
------ Other Trails
P Parking

Follow the creek along its lush bank, catching views of several picturesque waterfalls streaming down cliffs on the opposite shore. At 1.1 miles, cross a small bridge over the Mary Bird Branch and immediately begin a steep rise on a ridge between the side and main streams—one of two big elevation gains on the south fork. Drop back down to a grove of sycamores, and at 1.4 miles, reach the intersection with Turkey Run Ridge Trail.

Going straight, cross a bridge, a fire road, and then Scenic Drive, a 12-mile paved road circling the center of the park. Come to an area rich with knotty black birches, pass a spur trail that leads to Parking Lot B on Scenic Drive, and cross two small bridges over barely trickling side streams. This area is the fall line, where Quantico Creek plunges down erosion-resistant, gray-green boulders to the soft sedimentary rock of the coastal plain. Pass the spur to Parking Lot C and soon after, at 2.2 miles, cross another bridge over a side stream. Rise immediately on the second steep hill and return to the creek at a copse of holly, mountain laurel, and oak saplings. Continue as the creek becomes gradually more turbulent and boulder-strewn. Cross under Scenic Drive on a boardwalk, and at 2.9 miles, reach the intersection with Taylor Farm Road.

Birch trees arc over the south fork of Quantico Creek in Prince William Forest Park. Hikers along the river are sure to see evidence of beaver activity—fallen trees, gnawed tree trunks, and small lodges.

Turn right on the blue-blazed Taylor Farm Road and travel gradually uphill for 0.6 mile to High Meadows Trail. Turn right on this orange-blazed trail and meander downhill to Little Run. Turn left over the bridge, and begin a sharp rise on a ridge where beeches cling tenuously to the edge. At 3.9 miles, reach Old Black Top Road. Turn right toward the ranger station; go 100 yards and turn left onto the red-blazed Mary Bird Branch Trail. This 0.5-mile trail, named for an early homesteader, goes downhill to a bridge. Cross a short boardwalk, and climb the facing ridge, leveling out on top. Upon reaching Scenic Drive (the end of the Mary Bird Branch), cross the crosswalk and head to the right to a sign marking the start of Quantico Cascades Trail.

Follow the yellow blazes to Lake One Road, turning left at a double-blazed pine, and proceed 0.1 mile before turning right to reach the Dinosaurs and Volcanoes sign. Go steadily downhill, crossing North Valley Trail and continuing toward a hill in the distance. Reach the Fall Line sign and then head downhill on a series of tight switchbacks—the steepest elevation in the park. At 5.1 miles into the hike, drop onto the cascades and notice the Power of Water sign. The slick, almost putty-like rock here is part of the Chopawamsic formation, the result of volcanic eruptions 500 million years ago. Next, go south along the creek (to the right) toward North Valley Trail, making sure not to head north on an unmaintained trail.

At 5.3 miles, reach North Valley Trail at a Y intersection and turn left, heading south. Pass a Coastal Plain sign and continue along sharp bends in the creek, where massive upland boulders—more dramatic than the cascades to the north—create boiling mini rapids. Stop at a Pyrite Mine sign and observe the concrete ruins of old mine buildings. Next, reach the bridge over North Fork Quantico Creek and turn left across it to the north bank.

Follow the bank to a boardwalk bisecting a grove of tall pines. To the right is the denuded hill that was the site of the main pyrite mine, shut down in 1920. In 1995, the National Park Service built storm-water channels, planted 5,000 trees, filled the mine shafts, and buried the mine tailings in lime, all in an effort to regenerate plant and animal life. Continue on a boardwalk through more pines at the park's edge, following a depression from a narrow-gauge railroad that once serviced the mine. Turn right at a grove of rare redbuds, and cross a bridge back to the south bank of North Quantico Creek.

Twenty yards after the bridge, at 6.8 miles, turn left onto South Valley Trail. Travel for 0.9 mile back to the suspension bridge over South Fork Quantico Creek and return straight up the west edge of Laurel Loop Trail, reaching the parking lot at 7.9 miles.

MORE INFORMATION

In addition to the hiking trails, there are 21 miles of bicycle-accessible trails, two large picnic pavilions, five cabins constructed by the Civilian Conservation Corps, and four campgrounds.

The Prince William Forest Park website (www.nps.gov/prwi) has detailed information on trails accessed in this hike.

There is a fee of $5 per vehicle.

UNDER COVER: SPIES IN THE PARKS

In New Deal days, President Franklin Roosevelt's Civil Conservation Corps and Works Progress Administration built cabin camps at Chopawamsic Creek (now Prince William Forest Park) and Catoctin Mountain (Trip 14). These facilities offered outdoor experiences for less-fortunate urban youths until the new Office of Strategic Services, precursor to the Central Intelligence Agency, appropriated them in 1942 to train spies for work in World War II.

Roosevelt wanted an American special-operations and secret-intelligence force to rival Great Britain's MI6. However, as recently as 1929, Secretary of State Henry Stimson had insisted, "Gentlemen do not read one another's mail." Longstanding U.S. policy eschewed peacetime espionage. So, when establishing OSS (initially named COI, for Coordinator of Information) in July 1941, prior to Pearl Harbor's bombing, FDR had to proceed cautiously. He tapped an old law school classmate, decorated World War I hero Colonel William "Wild Bill" Donovan, to lead the new organization. But Donovan and his aides had no experience building a spy agency. They learned a few tricks from the Brits, then muddled through.

The cabin camps—close to Washington, yet semi-isolated, and offering plenty of rugged terrain—served OSS's top-secret needs well. Recruits, mostly young college-educated men, lived in the bugged, heavily guarded cabins (some of which are available today for camping), learning skills ranging from forgery to forest parachuting, covert radio operations to killing an enemy with a rolled-up newspaper. Forests in Maryland and Virginia provided literal cover for fledgling agents developing stealth in movement, concealment, and base-station setup. It was no cakewalk: Four men were killed and many were injured during training. (Future CIA Director William Casey sustained a broken jaw from a tripped booby trap.) In the dark of night, without warning, instructors rousted recruits from their bunks to face real-life, close-range pistol fire combat against "Nazi agents" hiding in a facility dubbed the House of Horrors.

Recruits practiced subtler covertness, too: befriending unsuspecting nearby townspeople, lock picking, black propaganda (spreading false information about an enemy), and sabotage tactics such as planting sham explosives under local bridges. Known by code names only, restricted to gathering in groups of four or fewer, they were forbidden to discuss their assignments. Their purported final exam involved infiltrating an industrial target—gathering information on production and supply, or planning sabotage. But at OSS "graduation" parties, liquor flowed liberally and candidates were unwittingly evaluated yet again, on how much they'd reveal under the influence. Utter loyalty was the ultimate test, and the final cover they would need to carry out their dangerous work.

TRIP 34
SKY MEADOWS STATE PARK

Location: Paris, VA
Rating: Moderate (some steep climbs)
Distance: 5.8 miles
Elevation Gain: 1,000 feet
Estimated Time: 3.0 hours
Maps: USGS Upperville; Potomac Appalachian Trail Club Map 8; sketch map available at park

Saved from development by noted philanthropist Paul Mellon in 1975, Sky Meadows State Park offers an incredible blend of pastures and woodlands on the eastern slope of the Blue Ridge Mountains.

DIRECTIONS
From I-495 (Capital Beltway), take Exit 49 west onto I-66 and take US 17 north (Winchester Road) via Exit 23 toward Delaplane/Paris. Go 6.5 miles, then turn left onto VA 710 into the park. The road ends at a parking lot near the Mount Bleak House and the visitor center. *GPS coordinates:* 38° 59.118′ N, 77° 57.523′ W.

TRAIL DESCRIPTION
Sky Meadows State Park has 1,500-plus mountain acres, on elevations ranging from 600 to 1,800 feet. The park's trails ascend steep, open meadows, and then travel through alternating woodlands and pastures at the top of the ridge. Throughout the hike, notice the great diversity in butterfly species, best enjoyed with close-focusing binoculars and a good field guide. Zebra swallowtails flutter across the trails with regularity, jolting a hiker's senses with majestic black-and-white stripes and a splash of red on the tail. The monarch butterfly is common in July and August, but the ultra-rare Giant Swallowtail can be spotted in August only.

Begin your hike at the northwest corner of the parking lot. The trail immediately veers left onto Boston Mill Road, which was constructed in the 1820s. After a few hundred feet, climb the stone steps to the right and begin the 0.7-mile ascent on the red-blazed Piedmont Overlook Trail. Pass a wooden bridge over a brook and an old farm building, and continue on to the top for a breathtaking view at Piedmont Overlook, where a patchwork quilt of pastures and

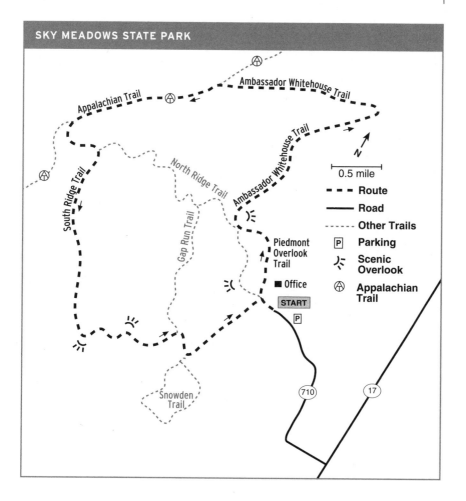

SKY MEADOWS STATE PARK

farm fields, interspersed with lakes and streams, stretches across the Crooked Run Valley. George Washington mapped this area in the 1740s, and in 1861, the valley served as the jumping-off point for Confederate soldiers en route to the Battle of Bull Run.

Continue into a patch of woods, then turn right and follow the blue-blazed North Ridge Trail for 0.2 mile. Next, turn right onto the 1.1-mile Ambassador Whitehouse Trail. This trail arcs northward, crosses a clearing between tree lines, and heads back into the woods. Keep your eyes and ears open for the ubiquitous red-headed woodpecker, a year-round resident; in spring and early summer, its drumbeat mating call reverberates through the park. Blue jays, mockingbirds, and cardinals also abound year-round. A sharp left turn puts you back on open ground. After half a mile, turn left on the white-blazed Appalachian Trail (AT), which stretches south along the ridgeline. The AT extends

Sky Meadows earns its name from this timeless view across Crooked Run Valley. Night sky observations are held at the park in the summer and autumn months.

for 2,167 miles between Georgia and Maine; for a sample, simply follow its rocky path for a single mile, through old-growth forest and then along a fence line. Pay attention to a wooden stepladder that climbs the fence to your left. (If you miss the ladder, however, you will reach a closed gate, where you can pick up Old Trail and reconnect to the AT.) Upon reentering the woods, travel a few hundred feet and turn left onto North Ridge Trail. Continue for 0.2 mile, until you reach where South Ridge Trail branches off to the right.

A bench marks this intersection, and it is a great spot to rest and have some lunch before beginning the descent. Turn right on the 1.6-mile South Ridge Trail and ease into a wide, soft-packed stretch that crosses a series of gentle streams. About halfway down, make a short side trip to see the ruins of Snowden Manor, a Federal-style house built in the 1860s and consumed by fire in 1913. A fireplace and chimney still stand. Just past this is another scenic spot for communing with the beauty of the Crooked Run Valley. Then you reach a small pond and finally an intersection with Boston Mill Road. Turn left here, and travel down this gravel road for half a mile to return to the parking lot. (Near the intersection of South Ridge Trail and Boston Mill Road is Snowden Trail, an optional 1.0-mile circuit hike through a mature oak forest.)

MORE INFORMATION

Sky Meadows, a popular bird-watching site, has a red-headed woodpecker sanctuary near the contact station at the southern end of the park, just off VA 710. The visitor center has nature and history exhibits, and a gift shop. Sky Meadows charges a $3 fee on weekdays and a $4 fee on weekends, per person. Visit www.dcr.virginia.gov/state_parks/sky.shtml or call 540-592-3556.

On weekends in the spring, summer, and fall, naturalists lead excellent 2- to 3-hour programs on the diverse butterfly, bird, and wildflower populations and the ecology of the streambeds. The park's Astronomy Days take place from spring to fall, in conjunction with the Smithsonian's Albert Einstein Planetarium.

NEARBY

The Strawberry Festival is held in the nearby hamlet of Delaplane every Memorial Day weekend. The G. Richard Thompson Wildlife Management Area (Trip 38) is a short drive from Sky Meadows.

TRIP 35
MASON NECK STATE PARK

$ 🐕

Location: Lorton, VA
Rating: Moderate
Distance: 5.4 miles
Elevation Gain: 250 feet
Estimated Time: 2.5 to 3.0 hours
Maps: USGS Fort Belvoir; sketch map available at visitor center

Mason Neck State Park provides sanctuary for a stunning array of winged predators, including bald eagles, ospreys, herons, and hawks. Its trails traverse sandy beaches, a tidal marsh, and dense woodland.

DIRECTIONS
On the Capital Beltway, from Exit 170 on the inner loop of I-95/I-495 (or from Exit 57 on the outer loop of I-495), go south on I-95 and take Exit 163 onto Lorton Road (VA 642). Turn left onto Lorton Road, travel 1.0 mile, turn right onto Armistead Road, and then take the second right onto Richmond Highway (US 1). Go about 1.0 mile and turn left onto Gunston Road, which heads east onto Mason Neck. Travel 4.5 miles past Pohick Bay Regional Park and Gunston Manor, and turn right onto High Point Road, which leads to both the state park and the wildlife refuge. Pass the park entrance and take the next right to the picnic area parking lot and visitor center. *GPS coordinates:* 38° 38.743′ N, 77° 10.330′ W.

TRAIL DESCRIPTION
Mason Neck State Park contains 1,813 acres of shoreline, marshland, and mature hardwood forest on a peninsula that juts into the Potomac River 18 miles south of Washington, D.C. The nearby Mason Neck National Wildlife Refuge (to the south and east), Gunston Hall plantation, Pohick Bay Regional Park (to the northeast), and Meadowood Special Recreation Management Area (to the north) combine to protect 6,400 acres on the 8,000-acre peninsula. Each offers hiking trails (in addition to canoe and kayak launches, bike paths, picnic areas, and nature overlooks), but the state park has the best-maintained and most extensive trail system. The park has one of the highest concentrations of bald eagles in Virginia, with approximately 30 pairs nesting year-round. Note

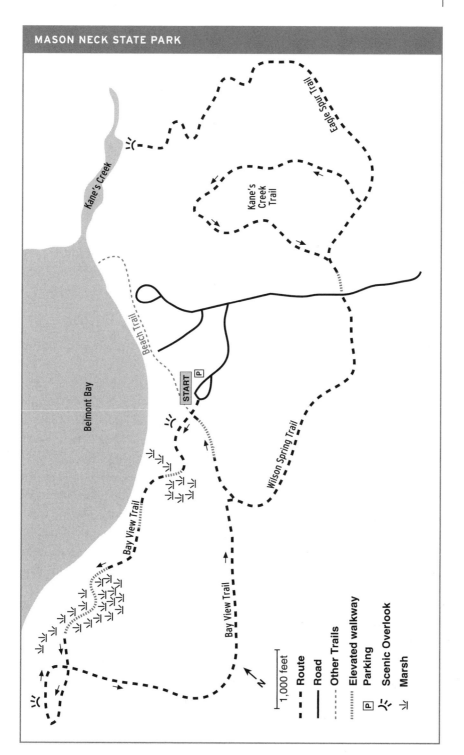

MASON NECK STATE PARK

Kane's Creek

Eagle Spur Trail

Kane's Creek Trail

Beach Trail

Belmont Bay

START

P

Wilson Spring Trail

Bay View Trail

Bay View Trail

N

1,000 feet

- - Route
—— Road
- - - - Other Trails
········· Elevated walkway
P Parking
Scenic Overlook
Marsh

that because federal law mandates a 500-foot berth for bald eagle nests in national and state parks, trails are often relocated. Check with the visitor center for recent changes.

Begin the hike on the 1.0-mile, red-blazed Bay View Trail, which can be entered at the back left corner of the picnic area parking lot. This trail traces the shoreline of Belmont Bay, follows a creek upstream to a large tidal marsh, then passes into the forest. Begin by following the broad dirt-and-mulch path a short distance along the cliff above the shore, and then ascend a series of wooden steps to a small bridge over an inland bog. Continue over the sandy trail, across a second wooden walkway where stands of honeysuckle enliven the meeting of land and water. The walkway affords an excellent view of Belmont Bay. Note the gabion nets shoring up the cliffs at this point. Mason Neck suffers from wave erosion caused by polluted waters, with many shore trees clinging to the tops of the sandy cliffs. Bay View Trail has to be periodically shifted inland because of cliff erosion. (Make sure to heed the postings for restoration areas.)

Arc back inland along a wooden fence and come to a boardwalk over a creek, where bay water flows into and out of the tidal marsh system, supporting a diverse wildlife population. Continuing on the boardwalk, enter a variegated tidal zone of spatterdock, wild rice, and cattail, punctuated by wood duck habitats constructed as part of an Eagle Scout project. Take time to spot birds and other wildlife. During high tide, large fish, including big-mouthed gar and carp, can be seen skirting underneath the planks of the boardwalk, while at low tide frogs, snakes, and salamanders can easily be viewed.

At the end of the boardwalk, enter the woods and ascend wooden steps that become gnarled roots; forge straight ahead to an observation blind for more views of the freshwater marsh. Next, loop back around and follow the trail's winding path through mature, old-growth hardwood forest, past an area of forest that bears the marks of a 1986 fire—burn marks can still be seen on the trees, and the reduced understory growth in this area has given rise to thriving blueberry and huckleberry bushes.

Continue on to the 0.5-mile, yellow-blazed Wilson Spring Trail, and bear right. Walk along the leafy and root-covered trail as it alternately gains and loses elevation and crosses two wooden bridges over swampy runoff. Until recently, Wilson Spring Trail was longer, circling farther to the south, but a bald eagle nest constructed near the trail in 2008 necessitated its shortening. Soon after the second bridge, cross the High Point bicycle trail, a parking area, and then the main entrance road. Continue on an elevated walkway, and veer

The tidewater marsh at Mason Neck State Park is a great place to spot songbirds, waterfowl, water snakes, and large fish like carp. Tides affect the Potomac's waters all the way to Washington, D.C.

right onto the 1.0-mile, blue-blazed Kane's Creek Trail. Travel a quick 200 feet, and turn right again onto the 1.25-mile, white-blazed Eagle Spur Trail. This is a straight out-and-back hike and the most strenuous section because the trail hovers along ridgelines and then plunges down into small valleys with intermittent flowing streams traversed via wooden planks. Oak, beech, and sweetgum trees—with their ubiquitous spiky-balled seeds—line the way, and ruby-throated salamanders swarm over dead logs and away from stomping feet (especially after a rainfall).

At the end of the Eagle Spur Trail is an observation blind over Kane's Creek, a year-round nesting and roosting area for the magnificent bald eagle. Bald eagles are best spotted in the morning hours or at dusk, when park rangers lead guided tours to assist in observation. When finished, retrace the 1.25-mile hike down Eagle Spur Trail, turning right when back to the circular Kane's Creek Trail. This pleasant loop is fairly level and returns to Wilson Spring Trail. Retrace the 0.5-mile hike down Wilson Spring Trail and turn right down Bay View Trail, over a boardwalk, and back to the starting point.

MORE INFORMATION

Mason Neck has trails open from June through November. There is a $4 fee to enter the park. Dogs are allowed. The picnic area parking lot can be full on weekends or holidays; if it is, you can start the hike at the Wilson Spring Trail parking lot a short distance south on the entrance road. The park also offers canoe and kayak rentals at $15 an hour for access to Kane's Creek, a perfect opportunity to spot bald eagles, ospreys, great blue heron, beaver, and even otters. Visit www.dcr.virginia.gov/state_parks/mas.shtml or call 703-339-2385.

NEARBY

Pohick Bay Regional Park has excellent recreational facilities, including a water park, Frisbee golf, and a mini golf course.

TRIP 36
LEESYLVANIA STATE PARK $ 🐕

Location: Woodbridge, VA
Rating: Moderate
Distance: 7.8 miles
Elevation Gain: 650 feet
Estimated Time: 3.5 to 4.0 hours
Maps: USGS Quantico and USGS Indian Head; free sketch map and interpretive maps in the visitor center

Leesylvania State Park offers well-marked and well-maintained trails on a peninsula surrounded by the Potomac River and two large tributary streams.

DIRECTIONS

On the Capital Beltway, from Exit 170 on the inner loop of I-95/I-495 (or from Exit 57 on the outer loop of I-495), go south on I-95. Take Exit 156 and go east on VA 784 (Dale Boulevard) to US 1 south. Turn right onto US 1, then turn left onto Neabsco Road (VA 610) east and go 2.0 miles into the park. *GPS coordinates: 38° 35.234′ N, 77° 15.427′ W.*

TRAIL DESCRIPTION

Leesylvania State Park consists of land once owned by General Robert E. Lee's father, "Lighthorse" Harry Lee. Be sure to pick up the Powell's Creek and Lee's Woods trail pamphlets at the visitor center because both of these interpretive trails are included in this hike. All trails are well marked with signs and colored blazes.

Depart from the visitor center, and go 200 yards toward the Potomac River, passing a structure that houses Purple Martin birdhouses. Turn right (south) at the yellow-blazed Potomac Trail. Follow it, keeping the picnic area to the right and beach to the left, taking in beautiful views of the Maryland shore across the Potomac. Continue across a small wooden bridge with the parking lots ahead on the right. Proceed along the dock area, and cross the top of the boat ramp to walk along the small seawall arriving at the start of Bushey Point Trail at the edge of the woods.

The green-blazed Bushey Point Trail is well maintained. Head west along the north bank of Powell's Creek as it crosses several long wooden boardwalks

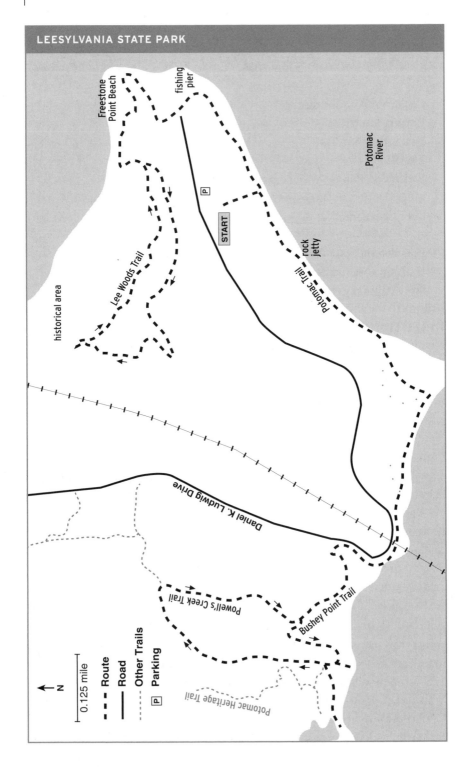

LEESYLVANIA STATE PARK

above marshy areas. On the left is a pole topped by a large wood duck bird-house protected by an inverted conical shield that prevents black rat snakes from eating the duck eggs. The trail also passes a canoe and kayak launch dock and then continues along a narrow path through an open area. The trail curves right following the road on the right and a deep ravine on the left before turning left down some steps into a ravine and up the other side. Go over a small ridge and back down steep steps into another ravine, as the path narrows following the side of the ridge.

Turn left on the blue-blazed Powell's Creek Trail to an overlook where acres of yellow pond lilies (also called spatterdock) are in bloom between June and August.

Go back 100 feet and then go straight through the trail intersection taking the west (left) fork of Powell's Creek Trail. Within a couple hundred yards, turn left (off Powell's Creek Trail) onto a trail marked with white blazes. Follow this trail for about 200 yards to a pond formed by a beaver dam, a marvelous sight well worth the short detour.

Now return to Powell's Creek Trail. As it heads north, it is marked with blue and white blazes because this section is also part of the Potomac Heritage Trail. After going north for almost a mile the path turns to the right and heads south, and the Potomac Heritage National Scenic Trail continues north. This section of Powell's Creek Trail (marked only with blue blazes again) is an interpretive nature trail (targeted at middle schoolers) and has numbered posts that correlate with the short lessons found in the pamphlet.

Powell's Creek Trail rejoins Bushey Point Trail near the ravines. From this point, go back on the path under the railroad bridge. At the historical sign explaining the Lee family tobacco crops, take the left fork to the marina area.

Walk back across the seawall through the marina area to the southern end of the yellow-blazed Potomac Trail. Continue between the large picnic area and the Potomac River beach. This is a good place to have lunch because it offers great views of the Potomac. At this point, the trail goes past a small fenced-in "controlled pond" to the point of land between Neabsco Creek and the Potomac called Freestone Point. Because most of the Potomac River is within the boundaries of Maryland, a walk halfway down the wharf takes you to another state. Return to the main trail and turn left to the beginning of the red-blazed Lee's Woods Trail.

This is a 2.0-mile loop with numbered signs correlating with the Lee's Woods Historical Interpretive Trail pamphlet and describing the history of Freestone Point. The trail moves about 100 yards up the hill into a wooded area. The first point of interest is a fireplace that is all that remains of a hunting lodge built in 1926. Turn right past the fireplace and amphitheater, and climb to the Civil War gun battery on the point. Leaving the battery, head west with Neabsco Creek to the right and a deep ravine to the left. The trail turns left down the ravine for 50 yards then goes right back up the ridge.

The woods open up to reveal the foundation blocks and a remarkably well-preserved chimney of the home of John Fairfax, a Confederate colonel. The trail follows an old road along the side of the ridge and turns left down the slope before turning right and moving back toward the top of the ridge.

A small clearing on the ridge marks the former location of the Henry Lee plantation, built 25 years before the American Revolution and named "Leesylvania," or Lee's Woods. The trail continues down the hill to a partial clearing. Head up a steep hill to the Lee-Fairfax cemetery on the top of the ridge. A wrought-iron fence and a large bronze plaque mark the burial site of Henry Lee and his wife. Near the plaque, take the trail heading left to the old railroad bed at the bottom of a 60-foot-deep ravine, a cut made to complete the railroad line across the peninsula in 1872. Return up the hill past the cemetery, turn left, and follow the red blazes trail along the top of the ridge. Go over the top and head downhill, crossing the previously traversed trail just east of the Fairfax House chimney. Continue on a wide gravel road down the hill, bending right past the turnoff to the Hunting Lodge and back to the north end of the visitor center parking lot.

MORE INFORMATION
Leesylvania is a very scenic park, with often used but well-maintained facilities, including a boat ramp, snack bar, fishing pier, group camp sites (tents only), and a large picnic areas right on the river. The park entrance fee is $5 on weekends and $4 during the week. Visit www.dcr.virginia.gov/state_parks/lee.shtml or call 703-730-8205.

NEARBY
Just a few miles west of Leesylvania State Park is the much larger Prince William Forest Park (Trip 33). Freestone Point in Leesylvania is only one stop along the county-spanning Prince William Civil War Heritage Trail. A must-do for history buffs, the trail also encompasses areas of Prince William Forest Park and Manassas National Battlefield.

TRIP 37
BULL RUN MOUNTAINS NATURAL AREA

Location: Haymarket, VA
Rating: Moderate
Distance: 3.5 miles
Elevation Gain: 810 feet
Estimated Time: 2.0 to 2.5 hours
Maps: USGS Thoroughfare Gap; free sketch map at trailhead

The Bull Run Mountains, the closest range to Washington, D.C., provide hikers with rugged—but not overwhelming—terrain.

DIRECTIONS

From I-495 (Capital Beltway), take Exit 49 west onto I-66. Go 27 miles and take Exit 40 (Haymarket). At the end of the exit ramp, turn left at the traffic light onto US 15 south (James Madison Highway). Go 0.5 mile to the next light, and turn right onto VA 55 (John Marshall Highway) west. Go 2.7 miles (crossing railroad tracks at 2.0 miles), and turn right onto Turner Road. Follow it a short distance across I-66, then turn left onto Beverly Mill Drive. Go 0.8 mile to Mountain House at the end of the road. *GPS coordinates:* 38° 49.516′ N, 77° 42.183′ W.

TRAIL DESCRIPTION

Bull Run Mountains Natural Area consists of 2,500 acres near Haymarket, Virginia. Bull Run Mountains Conservancy (BRMC), a private nonprofit organization, protects its unique ecosystem through education, research, and stewardship, and manages public access on the southern 800 acres of the natural area. Hikers are required to sign a waiver-of-liability form, which protects the conservancy from potential lawsuits. BRMC's trails are on the north side of Thoroughfare Gap and are available anytime during daylight hours.

At the trailhead kiosk, sign the liability-wavier form and pick up a map. The numbers on the map identify the trail intersections, and the legend at the bottom shows the trails by color code (except for Alternate Trail); hikers are cautioned to disregard any trail blazes painted on trees. Small colored disks identify trails leaving each intersection.

Cross the railroad tracks and follow Alternate Trail to the right. The trail is narrow but well defined and moves gradually up the ridge at a moderate

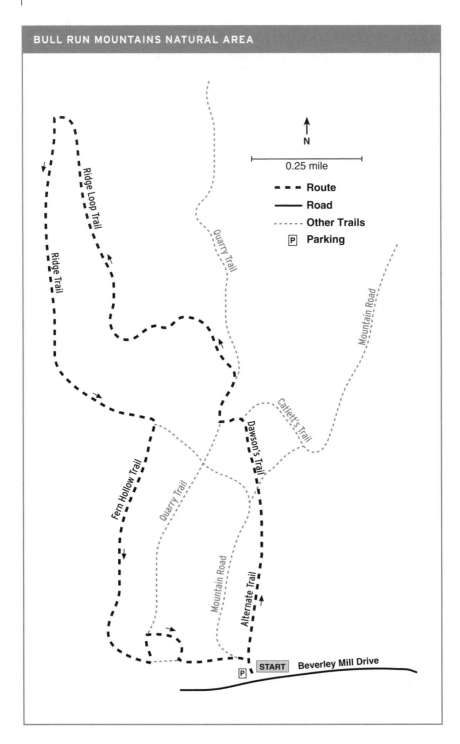

BULL RUN MOUNTAINS NATURAL AREA

N

0.25 mile

- - - Route
——— Road
········ Other Trails
Ⓟ Parking

Ridge Loop Trail

Ridge Trail

Quarry Trail

Mountain Road

Catlett's Trail

Dawson's Trail

Fern Hollow Trail

Quarry Trail

Mountain Road

Alternate Trail

Ⓟ START Beverley Mill Drive

The five-story Chapman's Mill, just northwest of the Bull Run Mountains Conservancy parking lot, once harnessed the waters of Broad Run to grind limestone and grist.

incline. At the large intersection marked with the 6 and 7 posts, follow the Dawson's Trail sign and go straight through the intersection down a wide path. Descend slightly into a small draw, then over a small ridge finger. Note a small beech tree with a sign pointing the way to Dawson's cemetery. Turn right and walk 100 yards to it. More than 150 years old, the carvings on the marker stones seem remarkably preserved, but BRMC personnel are certain they are authentic. Go back to Dawson's Trail, turn right, and go to intersection 11.

The trail map shows a left turn onto Catlett's Trail, but on the ground the path is generally straight ahead. Walk 150 yards past a small stream below and to the right to arrive at intersection 10. The brown sign on a large beech tree shows Quarry Trail (or road) to the left; turn slightly right here off Catlett's Trail. At intersection 13, Quarry Trail crosses the stream to the right; turn left here onto Ridge Loop Trail. Twenty-five yards up the trail, cross the stream and climb steeply for about 100 yards. Then climb less steeply up the side of the ridge on exposed, jagged rocks. Bend to the left and move up a draw at a moderate incline. Exposed ledges cover a wide area of the side of the ridge, ancient quartzite transformed by heating and pressure into hard metamorphic rock. At the top of the draw, still on Ridge Loop Trail, turn to the right and continue up the side of the ridge.

The ridge is the southern extension of High Point Mountain. At intersection 14, turn left down Ridge Trail along the spine of the ridge. After a little more than half a mile, the trail turns left down the steep side of the ridge. At intersection 9, turn right down Fern Hollow Trail and, within a few hundred yards, cross a short wooden walkway above a small stream. Descend gently down the hollow and cross a second wooden walkway above another small stream. (The small concrete box cistern was built in the 1930s to hold water for the mill worker's house.)

At the bottom of the hollow near intersection 4, in a grove of young beech trees, is an unidentified dilapidated wooden house with collapsed roof and walls. Until the nearby Chapman's Mill (built in 1742; also known as Beverly Mill) was closed in 1951, a mill worker resided in this building. At intersection 4, turn left and cross a marshy streambed area along a wooden walkway. The trail continues through more wet and muddy areas. However, the rocks, along with some logs, provide a way to cross the wet area. On the right are the railroad tracks crossed at the beginning of the hike. Approach intersection 3 and notice Broad Run and the high stone walls of Chapman's Mill. At intersection 3, turn left up Quarry Trail and walk a few hundred yards up a fairly steep hill to the Quarry Trench, site of the Battle of Thoroughfare Gap, a fierce Civil War battle that played an important role in the Second Manassas Campaign. Opposite the trench at Intersection 5, a brown sign shows Chapman Trail (not named on the trail map) to the right. The trail is not well defined, but following it about 800 yards down the hill leads to the Chapman Family Cemetery, surrounded by a stone wall. Go back about 100 yards and turn left down the hill along a narrow path to a large sycamore tree laced with crawling vines. At intersection 2, turn left and start down Mill Trail (also not named on the trail map) where there is a large stone-lined pit on the right. Continue down the trail, cross a crooked wooden walkway, go past intersection 1 (staying to the right), and then go over the tracks to the trailhead kiosk.

MORE INFORMATION

Visit www.brmconservancy.org to download a trail map, a release and waiver of liability form, a calendar with public programs, and other information. Chapman's Mill is open on weekends and some holidays. Visit www.chapmansmill.org to learn about restoration efforts.

TRIP 38
G. RICHARD THOMPSON WILDLIFE
MANAGEMENT AREA

Location: Delaplane, VA
Rating: Difficult
Distance: 8.8 miles
Elevation Gain: 1,750 feet
Estimated Time: 4.5 to 5.0 hours
Maps: USGS Linden and USGS Upperville; Potomac Appalachian
Trail Club Map 8: Snickers Gap to Chester Gap

**The trails at G. Richard Thompson Wildlife Management Area
crest the Blue Ridge Mountains to reach heights of 2,200 feet above
sea level, and in springtime are adorned with Virginia's best display
of trillium flowers.**

DIRECTIONS

From I-495 (Capital Beltway), take Exit 49 west onto I-66 and take US 17
(Winchester Road) north via Exit 23 toward Delaplane/Paris. Go 6.5 miles,
then turn left onto VA 688 (Leeds Manor Road) into the wildlife management
area. After 2.5 miles, turn right into the Lake Thompson parking area. Two
parking lots are off VA 688. Park in the northern lot near Lake Thompson.
GPS coordinates: 38° 57.47′ N, 77° 59.35′ W.

TRAIL DESCRIPTION

The Virginia Department of Game and Inland Fisheries stewards 36 wildlife
management areas (WMAs) across the state that encompass 200,000 acres of
public land. To maximize hunting and fishing opportunities, WMAs intro-
duce species, burn undergrowth, plant edible wildflowers, develop hedgerows,
and stock ponds. Hunting is allowed, but hikers can enjoy one of northern
Virginia's largest and best natural areas during open seasons by wearing bright
clothing and staying on designated trails.

G. Richard Thompson WMA is broken into two tracts; the much larger
southern tract has elevations between 700 and 2,200 feet above sea level, with
the Appalachian Trail (AT) spanning the ridgeline for 7 miles on its western
boundary. Generally speaking, as you go west, you go uphill. Eleven parking

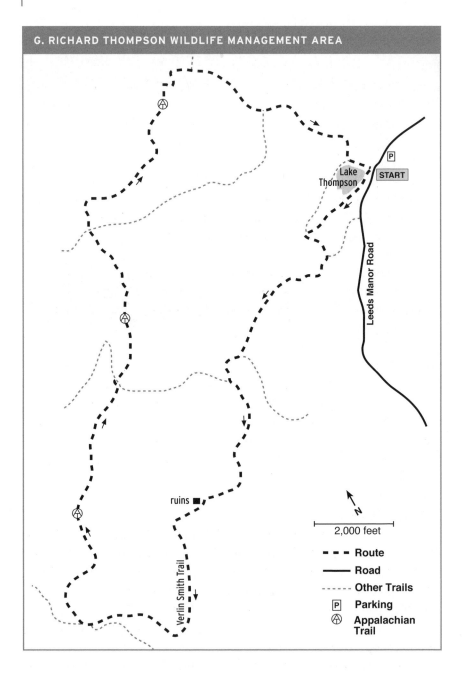

G. RICHARD THOMPSON WILDLIFE MANAGEMENT AREA

Lake Thompson

START

P

Leeds Manor Road

ruins

Verlin Smith Trail

N

2,000 feet

- - - Route
—— Road
----- Other Trails
P   Parking
Ⓐ Appalachian Trail

lots surround the area, and several trails running east to west connect the parking lots on either side.

One of this hike's main attractions is the literally thousands of large-flowered trillium that bloom along the trail from late April to early June. Added to

Hikers ascend a not-always-well-marked trail toward the ridge top at G. Richard Thompson Wildlife Management Area.

the trillium are dozens of other vibrant wildflowers, an impressionistic blend of showy orchids, yellow lady's slippers, sweet cicely, golden ragwort, louse-wort, wild hydrangea, buttonbush, and fleabane. The final feather in Thompson's bountiful cap is its 10-acre Lake Thompson, which is stocked with trout as well as bluegill, sunfish, catfish, and bass.

Walk 100 yards down the gravel path from the parking lot to the lake, and continue along the south shore. At the end of the lake, a deep ravine cradles the streambed, opening to the right. Gradually the ascent becomes steeper until, at 0.6 mile from the starting point, another trail joins from the right, signaling a sharp shift to the left and the beginning of steep and rocky terrain.

Turn right at a T intersection onto the unmarked Verlin Smith Trail. Here the trail runs along a wire fence on the border of the WMA. Beyond the fence are open hillsides with farms, vineyards, and solar-panel-equipped houses. Travel uphill along the fence for 200 yards, then veer right for a 0.5-mile climb, gaining 300 feet of elevation on a widening red-dirt trail to a convergence with another trail coming in on the left and a clearing. Continue past granite boulders and curve gently to the left. At a dilapidated sheet-metal shack, turn left to stay on Verlin Smith Trail.

Go downhill. Kettle Run glides across the path. This shaded stream is a good place to spot birds, boxer turtles, and snakes. Cross the stream and trek uphill again, passing through a clearing with dense, chest-high flowering plants. The trail levels out; at 0.2 mile from the clearing, it follows a rocky streambed for about 15 yards. Turn to the right to reach Wildcat Hollow Spring, which flows through granite boulders strewn across the path. Proceed on more sharp-edged rocks, traveling back uphill out of the ravine and along a gradual, narrow, and pleasant dirt trail. Then swing abruptly right at a large clearing that on nice days affords a view of the humpback, twin-peaked Wildcat Knob in the distance. Soon the trail widens and becomes gravelly.

Under a grove of large-leafed yellow poplars, the white-blazed AT comes in from the left to combine with Verlin Smith Trail. This point marks the beginning of the AT journey along the rocky spine of the mountain. The smooth rock makes a pleasant perch and pausing there offers a moment of tranquility at the convergence of trails. Make sure to turn right 50 yards or so ahead onto the AT as the wide Verlin Smith Trail continues straight to a parking lot. A little way ahead, the trail follows a rocky streambed along a gentle curve. Continuing ahead, the trail becomes rocky and steep as oaks, hickories, white ash, chestnut oaks, and a few sassafras trees—the leaves of which make a tasty seasoning much used by American Indians—crowd the path.

A blue-blazed trail (leading to more parking and a view of microwave/radio towers) breaks away to the left. Go straight toward a pin cherry tree standing directly in the trail. Start a descent until a wide, gravelly spur trail intersects. Turn left. (To the right, the trail returns to Verlin Smith Trail near the ruined shack.) Almost directly, double white markers on a tree to the right mark the scenic byway of the AT. Proceed down a level path lined with tall hickories spreading horizontal limbs of thick foliage overhead—what AT thru-hikers term the "Green Tunnel."

Just after an open clearing, another side trail intersects the path. Go straight, and pass a large, smooth boulder that looks like a Martian spacecraft. After an uphill stretch, a small, narrow trail breaks off to the left to yet another parking area. Again, stay on the larger AT as it goes right and begins a long, gradual, downhill descent. The ground alternates between sharp rocks and soft-packed dirt, with some dramatic granite boulders. At the Y intersection, go left to check out Dick's Dome shelter, before going on.

In the summer months this section, unofficially known as Stone Wall Trail, is overgrown, requiring extra efforts to move through the jungle-like mass of clothes-grasping raspberry bushes and devil's walking stick. At points, the trail is completely consumed, making it difficult to locate its twists and turns.

Scramble over some old stone ruins, and then a connecter trail spanning the WMA intersects from the right, opening a bigger, less-dense path ahead.

On this downhill stretch, the trail alternates between dense vegetation and open areas. Descend to the lake and turn left along its eastern edge to return to the parking lot.

MORE INFORMATION

If you have time, scenic US 50 is the best way to reach Thompson WMA because it goes through beautiful horse country. To learn more about the Thompson WMA, visit www.dgif.virginia.gov.

TRIP 39
RIVERBEND PARK AND GREAT FALLS PARK

Location: Great Falls, VA
Rating: Moderate
Distance: 6.8 miles
Elevation Gain: 1,100 feet
Estimated Time: 4.0 to 4.5 hours
Maps: USGS Seneca, Vienna, and Falls Church

A hike from Riverbend to Great Falls offers dynamic, changing views of the Potomac River as it churns through class 5 rapids at Great Falls and then flows into the narrow Mather Gorge.

DIRECTIONS

From downtown Washington, D.C., take US 50 (Constitution Avenue) west. Continuing as it becomes I-66, go over the Theodore Roosevelt Memorial Bridge and keep right at the end of the bridge, merging onto the George Washington Memorial Parkway north. Proceed 9.0 miles to I-495 (Capital Beltway), Exit 43. Cross I-495 and take the outer loop. Go 1.0 mile and take Exit 44 west, VA 193 (Georgetown Pike). Continue 4.6 miles on the Georgetown Pike, passing Great Falls Park on the right and turning right on River Bend Road. Go 2.0 miles on River Bend road and turn right onto Jeffery Road, and then right onto Potomac Hills Street, which ends at the visitor center. *GPS coordinates:* 39° 01.096′ N, 77° 14.735′ W.

TRAIL DESCRIPTION

Fairfax County's Riverbend and Great Falls parks, managed by the National Park Service , are only a few miles apart along the banks of the Potomac River. They are linked by the Potomac Heritage National Scenic Trail (PHNST). The main advantage of starting a hike at Riverbend Park is the free parking. (Great Falls charges an $8 entrance fee.) Starting along relatively calm waters at Riverbend, this southward journey takes you by the Great Falls of the Potomac River and, equally dramatic, the Mather Gorge. This trail also skirts the well-preserved remains of the eighteenth-century Patowmack Canal, a remarkable engineering feat begun by George Washington and now recognized as a National Historic Landmark.

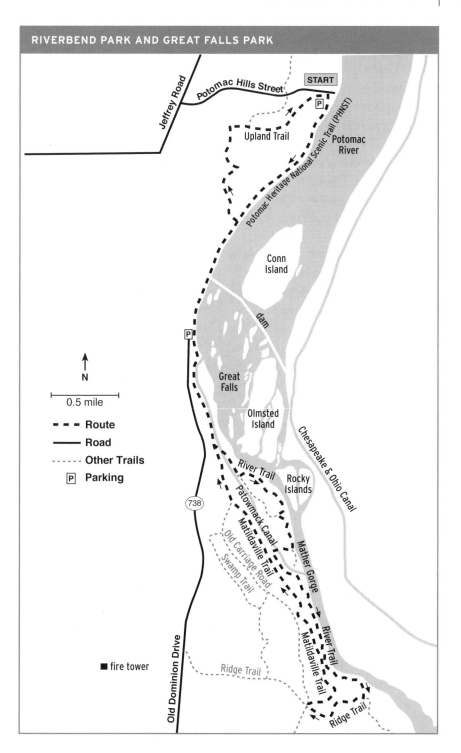

RIVERBEND PARK AND GREAT FALLS PARK

Jeffrey Road

Potomac Hills Street

START

P

Upland Trail

Potomac Heritage National Scenic Trail (PHNST)

Potomac River

Conn Island

dam

N

0.5 mile

- - - Route
—— Road
----- Other Trails
P Parking

Great Falls

Olmsted Island

Chesapeake & Ohio Canal

River Trail

Rocky Islands

Patowmack Canal

Matildaville Trail

Old Carriage Road

Swamp Trail

738

Mather Gorge

Old Dominion Drive

■ fire tower

Ridge Trail

River Trail

Matildaville Trail

Ridge Trail

From the parking lot, head toward the river and turn right on the PHNST, to begin the 1.75-mile segment to the Great Falls Visitor Center. Walk past the boat launch and picnic areas to enter the riverside forest where sycamore trees lean almost horizontally above the water, complementing the understory of tropical-looking paw-paw trees. At 0.5 mile, pass a side trail that leads to Weant Drive. Just after the intersection, ascend along a rocky ledge carved into the hillside, with exposed 500-million-year-old metamorphic rock, formed when the African continent pushed into the North American continent and lifted the ocean floor. At 0.6 mile, reach the intersection with Upland Trail, and at 0.9 mile, use a small bridge to cross a stream that marks the southern boundary of Riverbend Park. At the 1.0-mile mark is a small entrance sign for Great Falls Park. An overlook offers a clear view of the aqueduct dam—the southern limit for boat traffic—and of Conn Island in the center of the Potomac River.

After the dam, the trail follows a wide gravel service road. Abandon it at 1.3 miles with a slight left onto River Trail, a natural service trail that returns to the river (look for a river hazard sign at the split). At 1.5 miles, the remnants of the 200-year-old Great Falls Skirting Canal begin to appear on the left. The first structure encountered is the wing dam, which funneled water into the canal that the Patowmack Company built between 1786 and 1802. When completed, the canal was 1,820 yards long and had five lift locks to carry boats past the falls to the gorge below. Eventually, however, canals were displaced by railroads, as year-round maintenance was too difficult and could not meet the demands of commercial transportation.

Follow the trail along the canal inland, crossing a bridge over Mine Run and reaching the visitor center at 1.75 miles. The center is worth a stop for its collection of artifacts from the amusement park that once existed at nearby Matildaville. South of it, go left across the canal bed and onto Patowmack Canal Trail, which offers access to three overlooks on the falls. Churning rapids tumble 40 feet in 200 yards through a maze of jagged, weather-beaten rocks. At average flow, the river cascades to a 25-foot-deep pool just below the falls, but after a snowmelt or heavy rains, it can swell and overflow the narrow Mather Gorge. A sign on Patowmack Canal Trail marks the water level during serious twentieth-century floods, including the 1996 flood that put portions of Alexandria, Harpers Ferry, and the Chesapeake & Ohio Canal towpath underwater.

Proceed past a picnic area and turn left back to the blue-blazed PHNST as it forges uphill and begins to navigate around granite boulders. At 2.4 miles, descend to a wooden footbridge over a steep feeder stream, cross it, and climb back uphill to the cliffs above Mather Gorge, named for Stephen T. Mather, the

FAR AWAY IN TIME: THE GEOLOGY OF GREAT FALLS

If the rocky channel carrying the roiling Potomac River through Great Falls seems like a vision from a cruder world far away in time, that's only natural. More than 500 million years ago, the long-vanished Iapetus Ocean covered this spot. Its floor was a layer of greywacke—mud and sand coalescing into sandstone. The ocean's underlying crust eventually shifted and sank, scraping against the hard edge of Taconia, one island of a volcanic archipelago whose tectonic plate was on the slow move toward present-day North America. The ensuing collision helped build the Appalachian Mountains 450 million years ago. Meanwhile, the approaching crust acted like a bulldozer, pushing chunks of graywacke into an underwater heap. Tectonic pressure and volcanic heat churned and melted this sedimentary rock into metamorphic rocks: metagraywacke, gneiss, and schists.

Migmatite, 460 million years old, is medium-gray metagraywacke in heavily folded layers with wispy swirls of other rock types—granite, schist, quartz—injected by volcanic activity deep beneath Earth's surface, then cooled as pressure pushed the mass away from its heat source. Look also for 530-million-year-old amphibolite, a metamorphic hornblende rock with an igneous protolith (source rock) and a dark-gray "hammered" surface. Sedimentary greywacke still appears in bed formations; the coarser the grain of a layer within a bed, the longer ago the particles settled—as much as 600 million years.

The rocks of the Mather Gorge Formation, just downstream from Great Falls, contain veins of whitish quartz, pink feldspar, deep-red garnet, mica, and other minerals. Lamprophyre dikes—near-vertical layers of 360-million-year-old igneous rock forced upward by heat into cracks in surrounding rock—stretch across Mather Gorge from Maryland to Virginia, noticeably misaligned. One possible explanation for this is that a fault line beneath the river sliced through the gorge, making the lamprophyre shudder from side to side. Lamprophyre's presence is often linked with gold deposits; indeed, gold was mined for decades on the Maryland side of the falls.

But much of this geologic richness lay buried until the last Ice Age, 20,000 to 30,000 years ago. Before that time, the Potomac flowed across a higher, broad valley. Dropping sea levels and massive snowfalls caused the river to flow stronger and cut deeper, exposing the bedrock. Over millennia, erosion formed successive river terraces that are still visible today.

Great Falls National Park has three overlooks on the monumental rapids, where the Potomac River crashes down a series of falls for 75 feet before funneling through the narrow Mather Gorge.

first director of the National Park Service. At 2.6 miles, a sign signals a right turn to go back over the canal cut. Upon leaving the canal, turn immediately left to continue on the PHNST, following what becomes a tree-lined bluff above Mather Gorge. Soon the thin gorge widens into the larger Potomac Gorge, marking a point where the river crosses the fall line between the Appalachian Piedmont and the Atlantic Coastal Plain. At 2.9 miles, the blue-blazed trail reaches a road that leads down to Sandy Landing. Cross it obliquely to the right, and follow the trail into a small ravine and up the opposite side. Continue and pass through a notch in a spine of boulders. With the river to the left, follow the path along the slope and up to Cow Hoof Rock. From here, follow the blue blazes uphill past a faint intersecting trail from the right. Continue to a T intersection and turn right onto Ridge Trail. At 3.3 miles is a four-way intersection where turning right leads onto Old Carriage Road. After another immediate right, it becomes Matildaville Trail, which passes through the faint ruins of the town founded by Revolutionary War commander "Lighthorse" Henry Lee, who named it for his first wife. Just north of the ghost town, return to the Old Carriage Road and the visitor center.

Continue on the trail, and, at 5.8 miles, turn left where a sign marks the beginning of Upland Trail. Ascend a rocky trail away from the floodplain to an upland forest of oaks, hickories, and beeches. Cruise along the streambed to your right, and turn right onto a smoother trail. Next cross an east-west path that leads to Weant Drive. Go downhill here, and at 6.1 miles, come to a T intersection that faces a streambed with a ridge rising behind it. Turn left to stay on the marked Upland Trail. At the Y intersection, continue to the right and cross the streambed, climbing through a rich carpet of ferns to top the ridge. Upon arriving at another T intersection, go right, then turn right again at the Y intersection to travel back to the Riverbend visitor center.

MORE INFORMATION

Riverbend Park is open from 7 A.M. to dusk, and offers canoe and kayak rentals from May to October, as well as a number of exercise classes and expert-led bird-watching excursions at the nature center. Visit www.fairfaxcounty.gov/parks/riverbend or call 703-759-9018.

TRIP 40
HUNTLEY MEADOWS PARK

Location: Hybla Valley, VA
Rating: Easy
Distance: 1.5 miles
Elevation Gain: Minimal
Estimated Time: 1.0 hour
Maps: USGS Alexandria and USGS Mount Vernon; sketch map available at visitor center

Huntley Meadows is a 1,400-acre natural oasis in the heart of suburbia, less than a mile from the hustle and bustle of US 1. A prime birding location, it contains a large freshwater marsh that supports more than 200 species.

DIRECTIONS
From I-95/I-495 (Capital Beltway), take Exit 177 south onto US 1 (Richmond Highway). Travel 3.0 miles through a series of traffic lights, then turn right onto Lockheed Boulevard. Go 0.7 mile to a T intersection with Harrison Lane, then turn left into the park's main entrance. The visitor center parking lot is ahead. *GPS coordinates: 38° 45.611′ N, 77° 05.736′ W.*

TRAIL DESCRIPTION
Huntley Meadows trails do not cover great distances, but do feature scenic boardwalks in traversing the 500-acre freshwater marsh. Managed by the Fairfax County Park Authority, the park is located in Hybla Valley. This lowland area, formed by an ancient shift of the Potomac River, hasn't always been a nature lover's paradise. Human endeavors—farm fields and dairy pastures, a prospective airpark for zeppelins, a federal public roads test zone, a National Guard anti-aircraft site, and a Naval Research Laboratory radio communications test site—previously held sway over the land. In 1975, President Gerald Ford authorized the transfer of the land to Fairfax County for $1. Over the years, suburban development has increased surface runoff and, coupled with the introduction of enterprising beavers, greatly expanded the park's wetlands.

Begin the hike at the Lockheed Boulevard parking lot and walk a short distance to the visitor's center. Bird-watchers and photographers use the center as a rendezvous point. Check the nature logbook, peek at the bird feeder outside

BEAVERS AT WORK

Meet *Castor canadensis*: North America's largest rodents and nature's corps of engineers. Industrious enough to create an 850-meter-long dam—visible from outer space—in Canada's Wood Buffalo National Park, intelligent enough to build their dams arced into oncoming water flow, beavers are considered a keystone species: When they build dams, they also build local populations and enhance diversity of frogs, fishes, insects, and birds.

The beaver's anatomy is uniquely specialized: a flat tail for balance, steering, and communication (tail-slapping warns other beavers of danger); webbed posterior feet for paddling; and continuously growing incisor teeth. One beaver can gnaw down 200 trees in a year and its teeth will still be in fine working condition. The scaly tail is often considered a delicacy.

Castoreum, an oily substance long used in perfume making, is secreted by glands near a beaver's tail. Spread over the coat during grooming, castoreum waterproofs the fur, making the pelts excellent outerwear for the animals—and irresistible to trappers. Endangered in the 1930s, then reintroduced, beavers have come back strongly.

Beavers alter their surroundings by making dams and transport canals. A beaver family will also build a multiroom lodge, with underwater access tunnels, as its dwelling and operations base. The animals use various materials in construction: deciduous trees, stones, grasses, mud, waterlogged wood, even trash and animal carcasses. Beavers take turns chomping and resting; just a few hours' work will bring down a tree, leaving behind a telltale pointed stump.

Beaver dams, and the resulting ponds, help denitrification, the cleansing and filtration of waters containing toxins from farmland and highway runoffs. The ponds then provide beavers with wide, navigable waters offering safe harbor and escape from predators. Trouble can arise for people, however, when beaver dams cause flooding in agricultural lands, leading to crop losses; when beavers take down rare or valuable trees, as happened in Washington's Tidal Basin in 1999; and when resulting wetlands erode road-bridge foundations, levees, and railway trestles. Trapping and removal of the animals, however, is only a temporary solution. Other beavers are likely to move into the area, and any survivors tend to produce larger litters as compensation for the loss in numbers.

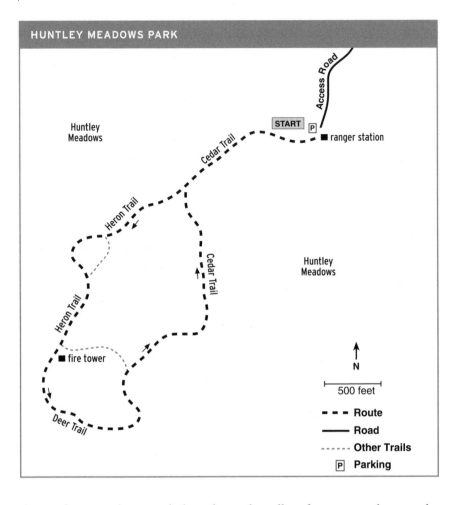

HUNTLEY MEADOWS PARK

Huntley Meadows

Access Road

START · P · ■ ranger station

Cedar Trail

Heron Trail

Cedar Trail

Huntley Meadows

Heron Trail

■ fire tower

Deer Trail

N

500 feet

- - - Route
—— Road
······ Other Trails
P Parking

the window near the main desk, and visit the gallery for rotating photography exhibits on Huntley Meadow flora and fauna.

Exit the visitor center and start on Cedar Trail, a gentle avenue through the woods to the wetlands. Cross a nineteenth-century ditch-and-berm used to drain the lowland for farming, and travel through young sweet gum and maple interlaced with shaggy-barked grape vines. This young edge habitat, preferred by marsh rabbits, house sparrows, and indigo buntings, soon gives way to mature, broad oaks. After passing five small location markers, turn right on Heron Trail and reach the wooden boardwalk at the wetland's edge.

On the right-hand side, a few feet down the boardwalk, stands one of the park's few sycamore trees, a stalwart sentinel over Barnyard Run as it enters the marsh. Loop around the wooden planks, taking time to enjoy the unique watery ecosystem. Dense stands of cattail, buttonbush, swamp rose, and lizard's

The ubiquitous red-winged blackbird alights upon a marshland plant at Huntley Meadows Park in suburban Virginia.

tail thrive here, natural filters for runoff from the surrounding suburbs that help protect the Potomac River and Chesapeake Bay. Watch for animals that feed on these plants—beavers, otters, muskrats, frogs, turtles, herons, ducks, geese, and songbirds.

Reenter the woods for a few hundred feet before returning to the open air. Follow the boardwalk to a two-story observation blind. Forest in every direction ensures the tranquility of this spot, where the park holds early-morning yoga classes in the spring. After leaving the blind, the serpentine boardwalk parallels the forest edge at the point where Barnyard Run exits the marshland and makes it way toward Dogue Creek (named for the American Indian Dogue tribe) at the western edge of the park. To the right, intricate beaver lodges nestle against the marsh edges. Beavers reentered Huntley Meadows in the 1970s and built this 450-foot-long series of dams that dramatically increased the volume of water in the wetlands.

Both the boardwalk and Heron Trail end at the edge of the forest, where the 0.4-mile Deer Trail begins. At the start of this loop, two informal trails break off in succession on the right. These untended 1.2-mile out-and-backs reach a fence on the western edge of the park, extending the hike but also guaranteeing muddy footwear. In any case, continue past a swale on the right where blue flag, a native iris, and rhododendron bloom as early as April, luring white-tailed deer to the area. Farther along, dead pines and live gray-barked beeches surround a meadow with bluebird nesting sites. At the next intersection, turn right back onto Cedar Trail, and make the return trip to the visitor center (or loop around again to the boardwalk). Dead oaks in this area, felled in the early 1990s by a rare disease, provide nesting sites for barred owls and several types of woodpeckers, including the large and quite awesome pileated woodpecker. Upon returning to the visitor center, take a break, mark any nature sighting in the logbook, and be sure to ask the resident naturalists about unknown species encountered.

MORE INFORMATION

Huntley Meadows features a 1.2-mile dual-use hiking and biking trail, accessed from South Kings Highway. The park has excellent educational programs for the entire family, ranging from site-specific bird-watching to teen night hikes. (Note that the visitor center is closed on Tuesdays.) There is no fee for parking. Visit www.fairfaxcounty.gov/parks/huntley or call 703-768-2525.

NEARBY

Restaurants, historic attractions, hotels, and parks can be found in Alexandria.

TRIP 41
FRASER PRESERVE

Location: Great Falls, VA
Rating: Moderate
Distance: 2.6 miles round-trip
Elevation Gain: 125 feet
Estimated Time: 2.0 hours
Maps: USGS Seneca; online at The Nature Conservancy's Fraser Preserve webpage

Lovely and peaceful, this secluded and somewhat hilly woodland escape rewards hikers with a plethora of wildflowers, a rushing clear stream, a cold-spring-fed marsh, and the chance to tread upon land long revered and inhabited by American Indians and later owned and farmed by Virginia gentry.

DIRECTIONS

From I-495 (Capital Beltway), take Exit 44 west, VA 193 (Georgetown Pike). Drive approximately 9 miles, then turn right onto Springvale Road (VA 674). Proceed 1.5 miles, and you'll see a Tudor-style restaurant, L'Auberge Chez François, on your left. Follow Springvale Road as it curves 90 degrees left around the restaurant property to merge briefly with VA 603 (Beach Mill Road), then make a quick right to continue on Springvale, which is also signed as VA 755 at this intersection. Drive approximately a half-mile through a residential area to the corner of Springvale and Allenwood Lane. The trailhead gate is just below at the foot of Springvale Road, but no designated or off-street parking is available. The Nature Conservancy recommends parking along the roadside at this corner; be sure not to disturb residents or block driveways. *GPS coordinates: 39° 02.097′ N, 77°18.580′ W.*

TRAIL DESCRIPTION

Truly a haven and very peaceful, this 220-acre preserve, with its wide array of natural habitats, is not widely or well known, except by local residents. (It doesn't even appear on some maps of the area.) The trail has three descents of 100 to 125 feet each, with three corresponding climbs of the same size—the final climb being at the very end of the hike. It is an excellent nature hike for older children (perhaps 8 and up), but because of its length, rugged surface,

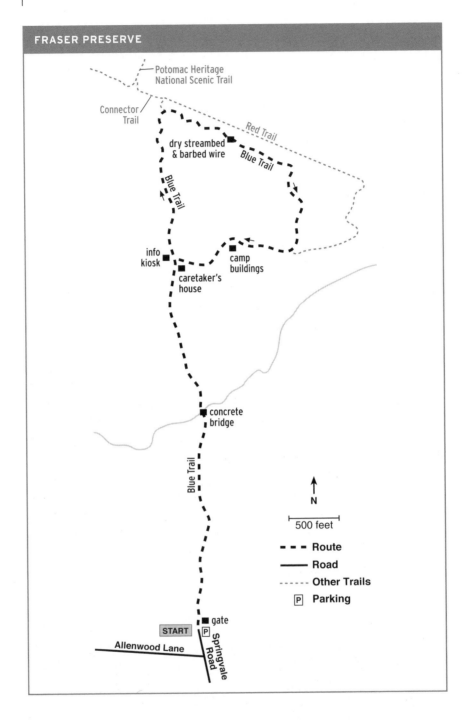

FRASER PRESERVE

Potomac Heritage
National Scenic Trail

Connector
Trail

Red Trail

dry streambed
& barbed wire

Blue Trail

Blue Trail

info
kiosk

camp
buildings

caretaker's
house

concrete
bridge

Blue Trail

N

500 feet

- - - Route
—— Road
- - - - Other Trails
P Parking

gate

START

P

Allenwood Lane

Springvale
Road

narrowness once off the gravel road, and several long climbs, it might not be suitable for smaller kids.

The former haunt of several American Indian tribes (Piscataway, Anacostan, Tauxenent), this land has yielded a wealth of artifacts—stone fishing weirs, arrowheads, and pottery—which now reside in the museum at American University in northwest Washington, D.C. The property formed part of a 5-million-acre land grant from Great Britain's King Charles II in 1649 to some aristocratic friends. In the 1700s, title to the land passed to several of the Virginia Fairfaxes and later the Lees, then eventually to Mrs. George (Bernice) Fraser, who gifted the acreage in 1975 to The Nature Conservancy and to the Calvary Baptist Church.

Approaching the trailhead gate, you'll see a sign for Camp Fraser, the Calvary Baptist Church's name for its children's camp within the preserve. Pass through the gate onto the gravel entrance road, noticing the abundance of wild grapevines festooning the trees here.

Fraser Preserve is known as a habitat for wildflowers (more than 300 species, some quite rare) and a year-round refuge for wild birds (more than 110 species have been identified here, including the bald eagle and ruby-throated hummingbird). The gravel road descends to a concrete bridge over a clear creek, where beavers and turtles may sometimes be seen, then meanders back uphill. Watch for wild climbing roses on the right as you begin this ascent. Some of this land is second- or third-growth forest, having been farmed in the past, but several large and venerable trees also grow here. Virginia bluebells abound in midspring, and mayapples a bit later.

As you reach the top of the hill, the caretaker's house will be on the right, and straight ahead is a sign for Fraser Preserve, pointing left to the information shed. Stop at this shed to pick up a trail map if desired, then continue left onto the loop portion of the trail, blazed with blue dots and markers. The surface becomes forest floor at this point, and the trail will be rather narrow (and possibly slippery) in places. The trail will descend a slope toward the cold spring-fed marshes. Just after a sharp veer to the left, which is also a small steep downslope, Blue Trail makes a sharp right turn, and Yellow Connector Trail to the left leads to the Potomac National Scenic Heritage Trail and to Fraser Preserve's Red Trail. (If you're up for a longer hike, consider taking this connector out along the utility right of way toward the river's edge for some lovely views of the Potomac River.)

Take the right turn to continue on the Blue loop. There may be downed trees here and there across your path, left from the 2010 snowstorms. You'll probably hear the music of trickling water from the marsh and pond below,

An adult female eastern tiger swallowtail butterfly (Virginia's state insect) browses the sun-drenched eastern bluebells (often called Virginia bluebells) for her lunch in northern Virginia's Fraser Preserve.

and deer tracks are common along here because of this available water nearby. After a bit, you'll cross a dry streambed faced with several rocks: Beware of some barbed wire on the left just past this point. The late-afternoon hoot of owls may startle you. Listen for spring peepers, too, if you're here later in the day.

The second ascent begins now, and if you're visiting in midspring, you might stumble upon a whole hillside of Virginia bluebells mixed with other wildflowers as you climb—there's a sort of magical, fairyland feeling of meadow and forest blended into one. Continue to the top of this ridge, and turn right (the Red Trail rejoins from your left at this spot) to complete the loop portion. The Blue Trail will pass among the Camp Fraser buildings, between the meeting hall and the caretaker's house, before leading back to the preserve sign. From here, take the gravel entrance road back downhill, across the clear creek, and up that last slope again to Springvale Road.

MORE INFORMATION

The trail and preserve are open daily, dawn to dusk. Dogs, cleated hiking shoes, and bicycles are not permitted. There are no rest rooms, water fountains, or benches available to the public. Fraser Preserve; 434-295-6106; www.nature.org/wherewework/northamerica/states/virginia/preserves/art1235.html.

Location: Warrenton, VA
Rating: Moderate to Difficult
Distance: 3.4 miles
Elevation Gain: 840 feet
Estimated Time: 2.0 hours
Maps: USGS Marshall; free map at parking area information kiosk

Little-used Wildcat Mountain Natural Area offers strenuous but scenic hiking in the Blue Ridge foothills. John Trail climbs to a 1,000-foot-high ridgeline where farmers once lived and worked.

DIRECTIONS

From I-495 (Capital Beltway), take Exit 49 west onto I-66. Go 31 miles and take Exit 28 (Marshall). Turn left at the end of the exit ramp onto US 17 (Winchester Road) south, and go a quarter-mile. Turn right onto VA 691 (Carters Run Road), go 5.0 miles, then turn left onto England Mountain Road (a private paved driveway). Follow the driveway past a house on the left with a pond, and park just after it at a small parking lot on the right near a kiosk. *GPS coordinates*: 38° 47.52′ N, 77° 51.90′ W.

TRAIL DESCRIPTION

Almost 50 years ago, The Nature Conservancy started managing 655 acres in the Broken Hills range in northern Fauquier County. Known as the Wildcat Mountain Natural Area, it is home to a wide variety of plant and animal life. There are stands of old oak and hickory trees mixed with younger pines, beeches, hickory, and oaks; foxes, deer, squirrels, raccoons, and even bobcats and an occasional black bear make their homes here.

The trail from the parking lot goes between England and Rappahannock mountains—it was cleared as a farm road over 250 years ago, when settlement begain in the region. Old stone walls marking homesteads can still be seen, though many of the small farms were abandoned after the Civil War. Logging and apple growing continued into the 1940s, and a nineteenth-century farmhouse and springhouse remain, both in surprisingly good condition.

The trail map shows a "preferred route" marked in yellow, and green-and-yellow diamond-shaped signs on the trees point out the direction of the trail.

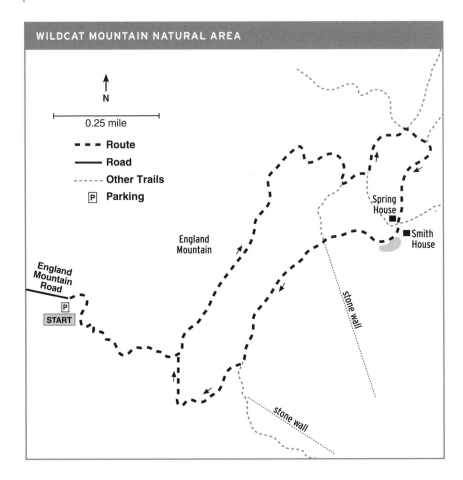

WILDCAT MOUNTAIN NATURAL AREA

Head up the gravel road about 500 yards to the T intersection, then turn right and walk 500 more yards to the trailhead. This is where it gets difficult. Turn left, and climb 100 yards almost straight up a steep, rocky, narrow trail. It sometimes goes straight up and sometimes cuts diagonally across the ridge. Turn sharply to the left where logs on the right mark the first switchback. The second switchback begins at a right turn around a large tree. Continue and take the third switchback back to the left. Trail marker signs guide you up the steep ascent, which is strewn with fallen logs and large rocks. In some sections, the trail consists of exposed rock ledges. This first third of a mile includes twelve switchbacks and 420 feet of elevation gain.

At the top of the ridge is a long, straight, high stone wall in good condition running to the right and left. Step through the disassembled section of the wall and take the trail to the left that leads down a gentle, wide, and well-marked path through the quiet, deep woods. The trail parallels a stone wall on the left,

This chimney is all that remains of a nineteenth-century homestead at Wildcat Mountain Natural Area.

and in some sections a barbed-wire fence marks the boundary of the nature area. England Mountain stands on private property, past the stone wall to the left, 200 yards through the woods. After walking half a mile down the broad, flat area, follow the gentle descent along a finger of the ridge.

The trail then goes down a short, steep section, and turns right onto an old farm road. Cross two streambeds, turn to the left, and move up a moderate incline. Next, turn to the right, continue up the hill, and turn left at the intersection. In about 50 yards, look for a green-and-yellow trail marker that confirms this as the main trail. Continue down into a ravine and back up to the next intersection. Here the preferred route is to the right, but another option is to take the farm road to the left and cross two more streambeds that are dry most of the year. At the John Trail sign, turn right, walk 100 yards up the broad path, and turn right at the T intersection.

Walk up a slight hill about 500 yards, passing several large yellow poplars, to reach the Smith House, probably abandoned for 50 years but in remarkably good condition. On the west side of the very old stone-and-mortar foundation, the plaster covering the stone used to form what looks to have been a map of the United States. However, weathering has caused the "Northeast" to crumble away. Behind the Smith House stands a fireplace and chimney that appears to mark the location of an older farm house. As you return to the trail, turn right down the small draw, and walk 60 yards to see the Spring House, used to keep meat, fruit, and dairy products from spoiling either with the use of pond ice or flowing water supplied by a spring that has since dried up.

Returning to the intersection in front of the Smith House, turn right and follow the trail across the top of the earthen dam. To the left is the dry bed of the former small reservoir that served the Smith House. Take the trail downhill and follow it, walking through the opening in another stone wall. The trail, which is actually an old farm road, slowly moves up the hill and turns right up a narrow path. Hike past oak trees, beech trees, and flat rock ledges until you come to another stone wall. Turn right at the stone wall and follow the path beside the wall for 200 yards. At the break, turn sharply left and head down the steep winding path that you climbed about an hour earlier. At the gravel road, turn right and then left to return to the parking area.

You can add 1.1 miles and about 220 feet of elevation gain to the hike by including a loop north of the John Trail sign, which is clearly depicted on the trail map.

MORE INFORMATION

Wildcat Mountain Natural Area is open year-round, dawn to dusk. Visit The Nature Conservancy website for more information on the history of the preserve and the steps the conservancy is taking to acquire surrounding portions of land and allow for natural succession. Visit www.nature.org/wherewework/northamerica/states/virginia/preserves/art1247.html.

TRIP 43
WASHINGTON & OLD DOMINION
TRAIL AND CROSS COUNTY TRAIL

Location: Vienna, VA
Rating: Easy
Distance: 12 miles
Elevation Gain: 230 feet
Estimated Time: 4.5 to 5.0 hours
Maps: USGS Vienna; official Northern Virginia Regional Park Authority W&OD trail guide; printable maps from www.wodfriends. org and www.fairfaxcounty.gov/parks/cct

This out-and-back covers a good distance of mostly flat ground on two county-spanning trails, ideal for setting a steady, easygoing pace. At its midpoint is a well-preserved eighteenth-century mill.

DIRECTIONS
From I-495 (Capital Beltway), take Exit 49 west onto I-66. Take Exit 62, VA 243 (Nutley Street), north toward Vienna. Go 1.0 mile, turn right onto Maple Avenue (VA 123), then go 1.0 more mile and turn right onto Park Street. Travel two blocks, and turn right into the Vienna Community Center parking lot. *GPS coordinates: 38° 54.037′ N, 77° 15.607′ W.*

TRAIL DESCRIPTION
Washington & Old Dominion (W&OD) Trail is a paved hike-bike path that follows the former roadbed of the W&OD Railroad for 45 miles through northern Virginia. The trail's southeastern end is at Arlington in the Shirlington business district, and the northwestern end is the small town of Purcellville, 9 miles from the Blue Ridge Mountains. The hike starts in Vienna and leaves W&OD Trail at Difficult Run to follow Cross County Trail, which was begun in 1999 and is still under development. The hike ends at the historic Colvin Run Mill. Keep in mind that portions of the Cross County Trail flood after heavy rains, so waterproof hiking boots are ideal.

From the community center parking lot, turn right onto the asphalt W&OD Trail, hiking below large electric transmission towers. At 0.2 mile, cross Maple Avenue (Chain Bridge Road), which is the main north-south artery through Vienna. One block beyond Maple Avenue is Church Street, site of the historical

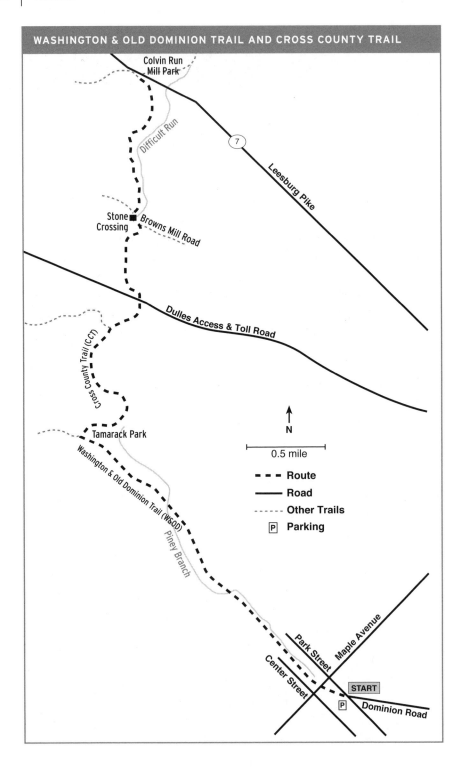

WASHINGTON & OLD DOMINION TRAIL AND CROSS COUNTY TRAIL

Difficult Run, which dumps into Potomac River at Great Falls, moves fast after heavy rainfall. It often overflows its banks to flood the adjacent Cross County Trail.

Freeman House the, a town museum and gift shop selling regionally produced books and handcrafts (open on afternoons from Wednesday to Sunday). At 0.6 mile is another well-preserved building, the eye-catching, circa-1859 Vienna train station, which features a brightly painted mural. The last train departed from the station in 1967. Now it houses items from its heyday and a scale-model version of the W&OD line through Vienna in the era of steam locomotives, open to the public only ten Saturdays a year. (Go to www.nvmr. org for more information.)

At mile marker 12 (12 miles from its start in Alexandria), an equestrian trail begins, paralleling the asphalt trail and, in sections, offering a nice alternative path with some elevation change. Pass the entrance to Northside Park at the 1.0-mile mark of this hike. Here the trees are nestled close to the trail on the right, but an open hill studded with power lines falls away to the left and offers little shelter on sunny days. Informative signs about the flora and fauna of Virginia's northern Piedmont make it worthwhile to stop on this portion of the trail. You may view dragonflies, for instance, and learn that their wings beat 50 times per second.

The circa-1813 Colvin Run Mill, in the shadow of traffic-laden VA 7, is the halfway point for the out-and-back W&OD–Cross County Trail hike. Tours of the mill and adjacent house are offered twice a day in the warmer months.

Two miles into the hike, the green space increases on either side of the trail, indicating Clarks Crossing and Tamarack parks. At 3 miles, cross a bridge over Difficult Run and go about 100 yards before swinging right onto Cross County Trail (CCT). This 40-mile-long, still-under-construction trail connects Fairfax County north to south, and this section is known as Difficult Run Stream Valley Trail because it adheres to its namesake stream until its confluence with the Potomac River in Great Falls. The trail is red-blazed and well marked with metal poles sporting the CCT logo. The trail is intermittently maintained, but expect some overgrowth and don't expect snow to be cleared in the winter. And snow isn't the major obstacle—in the spring and after heavy rains, Difficult Run often overflows and leaves low-lying sections of the trail under several inches of water. It is advisable to wear solid, waterproof boots for the slogs through these sections.

For the first mile after leaving W&OD Trail, the trail snakes along the side of a hill with nice views of Difficult Run below to the right and suburban homes above to the left. After crossing a tributary of Difficult Run, turn right on a gravel path, then cross fast-moving Difficult Run over a series of round concrete steps. Walk onto a small bridge over swampy lowland before forging across another trail intersection to reach the Dulles Toll Road overpass. North of the toll road, turn left at a T intersection in a suburban neighborhood and follow a fairly level asphalt trail. At about three-quarters of a mile north from the toll road, recross Difficult Run for the final time, over a series of boulders, and immediately after, pass Browns Mill Road. The trail gradually edges westward away from Difficult Run and soon reaches a pleasant grove of pines and cedars that makes for the quietest and most secluded section of the hike. At the 6-mile mark, come to Colvin Run Road and its intersection with the busy Leesburg Pike. This run once powered Colvin Mill, a restored early eighteenth-century mill just across the pike and up Colvin Run Road. Decide here if you'd like to make a stop. Whether visiting the mill or not, turn around at this point to make your return.

MORE INFORMATION

The park is open year-round, from dawn to dusk. A 63-page guide that contains route information, maps and location guides, history, and safety information is for sale at www.nvrpa.org/park/w_od_railroad. Visit the Friends of W&OD Trail at www.wodfriends.org or call 703-729-0596.

NEARBY

Colvin Run Mill Park includes a miller's house, general store, and barn and is open Wednesday to Monday from 11:00 A.M. to 5:00 P.M. There is a $6 charge for a worthwhile, hands-on tour of the milling process, and at certain times of the year, actual wheat milling, open to the public, occurs at the site. The general store has the wheat for sale, as well as refreshments.

TRIP 44
BULL RUN–OCCOQUAN TRAIL

$ 🐕

Location: Manassas, VA
Rating: Moderate
Distance: 7.8 miles
Elevation Gain: 470 feet
Estimated Time: 4.0 hours
Maps: USGS Manassas; map in NVRPA brochure, available at entrance booth

Traveling through a swath of rural land in the Bull Run and Occoquan watersheds, Bull Run–Occoquan Trail can seem as remote in places as the Appalachian Trail.

DIRECTIONS

This hike requires a car shuttle between two points—Bull Run Regional Park and Hemlock Overlook Regional Park. Head for Hemlock Overlook first. From I-495 (Capital Beltway), take Exit 49 west onto I-66 and from I-66, take Exit 53 (Centerville), VA 28 south. Stay on 28 (Centerville Road) for 2.5 miles, then turn left onto Compton Road, and then, at a T intersection, turn right onto Clifton Road. Go 1.8 miles, through the town of Clifton, then turn right onto Yates Ford Road, and travel 1.4 miles to the parking lot at the Hemlock Overlook park entrance. *GPS coordinates*: 38° 46.007′ N, 77° 24.302′ W.

To reach Bull Run, return north on 28, and turn left onto US 29 south (Lee Highway). Go 2.3 miles, then turn left onto Bull Run Post Office Road. Stay straight where the road jogs slightly left (avoiding a sharp left), and go over I-66 and past the entrance station. Continue 1.6 miles, then park at the swimming pool on the left (the trail begins just ahead to the right). *GPS coordinates*: 38° 48.13′ N, 77° 28.60′ W.

TRAIL INFORMATION

This 17.5-mile path follows Bull Run in the north and the Occoquan River farther south, through the longest stretch of undeveloped land within an hour of Washington, D.C. The Northern Virginia Regional Park Authority manages 4,000 woodland acres in these watersheds, including, from north to south, Bull Run, Hemlock Overlook, Bull Run Marina, Fountainhead, and Sandy Run regional parks. Bull Run–Occoquan Trail, maintained by the Potomac

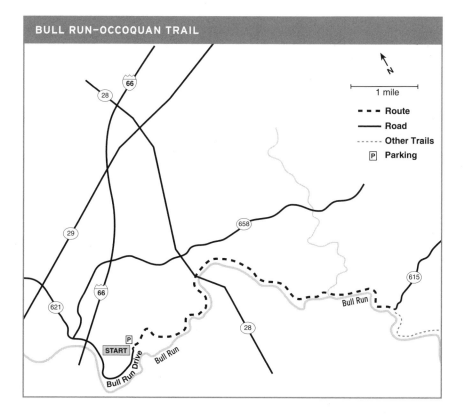

BULL RUN–OCCOQUAN TRAIL

Appalachian Trail Club, goes through all the parks except Sandy Run. The trail's terrain alternates between flat river bottomland and rocky hills and ravines, with dramatic elevation especially evident in the northern section described in this hike, between Bull Run and Hemlock Overlook regional parks.

From the swimming pool parking lot, proceed 100 feet down the road to an information sign and small wood bridge beneath a willow oak. This is the start of the blue-blazed Bull Run–Occoquan Trail. Begin on the wide dirt trail, taking wooden ramps over swampy areas, and turn right at the T intersection with Cub Run. In April and early May, the forest floor around this portion of the trail erupts in thousands of Virginia bluebells, shade-loving wildflowers that American Indians used as a dye. The purple flower of the pawpaw tree—dark and mournful like a dying rose—and white flower of the dogwood tree add springtime color here and elsewhere on the trail. Cross a clearing for electricity pylons, and after 0.8 mile, turn left at a second T intersection and cross Cub Rub on a suspension bridge near its confluence with Bull Run. Notice the steep, rocky opposite bank of Bull Run—the uneven terrain here differs from the gentle course of the river near its origin west of Dulles Airport. From its headwaters, Bull Run drops 1,280 feet through the Piedmont plateau to the coastal plain of the Potomac River.

Start along Bull Run's eastern shore, alive with scraggly river birch, tall sycamore, and stout Shumard oak. At 1.4 miles, go under Ordway Road and across a warped bridge. Several hundred yards on, at a point where the husk of a sycamore stretches halfway across Bull Run, follow the blue blazes left and uphill. Climb to a cedar grove and then descend back to Bull Run as it flows under Centreville Road (VA 28). This junction was the site of the Civil War battle of Blackburn's Ford, where inexperienced New York troops under Israel B. Richardson stumbled into a brigade of Confederates concealed in the woods. Richardson was later mortally wounded at the Battle of Antietam (Trip 15).

Continue to a T intersection and turn left uphill (marked by double blazes). Moving from the water, proceed up and down steep terrain, following a twisting trail. Pass a Civil War artillery emplacement under large tulip trees, and then, at 3.7 miles, cross concrete steps over fast-flowing Little Rocky Run, where clear water snakes its way around dirt shoals. Turn left at double blazes, and cross a fire road several hundred yards on, under old-growth giants. Proceed up and down a series of broad hills carved by trickling, rocky streams. A bed of brown leaves and a shimmering green canopy of chestnut oaks, paw-paw, and mountain laurel color the steep landscape.

Reach Bull Run again a little past the 5-mile mark—more bluebell patches here in the spring—and follow the riverside hornbeam, birches, sycamores, and oaks for 0.3 mile, before veering left away from the horse trail that follows the river. Climb astride gurgling mini waterfalls, cross the rocky stream on wood planks, and climb wood steps up a steep-sided draw, then loop over a small hilltop and head back downhill. Reach a low floodplain where old rusty engine parts share the forest floor with low-growing, foul-smelling skunk cabbage. At 5.7 miles, cross Johnny Moore Creek on stone pillars.

Come back to Bull Run at an embankment where a side stream comes in, and at the 6-mile mark, reach the rusting but still operating railroad bridge of the Norfolk Southern Railroad (Amtrak and Virginia Railway Express trains cross here on their way to Washington). Inspect the crumbling stone foundations of the Civil War Orange & Alexandria Rail Road trestle, a strategic point only a few stops from the vital hub of Manassas Junction. Go underneath the trestle past small but sporting rapids, then traverse a grassy open expanse with the tracks on the left and Bull Run on the right. Reach and cross Pope's Head Creek near its confluence with Bull Run, taking care on its steep banks and slick stone pillars.

Birch- and sycamore-lined Bull Run is a constant companion on Bull Run–Occoquan Trail between Bull Run and Hemlock Overlook regional parks. Bull Run is part of the 40-mile-long Occoquan Water Trail, which flows into Belmont Bay and Potomac River.

Continue on crumbly substrate at the bottom of a sharp, hemlock-lined cliff to the left. The dark-green, conical-shaped hemlocks—not poisonous, the leaves are used in tea—are complemented by diamond-barked, flowering dogwoods. At 7.1 miles, come to what looks like a hollowed-out concrete bunker—the remains of the first hydroelectric plant in Virginia, built in 1925. This plant supplied power to Clifton, the first town in Fairfax County to receive electricity.

Go uphill alongside the plant (downriver), and then head left uphill at a blue blaze on a sharp rock. Curve along a narrow stretch lined with mountain laurel and go left at the sign Hemlock Overlook/Yates Ford Road, leaving the blue blazes to follow yellow blazes directly atop a rocky streambed. Go 0.5 mile uphill to the parking lot at Hemlock Overlook Regional Park.

MORE INFORMATION

Bull Run–Occoquan Trail is accessible to horseback riders as well as hikers. Biking is prohibited. Dogs are permitted, but must be leashed. Bull Run and Hemlock Overlook regional parks are open year-round; admission to Bull Run is free to Fairfax, Loudoun, and Arlington county residents, $7 for nonresidents. (Both Bull Run and Hemlock Overlook regional parks have shooting centers, and rifle reports can be heard in the vicinity.) Visit www.nvrpa.org/park/bull_run and www.nvrpa.org/park/hemlock_overlook.

NEARBY
Occoquan Water Trail comprises 40 miles of Bull Run and the Occoquan River. There are five access points along Bull Run–Occoquan Trail: at Bull Run Regional Park, the VA 28 intersection, the Bull Run Marina, Fountainhead Regional Park, and Lake Ridge. The water trail continues around Mason Neck to Pohick Bay Regional Park. Visit www.nvrpa.org/parks/occoquanwater/ for more details.

TRIP 45
SCOTT'S RUN NATURE PRESERVE

Location: McLean, VA
Rating: Difficult
Distance: 2.8 miles
Elevation Gain: 710 feet
Estimated Time: 2.0 to 2.5 hours
Maps: USGS Falls Church; downloadable trail map at www.
hikingupward.com/OVH/ScottsRun/images/Map.pdf

Scott's Run Nature Preserve offers strenuous hiking along bluffs and ridges overlooking the Potomac River near Washington, D.C.

DIRECTIONS
From I-495 (Capital Beltway), take Exit 44 west, VA 193 (Georgetown Pike). Proceed past the first small parking lot for Scott's Run Nature Preserve (on the right, 0.3 mile from I-495) and turn right into the second main lot (1.0 mile from 1-495). The turnoff is hidden from view just after the Swinks Mill Road sign on the left and just before a large sign on the right for Betty Cooke Bridge. *GPS coordinates:* 38° 57.57′ N, 77° 12.32′ W.

TRAIL DESCRIPTION
The swath of wilderness now called Scott's Run Nature Preserve, once known as the Burling tract, was the scene of controversy in the 1970s when housing developers came knocking. Determined local environmentalists and high school students saved it from suburban sprawl. This 385-acre preserve has scenic views of Scott's Run, the Potomac River, a small waterfall, the remains of an old homestead, and a grove of old-growth Eastern hemlocks. Trailing arbutus, Virginia bluebells, and trillium bloom on the steep hillsides. Scott's Run itself starts near the parking lots of the Tyson's Corner shopping center, flows north through business parks and condominium complexes, and finally through the nature preserve and over the waterfall as it empties into the Potomac.

Scott's Run Nature Preserve is interlaced with trails—about 25 intersections and 40 segments ranging from easy to very difficult. The Fairfax County Park Authority doesn't blaze or name any of them, but posted maps at the parking lots do identify River Trail along Scott's Run and a network called

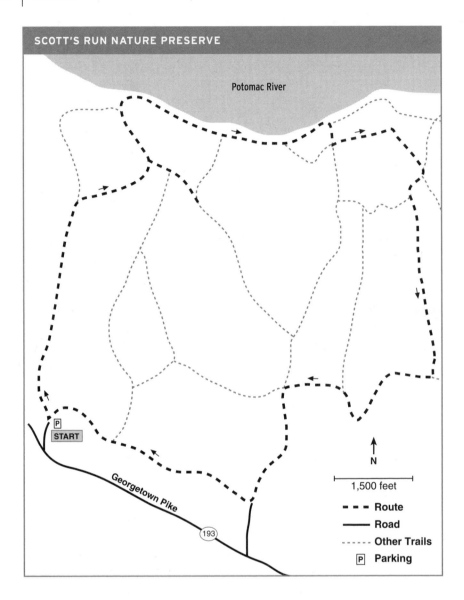

SCOTT'S RUN NATURE PRESERVE

Potomac River

START

Georgetown Pike

193

N

1,500 feet

- - - Route
——— Road
----- Other Trails
P   Parking

Woodlands Trails. Use the map in this guide in conjunction with the posted map and signs at some of the intersections. Note that on weekends, the easier trails can be crowded with families and groups.

From the main parking lot, start on the wide, rocky trail that runs parallel to Scott's Run through a small, steep-sloped valley. The wooded slopes are crowded with sycamore, yellow poplar, chestnut oak, American beech, and various pines. In 400 yards, the trail crosses Scott's Run via short concrete

The tough riverside terrain of Scott's Run Nature Preserve offers sweeping views of the Potomac as it flows east toward Washington.

posts that act as stepping-stones. Continue with the streambed on the right for 600 yards until the trail splits. Take the right fork across Scott's Run again by means of concrete posts, and climb a moderately steep hill.

A sign at the next trail junction describes the community protests that blocked development in the area. Take the wooden steps on the right for a 300-yard out-and-back to a hilltop, where the chimney is all that remains of the old Burling house. Edward Burling was one of the founders of the Washington law firm Covington and Burling, and the house here hosted politicians seeking to escape the pressures of the capital during the early 1900s. Return to the steps and turn right downhill, following the wide trail to the Potomac River bank. At water's edge, look back to the left to see the 30-foot-high waterfall where Scott's Run flows over the rock ledges into the Potomac River.

Turn around and walk the narrow trail on the riverbank, taking in the scenic views of the Potomac, where strong river currents flow through the Stubblefield Falls. The trail next shifts from the river through a grove of large pawpaw trees and past steep rock ledges on the right. Pass the intersection with a small trail that leads uphill to the Burling house ruins, and in a few hundred yards, pass a second trail that leads uphill. Continue along the river-bank, across an intermittent stream, and up a narrow trail, carefully stepping over logs and rocks.

On the far side of a small point of land, reach an impassable, exposed rock ledge, and bend right with the trail between two small ridges, climbing to a point 100 feet above the river. This uphill is difficult and requires clambering over roots and rocks on all fours. Just after the steepest section, come to an intersection and turn left to follow the narrow path past mountain laurels across the face of the steep hillside. The trail scrambles up and down the hillside over rock outcroppings that again require quadrupedal motion. Crawl across a stream running through the rocks, and hike up the side of the hill, then back down the hill past tulip and beech trees near the river. At two small brown fiberglass trail markers, turn right up the hill away from the water.

Continue up this more moderate hill and turn right at the four-way intersection, keeping the small draw to your left. Near the top, take the left fork downhill past two trail markers. Continue straight (avoiding the narrow path to the right), hike past two more trail markers, and proceed up a gradual incline. The trail continues slightly uphill, curves to the left past more trail markers, and comes to a T intersection. Turn right away from the traffic noise of I-495 on a trail that leads through a grove of large tulip trees. Continue down a gradual decline, turn to the left into a small ravine, and then turn back to the right over a wooden bridge. After crossing the small creek, take the left fork uphill.

Hike to the top of the ridge and turn left at a major four-way intersection, cutting between a large oak to the left and yellow poplar to the right. Walk along the top of the ridge up a slight incline, take the left fork at the next intersection, and pass several large homes as the trail comes close to the preserve boundary. Arrive at the first, smaller parking lot on Georgetown Pike, and then turn right on a trail leading back into the woods. This poorly marked trail parallels the road down a shallow ravine. Cross the streambed and walk up the other side of the ravine through beech, poplar, and oak trees. Where the trail drops down into a second ravine, take the left fork to avoid crossing the stream at the bottom of the gully. Continue with the streambed to the right and a small ridge sloping up to the left, blocking the sound of traffic on the pike. End at the long set of wide, wooden steps leading down a steep hill to the big parking lot.

MORE INFORMATION

Both parking lots are often full on weekends, so arrive early. Despite its splendor, Scott's Run is polluted and swimming or wading is prohibited. Visit www.fairfaxcounty.gov/parks/ for more information.

NEARBY

For a longer hike, try combining a circuit at Scott's Run with an out-and-back on the Potomac Scenic Heritage Trail, either west toward Riverbend Park and Great Falls Park (Trip 39), or east toward Turkey Run Park, Potomac Overlook Regional Park, and Theodore Roosevelt Island (Trip 25). Meadowlark Botanical Gardens (Trip 50), the Washington & Old Dominion and Cross County trails (Trip 43), and Fraser Preserve (Trip 41) are also nearby.

TRIP 46
MOUNT VERNON TRAIL–
FORT HUNT PARK TO MOUNT VERNON

Location: Mount Vernon, VA
Rating: Moderate
Distance: 8.2 miles
Elevation Gain: 400 feet
Estimated Time: 3.5 to 4.0 hours
Map: USGS Mount Vernon

The southern end of Mount Vernon Trail connects Fort Hunt Park to George Washington's Mount Vernon estate and offers continuous views of the Potomac River.

DIRECTIONS

From I-95/I-495 (Capital Beltway), take Exit 177B onto northbound US 1. At the first light, turn right onto Franklin Street, drive three city blocks, and turn right onto South Washington Street, which becomes the George Washington Memorial Parkway. Proceed on the parkway for almost 6.0 miles, take the right exit into Fort Hunt Park. Turn right at the T intersection onto the road that circles the park, then take the first left into the parking lot. If it is full, proceed to the next lot along the circle. *GPS coordinates:* 38° 43.00′ N, 77° 03.10′ W.

TRAIL DESCRIPTION

The 3.4-mile stretch of Mount Vernon Trail from Fort Hunt Park to Mount Vernon follows the scenic George Washington Memorial (GW) Parkway along a gentle bend in the Potomac River, over land that once constituted Washington's 8,000-acre Mount Vernon plantation. The GW Parkway, built with limited access in a time before wide-lane interstates, opened in 1932 to connect the capital with Mount Vernon. The 18.5-mile-long trail described here was built in 1973, giving nonmotorized travelers a chance to enjoy the parkway. The National Park Service (NPS) manages both.

The hike starts with a loop around Fort Hunt Park before going out-and-back to Mount Vernon. Start at the first parking lot on the circle. Turn left onto the paved circle and pass a tiny brick outbuilding, staying to the left where the road becomes one-way to allow vehicular traffic to pass on the right. After passing horse stables for the U.S. Park Police on the right, come to a parking

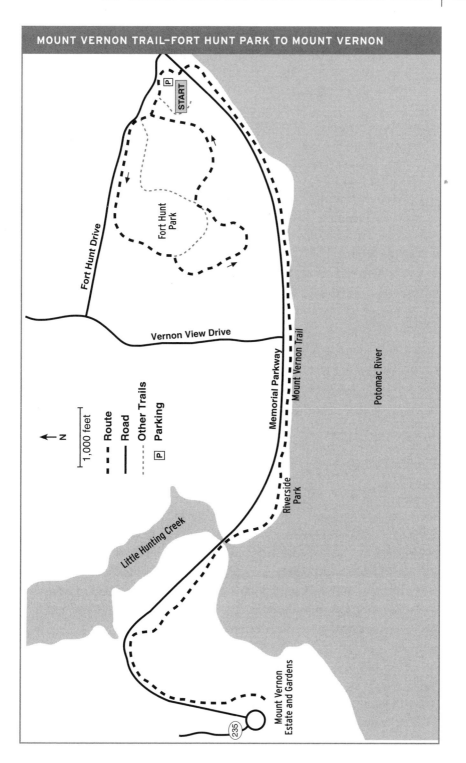

MOUNT VERNON TRAIL–FORT HUNT PARK TO MOUNT VERNON

P

START

Fort Hunt Drive

Fort Hunt
Park

Vernon View Drive

Memorial Parkway

Mount Vernon Trail

Potomac River

N

1,000 feet

- - Route
—— Road
······ Other Trails
P Parking

Riverside
Park

Little Hunting Creek

Mount Vernon
Estate and Gardens

235

lot and turn right onto a side road. After a few hundred yards, turn right at a conspicuous yellow-blazed oak tree onto a dirt trail that enters the woods. Follow this well-marked and maintained trail for a short corkscrew stroll. Stay straight ahead at a point near a picnic table where the trail forks in three directions (no blazes here). After a few more turns and a bridge crossing, the yellow-blazed trail ends. Turn right and enjoy an easy uphill for a quarter-mile before taking another right back onto the paved circle. Break the circle with a right onto the entrance/exit road that leads to the GW Parkway.

Watch for a concrete bunker on the right, an imposing reminder that the park was once Fort Hunt. It was built in 1893 to protect Washington, D.C., from sea invasions. In the 1930s the fort-quartered Civilian Conservation Corps (CCC) workers planted trees along the GW Parkway. In World War II, the fort reverted to the U.S. Army, serving as a detention and interrogation center for Axis POWs.

Walk just past the intersection with Fort Hunt Road, then turn right on Mount Vernon Trail toward the benches and information kiosk—a good place to pick up NPS maps of Mount Vernon Trail and GW Parkway and prepare for the 6.8-mile round-trip. Continue underneath a Depression-era stone bridge and over a long wooden boardwalk with views of Fort Washington through the trees to the left. This circa-1809 fort was destroyed by its fleeing garrison during the War of 1812 and later rebuilt to resume guard of this narrow channel of the Potomac. Fort Hunt was constructed to complement it.

Mount Vernon Trail has an exciting, almost metropolitan feel—bicyclists and joggers, picnickers and anglers comingle, making people-watching a fun element of the trail. The trees offer intermittent shade; many were planted by the CCC in the 1930s, including oak, maple, beech, elm, cherry, and sycamores. Birds of prey such as ospreys and red-tailed hawks perch in the trees or patrol the water, and occasionally a resident pair of bald eagles dubbed George and Martha (the names stay the same even when a new pair forces out the old) can be seen. Continuing on the trail, you pass mile markers, boardwalks over pungent swampland, stately homes, the Cedar Knoll restaurant, Riverside Park, and a large stone bridge over Little Hunting Creek (a Potomac tributary that begins at Huntley Meadows Park—see Trip 40).

Much of this area was part of Washington's "River Farm." He lived at Mount Vernon from the 1750s until his death in 1799, and the grounds became a laboratory for his economic and agricultural experiments. The first president worked his entire adult life to make the Potomac River the preeminent trade corridor in the nation, connecting Washington, D.C., with frontier settlements to the west.

Now turn uphill and away from the river, passing a series of boardwalks lined with majestic beech trees. The uphill becomes steep, and then reaches benches, a water pump, and an information kiosk next to one of Mount Vernon's large parking lots. Continue to Mount Vernon's large circular driveway and directly to the entrance gates. Then retracing the route, return to Fort Hunt Park.

MORE INFORMATION

Fort Hunt Park, a unit of the George Washington Memorial Parkway, is open year-round from 7 A.M. to sunset. There are several picnic areas for families or small groups. Visit www.nps.gov/gwmp/fort-hunt.htm or call 877-444-6777.

NEARBY

A visit to Mount Vernon's inner grounds, mansion, and tomb costs $15. This in itself can take a full day, so if time or money is a factor, stop instead at the free visitor center, which has exhibits, a gift shop, a cafeteria-style restaurant, and bathrooms. In 2007, Mount Vernon opened a fully functional reconstruction of Washington's eighteenth-century distillery, which can be toured for $4 for adults and $2 for children ages 6–11; it is free for children 5 and under (when combined with Mount Vernon admission, it is $2 for adults, $1.50 for children ages 6-11, and free for children 5 and under). Visit www.mountvernon.org or call 703-799-8688.

TRIP 47
OLD RAG

$

Location: Etlan, VA

Rating: Difficult

Distance: 8.8 miles

Elevation Gain: 2,510 feet

Estimated Time: 5.0 to 5.5 hours

Maps: USGS Old Rag Mountain; Old Rag Road and Trail map available at fee station in lower parking lot. The USGS has a detailed geologic history of the mountain, available on the Web at pubs.usgs.gov/of/2000/of00-263/of00-263.pdf.

Old Rag Mountain is a strenuous rock scramble on an eastern spur of the Blue Ridge Mountains in Shenandoah National Park and one of the most popular hikes in the Mid-Atlantic region.

DIRECTIONS

From I-495 (Capital Beltway), take Exit 49 west onto I-66. Go 11.5 miles, and exit onto westbound US 211. After 29 miles, turn left onto US 522 in Sperryville; drive 0.8 mile and turn right onto VA 231. Go 7.5 miles, turn right onto Sharp Rock Road, proceeding 1.2 miles and turning right on Nethers Road. After 2.0 miles, reach the lower lot and fee station. (Please note: The upper lot has been permanently closed.) *GPS coordinates:* 38° 34.255' N, 78° 17.145' W.

TRAIL DESCRIPTION

Old Rag Mountain is a solid hour and a half from Washington, D.C.—the farthest afield of all the trips in this guide. However, the unique challenge of hiking to its summit is worth traveling the distance. Old Rag is an outlying mountain on the eastern edge of the Blue Ridge. It is an extremely old formation, the result of tectonic forces in play more than a billion years ago during the Grenville Orogeny. For the last 200 million years, the crystallized granite has been exposed to weathering at the surface, and for the last 50 years or so, recreational hikers have made Old Rag the most popular destination in Shenandoah National Park.

To avoid the largest crowds, it is best to do this hike in the middle of the week or in wintertime. During weekends in the summer and the autumn "leaf season," expect large crowds and queues forming at the difficult tunnels

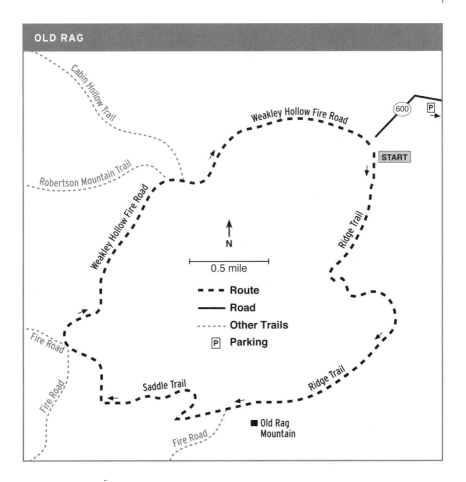

and ledges. Also, to mitigate the effects of overuse at Old Rag, avoid camping anywhere along the route (camping is specifically prohibited above 2,800 feet of elevation). Note that the narrow passes make for tight squeezes even for an average-sized adult.

From the lower parking lot, hike 0.8 mile up Nethers Road, keeping the Hughes River on the right until arriving at the trailhead for the blue-blazed Ridge Trail. From here, it's a 2.7-mile climb to the summit, with the first 0.7 mile on a gently ascending trail through a dense hemlock forest. At this point, the trail narrows into a rock-studded path lined with large boulders—hints of the demanding terrain to come. Finally, proceed along swooping, mountain-laurel–lined switchbacks, past several overlooks at treeline.

The 2,800-foot elevation mark is indicated by a No Camping sign, and the path becomes composed entirely of granite at this point. Here the real fun be-gins! At first, simply step from boulder to boulder, but then, after rounding a

ROOSEVELT'S TREE ARMY: THE CIVILIAN CONSERVATION CORPS

In March 1933, new President Franklin D. Roosevelt knew unrest was brewing nationwide among unemployed youth and World War I veterans, who were caught in an economic depression growing ever more severe. The previous year, his predecessor, Herbert Hoover, had faced a desperate band of 17,000 former soldiers marching into Washington, insisting upon immediate payment of a service bonus promised to them but not redeemable until 1945. The regular Army soon forcibly evicted this "Bonus Army." Several people were killed, including at least one child, and many wounded.

A landed gentleman himself, Roosevelt also felt grave concern about the soil erosion then decimating midwestern farmlands (due largely to logging and plowing), leaving their inhabitants in a swirling dust bowl without livelihood or sustenance. Appreciative of outdoor life, FDR also wished to make nature's benefits accessible to more Americans. He now perceived a supply of hungry young men who could help him address these issues, and quickly proposed the Emergency Conservation Work Act, providing for "a civilian conservation corps, to be used in simple work...of definite practical value." A month later, the first work camps began springing up within a day's drive of Washington—ideal for showcasing Roosevelt's brainchild to VIPs foreign and domestic. Camps were soon established in all 48 states and several territories.

Members of the new corps were paid $30 a month ($25 of which was sent directly home); they lived under military-style conditions. Single men aged 18 to 25 from needy families could and did enlist eagerly for six-month tours, for up to a total of two years. Veterans of World War I, single or married, soon were also allowed to join. By summer 1933, 250,000 men had been mobilized. While integration had been stipulated, the corps's 200,000 black workers were primarily housed in separate (but, progressively for the time, equal) camps, at equal pay. A distinct division, mostly working in western states, was also established for 85,000 American Indians.

Organized labor objected to low CCC wages and government-paid skills training that allowed these young men to compete unfairly with union members, so FDR cleverly appointed a union leader to head the program. Some complained that CCCers would bring trouble to host communities; camps were placed strategically to win support. Others, fearing the totalitarian wave engulfing Europe, saw in FDR's plan shades of Hitler's *"Arbeit macht frei"* ("Work sets one free") propaganda, or of Mussolini's private army.

But most CCC workers and their families were simply grateful. About 70 percent of enrollees arrived malnourished and poorly clothed. Interviewed later, they universally recalled the muscles, skills, and pride they developed; the tangible results of their work; and the abundant, tasty food provided to them. One laborer reminisced that it was "the only time in my life I'd ever had two pairs of shoes! And three squares [meals] a day...I really had it made!"

In today's Shenandoah National Park, home of the Old Rag trail, the CCC established ten camps. Their members initially worked to build fire towers, log comfort stations, trails, and picnic areas. They also cleared understory forest growth, transplanted nursery and wild stock into eroded spots, and removed blight-damaged chestnut trees. CCCers later labored "straightenin' the curves, flattenin' the hills" of Skyline Drive, and constructing roadside scenic overlooks that had not been included in the parkway's initial plans. They also erected many of the park's buildings, from chestnut they felled nearby and from handmade wood-grain concrete shingles. They engraved the park's trademark chestnut-wood signs and forged iron hinges, latches, tools, and sign brackets still in use today.

Strenuous objections came from farmers and other rural residents whose lands the state and federal governments seized to create these new recreation areas. The issue went to the Supreme Court; landowners lost. A very few residents were granted life interests in their properties, but many whole towns and settlements died out.

Nationwide, CCC workers planted more than 3 billion trees, fought forest fires, carved erosion-control channels, built retaining walls, dug irrigation waterways, erected fire towers, quarried stone, stocked fishponds, and aided in disaster relief and cleanup. They helped build the presidential retreat Shangri-La (now Camp David) and portions of the Appalachian Trail. They created 800 parks.

The CCCers came, 3 million strong, to grow stronger. Then came another world war; many CCC workers joined the armed forces as their corps was demobilized. CCC camps were used to house conscientious objectors, interned Japanese-Americans, and German POWs. But, as FDR intended, the corps's good works remain for outdoor lovers today.

broad slab providing an eastward vista, begin a mile-long scramble west through a challenging granite obstacle course. For this section, it is necessary to variously crawl on all fours beneath rock overhangs, drop into crevices, clamber up narrow chutes, leap over cracks, shimmy along edges, and hoist yourself up onto ledges. Make sure to locate the next blue blaze before making a move, and on crowded days, be conscious and considerate of other hikers.

At 3.2 miles, emerge from the first stretch of rock labyrinth onto the minor summit, a large flat area with views in all directions. Next, continue on a less-intense rock scramble for 0.3 mile to reach the 3,268-foot summit of Old Rag. Climb one of the series of steep rock piles on the right to reach the mountain's highest point (3,291 feet), being especially careful on windy days. Take time to eat lunch and bask in the views.

The remaining 5.3 miles are downhill. From the summit, continue the circuit on the blue-blazed Saddle Trail. After 0.4 mile, pass Byrds Nest Shelter #1, and following another 1.1 miles of bracing switchbacks through heavy forest, reach Old Rag Shelter. From here, the trail widens and follows a forestry road for 0.4 mile to the intersection of the Berry Hollow fire road (left), Old Rag fire road (straight), and Weakley Hollow fire road (right).

Turn right on the yellow-blazed Weakley Hollow fire road, and after 1.4 miles, pass Robertson Mountain Trail and, within 200 yards, Corbin Hollow Trail. Continue for 1.1 miles on the broad path through old-growth forest, making several crossings over Brokenback Run, before returning to the upper parking lot.

MORE INFORMATION

There is a $15 per vehicle entrance fee ($10 December–February), good for one week of access to Shenandoah National Park. Dogs are not permitted on Old Rag. For more information about the Old Rag area, visit www.nps.gov/shen/planyourvisit/upload/old_rag_area.pdf.

NEARBY

From the junction with Robertson Mountain Trail, it is 1.0 mile to the 3,296-foot summit of Robertson Mountain. White Oak Canyon and Cedar Run trails are also nearby; they follow steep, cascading rapids on the east side of the Appalachian ridge.

Location: Harpers Ferry, WV
Rating: Difficult
Distance: 7.6 miles
Elevation Gain: 1,670 feet
Estimated Time: 4.0 to 4.5 hours
Maps: USGS Harpers Ferry; Potomac Appalachian Trail Club Map 7: Harpers Ferry to VA-7; Harpers Ferry National Parks Service map

This hike from downtown Harpers Ferry to Maryland Heights across the Potomac is as challenging as it is gorgeous.

DIRECTIONS

From I-495 (Capital Beltway) inner loop, take Exit 38 (or from outer loop, take Exit 35) onto I-270 toward Frederick. At Exit 32, take I-70 west, but immediately take Exit 52, US 340 west (also US 15 south). Continue on 340 west toward Charles Town. Cross one bridge over the Potomac River into Virginia, then take the second bridge back over the river into West Virginia, and take the second right onto Union Street. Next take a right onto Washington Street, a right onto Storer College Place (at the Appalachian Conference Headquarters), a right onto Filmore Street, and then an immediate left into the center's parking lot. *GPS coordinates:* 39° 19.42′ N, 77° 44.60′ W.

TRAIL DESCRIPTION

Harpers Ferry is the site of abolitionist John Brown's unsuccessful attempt to incite a slave insurrection. Brown and 21 men—including two of his sons—raided the U.S. arsenal here in October 1859, hoping to capture the rifles and distribute them to zealous slaves and antislavery whites. Robert E. Lee led the U.S. reprisal, representing the government he would soon disavow. Ten of Brown's men were killed, five fled, and the rest were captured. The state of Virginia tried and hanged the prisoners at nearby Charles Town.

This 7.6-mile hike visits sites of past violence as well as those of pristine beauty. It starts at the National Park Service (NPS) parking lot near the US 340 bridge in West Virginia, descends into old-town Harpers Ferry and past John Brown's Fort, crosses the Baltimore & Ohio (B&O) railroad bridge into

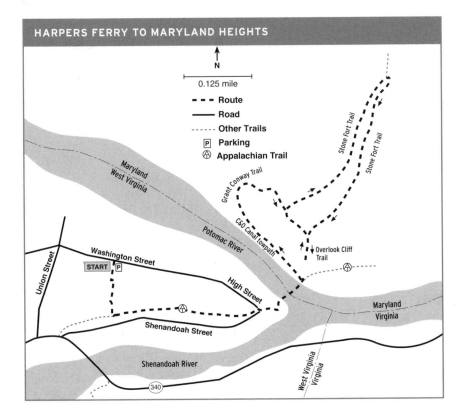

HARPERS FERRY TO MARYLAND HEIGHTS

Maryland, follows the Chesapeake & Ohio (C&O) Canal towpath west, and ascends Maryland Heights to the ruins of a Union stone fort.

From the NPS parking lot, start the hike by walking down the steps (in the direction of the Shenandoah River) to the white-blazed Appalachian Trail. Take a left. At 0.3 mile, pass an intersection with a blue-blazed trail, and continue along the ridgeline with the Shenandoah River 200 feet below to the right. Come to another short side trail at 0.6 mile that goes left to Harper Cemetery—a worthwhile stop to see where Robert Harper, a Pennsylvania architect, set aside 4 acres on the hilltop in 1782. The next stop is Jefferson Rock, a beautiful overlook of the Potomac and Shenandoah rivers.

Pass the remnants of St. John's Episcopal Church, the earliest church in town, and drop down to the circa-1833, neo-Gothic St. Peter's Roman Catholic Church, which is open to visitors. Continue the descent down smooth stone steps carved from the hillside in the early 1800s, and turn right at the bottom of the hill into downtown, going left on Shenandoah Street. Pass John Brown's Fort on the right. This structure was the guardroom and fire engine house of the original "United States Armory and Arsenal at Harper's Ferry," the build-

The neo-Gothic spire of St. Peter's Roman Catholic Church stands as a silent sentinel above Harpers Ferry, where the Shenandoah and Potomac rivers converge. The US 340 bridge and the looming bulk of Loudoun Heights are in the distance.

ing that Brown and his cohorts retreated to for their final stand. Continue over the B&O Railroad footbridge (the 1.0-mile mark) to Maryland, and descend the spiraling steps to the C&O Canal towpath.

Turn left on the towpath and pass the stone remnants of Lock 33, the unloading point for goods bound for Harpers Ferry. Tread the preserved towpath where workers once struggled to maintain the water levels and keep the barges moving. The C&O Canal began operation in 1836, but after years of decline, a flood in 1924 spelled its end. Continue on the towpath for 0.25 mile, then turn right onto the green-blazed Grant Conway Trail to begin the tough ascent to Maryland Heights.

Follow the Grant Conway Trail uphill and to the right away from the river. After about a half-mile, turn left on the blue-blazed Stone Fort Trail, which leads to the Union stone fort atop 1,000-foot-high Maryland Heights. Proceed up a very steep stretch—over 500 feet of elevation gain in 0.5 mile.

Upon reaching the plateau, continue as the path winds through a level area, with circular earthen platforms that mark Civil War campsites. Stay to the right of a long stone-and-earth breastwork, one of two parallel rifle pits erected in June 1863. These fortifications were erected too late to prevent one of Lee's masterstrokes in September 1862—a three-pronged attack on Harpers Ferry that netted 10,000 prisoners. The green Union defenders surrendered in

JOHN BROWN AND THE ASSAULT ON HARPERS FERRY

Born in 1800, young John Brown found inspiration in the Bible and sought to enter the ministry. But after a failed stint at prep school, he went to work for his father, a respected tanner and one of the earliest known fugitive-slave helpers in Ohio. John preached antislavery and dabbled in Underground Railroad work himself. Still, he longed to do more.

Business failures hampered Brown as the years passed, and he found himself bankrupt in middle age. He decided to join five of his sons, who, in 1854 and '55, had emigrated to Osawatomie, Kansas where pro- and anti-slavery factions were fighting a bloddy struggle over the future of that soon-to-be state. When proslavery men sacked the free-soil town of Lawrence in May 1856, Brown and several of his sons retaliated, routing five proslavery leaders from their beds near Pottawatomie and executing them posthaste with broadswords.

Other confrontations followed. One of Brown's sons, Frederick, was killed. But Brown gained national notoriety, and great credibility among black abolitionists, as a white man taking up arms to end slavery. "Old Brown" also managed to escape prosecution. These factors, plus Brown's gift for gaining the trust of strangers, opened doors to big-name financing in the North. Even to most of his donors, however, Brown was secretive about his next move. He had long plotted to open a slave-revolt campaign at Harpers Ferry, Virginia (now West Virginia). Brown hoped to arm liberated blacks with weaponry looted from the federal armory there, then strike southward, enticing more slaves to revolt against their masters and join his liberation army.

In the summer of 1859, Brown (using the name Isaac Smith, for operational security) rented a Maryland farmhouse 5 miles from Harpers Ferry. Here his group clandestinely gathered and trained. But neighbors grew inquisitive, finances dwindled, and his friend Frederick Douglass—himself an escaped slave, now a renowned abolitionist leader—refused to join the attack. Nervous, Brown moved to strike, although he did not feel ready. On Sunday night, October 16, his band of sixteen white and five black men crossed the Potomac into Harpers Ferry, taking hostages and cutting telegraph wires. Raiders also captured local planter Colonel Lewis Washington (George Washington's great-grandnephew), his slaves, and the first president's heirloom ceremonial sword, which Brown buckled reverently around his own waist.

JOHN BROWN AND THE ASSAULT ON HARPERS FERRY (continued)

Ironically, the first casualty of Brown's slave-freeing campaign was a black man already free: a baggage porter who confronted raiders seizing a passing train. Unaccountably, Brown allowed the train to continue down the line, where crewmembers spread alarms about the attack. President James Buchanan quickly summoned a respected Virginia officer, Lt. Colonel Robert E. Lee, to lead U.S. troops to the raid scene.

Monday went badly for Brown. Local militia, some reportedly drunk, swarmed the armory, firing on raiders, mutilating casualty corpses, surrounding buildings, and cutting off escape. Two of Brown's three raider sons lay dying in the brick firehouse, now known as "John Brown's Fort," to which the raiders had retreated with their hostages. But Brown remained determined.

As Tuesday dawned, Lee sent another Virginian and future Civil War icon, Lieutenant J.E.B. Stuart, to offer the mysterious "Smith" and his men fair treatment for peaceable surrender. From his own Kansas service, Stuart recognized "Smith" as the infamous "Osawatomie Brown." When Brown refused to surrender, troops battered down the firehouse door. One Marine rushed Brown, slashing him with a dress sword. The abolitionist and surviving raiders were taken prisoner.

Savior? Terrorist? Fanatic? Fool? Brown has been called all of these things and many more. Prophet, even. In his determination to use violence in the abolitionist cause, Brown certainly foreshadowed the bloody sectional war that followed 18 months after Harpers Ferry, as well as the end of slavery that conflict eventually heralded. Then again, friends both black and white warned Brown that he and his few men could not conquer the whole South, and that many slaves would not take up arms against their masters. And Douglass insisted that Brown was leading his men into a "steel trap" at Harpers Ferry. Brown's friends then, too, were reluctant but clear-eyed prophets of the age.

His Bible, Brown explained at his treason trial, bade him "remember them that are in bonds as bound with them." Many blacks held him as a martyr for this courageous, principled stance. Funereal bells tolled in many Northern states, while Southern slaveholders grimly gloated, as John Brown's body swung from a gallows on December 2.

droves, enabling the Confederate detachment to rejoin the main force just in time for the Battle of Antietam (Trip 15).

Follow the path uphill on log steps and cross a stone wall, turning left and continuing to the northwest corner of the interior fort. The parapet here was the largest earthwork constructed on Maryland Heights. Continue 250 feet, passing the northbound Elk Ridge Trail on the left (do not take this blue-blazed route), and turn right to follow the blue blazes on the rocks a short distance to the stone fort. A row of large foundation stones offers an excellent view, especially in winter months.

Follow the blue blazes southward down the mountain on the Stone Fort Trail. At 0.5 mile from the top, reach the former site of a giant Parrott rifle, which weighed 9,700 pounds and took 300 men to haul up the mountain. It was mounted on a 360-degree swivel and could hurl its projectiles more than 2.0 miles at the opposing high grounds of Loudoun Heights (in Virginia) and Bolivar Heights (in West Virginia). Go left where the trail splits, and pass the pits of old, collapsed powder magazines. Walk on the spine of the rocky ridge downhill, and take another left where the two trails become one again. Continue downhill and turn left onto the red-blazed Overlook Cliff Trail. Follow the path down a series of winding switchbacks to the cliff-top overlook above Harpers Ferry. It is a stupendous, worth-every-muscle-ache view of the two rivers, the railroad bridge, and the historical downtown. After enjoying the view, retrace your steps on Overlook Cliff Trail to the Grant Conway Trail (site of another gun emplacement). Turn left downhill and return to the C&O towpath and from there to Harpers Ferry.

MORE INFORMATION

The historic sites at Harpers Ferry are open daily (except Thanksgiving, Christmas, and New Year's Day), from 8 A.M. to 5 P.M. Visit www.nps.gov/archive/hafe/home.htm or call 304-535-6298.

NEARBY

Hiking all three of the heights—Bolivar, Loudoun, and Maryland—would make for an extremely ambitious day hike. For additional exciting adventures, be sure to check out whitewater river trips on the Shenandoah and Potomac rivers: Historical River Tours, Inc. combines river tours with local history. Visit www.historicalrivertours.com to learn more.

TRIP 49
MANASSAS NATIONAL
BATTLEFIELD PARK

Location: Manassas, VA
Rating: Moderate
Distance: 5.4 miles
Elevation Gain: 900 feet
Estimated Time: 3.0 to 3.5 hours
Map: USGS Gainesville

**The rolling hills of Manassas National Battlefield Park offer the
perfect mix of nineteenth-century historical interpretation and
opportunities for forested solitude.**

DIRECTIONS
From I-495 (Capital Beltway), take Exit 49 west onto I-66 to Exit 47 (Masassas). Go north on VA 234 (Sudley Road). The park entrance is 1.0 mile ahead on the right. *GPS coordinates: 38° 48.79′ N, 77° 31.29′ W.*

TRAIL DESCRIPTION
The open hills and forested patches of Manassas National Battlefield Park offer the intrepid hiker food for thought as well as a physical workout. The terrain in this hike had an important effect on the Battle of First Manassas on July 21, 1861—the first major battle of the Civil War. Bull Run forced advancing Union troops to waste valuable time searching for a ford, and the hills to the south offered the Confederates high ground on which to inflict punishment and eventually drive the bluecoats back. First Manassas Trail, a 5.4-mile trek over this terrain, visits Bull Run and several of the most hotly contested points of the battle. Even those not interested in military history will feel a tangible link to the past standing on ground where 38,000 Federals and 32,000 Confederates fought with savage intensity.

First Manassas Trail starts to the right of the visitor center, between a stand of oaks on one side and the statue of Confederate General Stonewall Jackson on the other. Follow the broad, grassy path straight ahead toward a line of cannons. The higher, unmowed grass on either side recreates the sea of weeds that the soldiers waded through during the fighting. Upon entering the woods

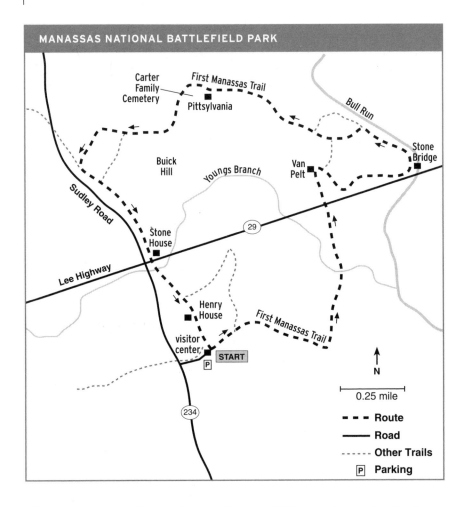

MANASSAS NATIONAL BATTLEFIELD PARK

Carter Family Cemetery
First Manassas Trail
Pittsylvania
Bull Run
Stone Bridge
Buick Hill
Youngs Branch
Van Pelt
Sudley Road
29
Stone House
Lee Highway
Henry House
First Manassas Trail
visitor center
START
P
N
234
0.25 mile
- - - Route
— Road
----- Other Trails
P Parking

where Jackson earned his nickname "Stonewall" for shoring up the Confederate line, bear right on the mulch path denoted by a blue-blazed marker. The cool, shaded covering here is courtesy of a diverse range of pines, cedars, hickories, American elms, persimmons, and a few black walnut trees. Soon the mulch changes into gravel, with ash trees set directly in the path. Cross two wooden bridges over dry-in-the-summer streambeds. An old bench sits right before the bridges.

Turn 90 degrees left at the clearing, making sure to take the first left onto the small dirt path rather than the second left onto a wider gravel road. A little way ahead is a concentrated pine grove, and then cedars, oaks, and a few sassafras shrubs mark the way on the right, and a small clearing opens on the left. The trail returns to gravel here. Trees pop up here and there in the clearing on the left, marking the early succession of field to forest. At the

The Stone House at Manassas National Battlefield served as a refuge for the wounded during the 1861 battle and today stands flanked by twin silver maple trees.

end of the clearing, where a large black walnut unfurls its canopy of crowded compound leaves, turn left over a dry streambed toward another open clearing, and then immediately right (a marker denotes the turn). Travel over the Youngs Branch (a tributary of Bull Run) on a wooden bridge shaded by elms and hickories. Turn left onto a gravel path near another marker, and arrive soon in the middle of a large, open field. Rows of cedars and pines come and go on the right, and two benches sit under the shade of a single cedar—a perfect spot for lunch. Cross US 29 (Lee Highway—a major thoroughfare) and go up a short rise. Make sure to go straight where a dirt path diverges sharply to the right. Pass a squat tree that gives off a silver sheen—an illusion maintained by the silvery underside of its leaves—and turn right up a rise to the Van Pelt House site, a small clearing surrounded by big-leafed redbud trees. This site served as the battle headquarters of Confederate General Nathan Evans, whose South Carolinians cleared the ridge on the western slope all the way to Bull Run to enable fields of fire. Follow a sign for the Stone Bridge pointing right, and descend a sharp slope to a raised walkway over damp lowland. This leads to the Stone Bridge, the original structure defended by the Confederates.

Turn left on the gravel road in front of the bridge and follow Bull Run. Go left at the Farm Ford, and ascend the gravel slope. Turn left again at the top of the hill, then turn right back onto the larger trail that comes directly from the Van Pelt House. This habitat where trees and grass meet is replete with chickadees, bluebirds, mockingbirds, sparrows, robins, and red-tailed hawks. Travel slowly downhill past a law enforcement office on the left and plunge into the woods on a mulch path that travels past giant yellow poplars, a few sycamores, and, even rarer, a chestnut oak. The trail passes the Carter House, a few ruins in a depression. After 4.0 miles on the hike and 0.75 mile on the broad mulch path in the woods, on the left pass the George Stovall Marker, for a Georgian who died on the spot and whose last words, according to the marker, were "I am going to heaven." This is the wooded saddle of Matthew's Hill. Markers to the 8th Georgia, 4th Alabama, 71st New York, and 2nd New Hampshire commemorate the tough fighting. Emerge from the woods and proceed straight onto a mowed portion of grass. Head toward a few of cedars on the rise ahead and continue down Matthew's Hill to the Stone House, an original antebellum home, which was in the thick of the carnage and served as a Union hospital through numerous engagements. Cross US 29 at the traffic light, then cross a wooden bridge over Youngs Branch again, heading uphill over ground where Union forces retreated. Arrive at Henry House, a postwar stand-in for the original, where octogenarian Judith Henry was killed by a bullet aimed at snipers firing from her home, and continue past it, back to the visitor center.

MORE INFORMATION

There is a fee of $3 per person for park entry, but children under sixteen are admitted free. The National Park Service gives daily tours of both the First Manassas and Second Manassas battlefields. Visit the website at www.nps.gov/mana for a tour schedule and to download podcasts about the two battles.

During winter, the hiking trails, rolling hills, and bridle paths draw cross-country skiers and snowshoers.

"FIRSTS" OF THE FIRST BATTLE OF MANASSAS

The rolling hills around Manassas Junction, or Bull Run, were the site of many military "firsts."

The first major land engagement of the War Between the States took place here on July 21, 1861. It was expected by many—whether Confederate or Union—to be an occasion for celebration. Each army was certain that it could easily beat the enemy in one battle, although the sides were, in President Lincoln's words, "green alike." Drilling, discipline, and practice were sorely needed, but the feverish public on each side demanded a swift victory.

Major changes to battlefield strategy and tactics were also needed, and possible, since railroads had recently become an important aspect of the American landscape and economy. Military leaders were just beginning to appreciate the iron lines' value and utility in wartime. Wishing to control the railroads as a step toward capturing the enemy capital at Richmond, Union General Irvin McDowell moved his army of 35,000 volunteers—the largest army ever fielded in America at that time—southwest from Washington toward the Manassas rail junction, where 21,000 Confederates under Brig. General Pierre G.T. Beauregard (McDowell's West Point classmate) were encamped.

Some of those Union soldiers, marching slowly toward their first face-off with the rebels, dawdled like schoolboys in the sultry heat to pick blackberries. But at their first taste of war, they and their counterparts in gray quickly realized the seriousness of their situation. The ensuing battle demanded the first train movement of troops into combat in U.S. history, as the Confederates hurried General Thomas J. (soon to be known as "Stonewall") Jackson's brigade in from the Shenandoah Valley to reinforce Beauregard. Well-to-do civilians, including members of Congress, drove out to the battlegrounds in carriages laden with picnic baskets and champagne, then—as defeat loomed—clogged the roads while fleeing alongside frantic Union soldiers toward the safety of their capital (in perhaps the earliest recorded American traffic jam). Routed, the Yanks handed the Southerners their first major land victory, although both sides made serious errors and sustained unexpectedly heavy losses.

Another transportation mode came into American military use at the First Battle of Manassas, when McDowell requested aerial reconnaissance by Professor Thaddeus Lowe's balloon *Enterprise*, which was then on a

"FIRSTS" OF THE FIRST BATTLE OF MANASSAS (continued)

demonstration tour in Washington. Lowe was one of several aeronauts seeking a Union government contract to create an Army Balloon Corps. From a tethered balloon, airborne telegraphy was even possible. On July 24, after the battle, a second balloon recon mission by Lowe relieved Northern terrors by reporting that the victorious Confederates weren't massing for attack, and President Lincoln appointed Lowe the Union Army's chief aeronaut.

Back on the ground, wig-wag semaphore signaling—the use of large, square, colored flags waved in code patterns—was being employed in combat for the first time. And the battle's chaos, smoke, and blunders impacted another sort of flag: Confederates realized that their original "Stars and Bars"—a blue field and white stars upper left, with three horizontal red-white-red stripes—resembled much too closely the U.S. banner. The Rebel battle flag design was soon changed to the red field with diagonal stars-and-bars still recognized today.

First mentioned in accounts of the 1861 battle was the Confederates' infamous, unnerving Rebel yell. No one is sure today how the yell really sounded. Union soldiers in the field described it as like a rabbit's scream, or an Indian war whoop, or a Highlander's attack cry. One insisted that when it sounded, "a peculiar corkscrew sensation ... went up your spine," and another taunted, "If you claim you heard it and *weren't* scared, that means you never heard it!"

Local grocery merchant Wilmer McLean also learned about wartime beginnings, and endings, in a very personal way. McLean and his wife lived on the Manassas battlefield at the time of the first battle there. They later moved south to Appomattox—to a house chosen to host Lee's formal surrender to Grant in 1865. After the surrender, McLean reportedly quipped, "The war began in my front yard, and ended in my front parlor." Actually, both McLean houses hosted generals. During First Bull Run, the McLeans' home was commandeered as a headquarters for Beauregard, who later recalled, "A comical effect of this artillery fight was the destruction of the dinner of myself and staff by a Federal shell that fell into the fireplace of my headquarters at the McLean House." But by the time Second Manassas occurred, in late August 1862, both armies had learned in their bones the true cost of war—and for many, it wasn't so easy to joke about.

TRIP 50
MEADOWLARK BOTANICAL GARDENS

Location: Tysons Corner, VA
Rating: Easy
Distance: 3.8 miles
Elevation Gain: 360 feet
Estimated Time: 2.0 hours
Maps: USGS Vienna; free sketch map in visitor center

Meadowlark Botanical Gardens offers trails that wind past trees, shrubs, and wildflowers indigenous to Virginia's wetlands and piedmont.

DIRECTIONS

From I-495 (Capital Beltway), take Exit 47 (Tysons Corner) west onto VA 7 (Leesburg Pike). Drive 3.0 miles (passing Tysons Corner) and turn left onto Beulah Road. Then drive 1.0 mile to the garden entrance on the right. *GPS coordinates:* 38° 56.250′ N, 77° 16.955′ W.

TRAIL DESCRIPTION

Meadowlark Botanical Gardens, 3.0 miles west of Tysons Corner in the heart of northern Virginia, is a small suburban park (95 acres) that combines the beauty of botanical gardens with several miles of wooded trails. Managed by the Northern Virginia Regional Park Authority, Meadowlark has a unique native plant collection. A camera is a must.

This hike is 3.8 miles long and includes a short inner loop as well as a longer outer loop. Exit the visitor center through the side door near the small gift shop, walking around the garden area to the atrium building. Follow the path to the seasonal plantings and the herb garden, using the tour map and the numbered signs along the path.

From the herb garden at the top of the knoll, look to the southwest for a picturesque view of the "Great Lawn" area—three small lakes, gazebos, and more gardens and nature areas. Head left toward Lake Gardiner and take the path to the right around the lake. On the other side of the lake, turn left and take the bridge to the tiny island in the lake. Follow the path to the other side of Lake Gardiner and turn left up the hill, back to the herb garden. Then head down the slope along the path toward Lakes Carolyn and Lena. The

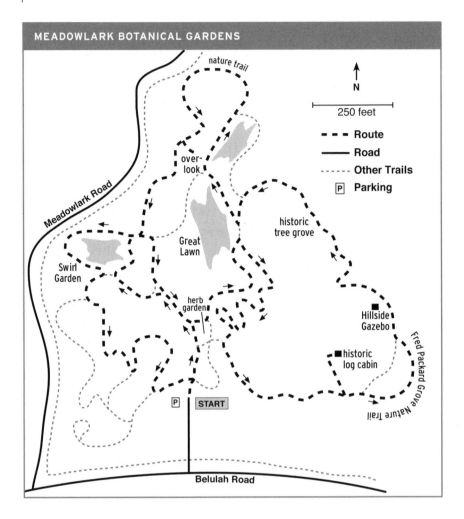

MEADOWLARK BOTANICAL GARDENS

nature trail

N

250 feet

- - - Route
—— Road
...... Other Trails
P Parking

over-
look

Meadowlark Road

historic
tree grove

Great
Lawn

Swirl
Garden

herb
garden

Hillside
Gazebo

Fred Packard Grove Nature Trail

historic
log cabin

P START

Belulah Road

path curves to the right and then to the left, passing two intersections. Stay to the left each time. Near the corner of Lake Caroline (with the gazebo in the middle), turn sharply right to the Conifer Collection, and walk a couple of a hundred yards past the collection on your left, turning right and then left to the Springhouse and Hosta Gardens. On the left side of the path down in the creek bed are the ruins of the eighteenth-century springhouse that supported the farmhouse up the hill. Leaving the springhouse, the path zigzags through the wooded area until it reaches the Perennial Color Border area.

Follow the path to the left, keeping the atrium to your right. Continue to follow the path as it curves to the left and then to the right until it crosses a service road. In this area of rare chestnut trees, find signs about the husband and wife team, economist Gardiner Means and social historian Caroline Ware,

Meadowlark Botanical Gardens packs a lot of worthwhile hiking into its 100 acres, including sweeping arched bridges over artifically made lakes.

who bought this farmland in 1935. About 30 years ago, Ware donated the land to the Northern Virginia Regional Park Authority, which added a 21-arce parcel to the Means-Ware farm. The resulting public gardens and park wonderfully display the beauty of the Virginia Piedmont region.

After visiting the cabin return to the asphalt path, turn left and follow the path about 30 yards to the start of Fred Packard Grove Nature Trail. (Packard was an executive director of the Northern Virginia Regional Park Authority.) On the right is the dirt trail leading into the woods. Climb slightly, and then turn left down the hill and across a bridge over a dry streambed. Follow the path, continue up the hill, across another bridge, and go back out to the asphalt. Turn right on the path and pass the Hillside Gazebo on your left. Next, pass an area on the left of trees native to Virginia, several of which are identified by signs.

The path curves to the left around a large meadow. Two-thirds of the way around, bear left at the Y intersection. Where the four paths come together at the southern end of Hosta Garden, turn right 180 degrees and follow the path along the bank of Lake Caroline. Near the gazebo bridge, turn right toward Lake Lena and the Virginia Native Wetlands area. Walk along the boardwalk

Exploring the nooks and crannies of Meadowlark often yields surprising finds, like this Russian-doll totem.

beside the lake and take in the numerous bald cypress trees. Native water plants flourish during the summer, and pitcher plants, cardinal flowers, iris, rush, aromatic bayberries, cattails, and numerous sedges line the shores. The wetlands are also habitat for turtles, brown water snakes, frogs, native fish, and several types of herons and perching birds.

As the trail leaves the Virginia wetlands, look for a sign for a nature trail that enters a young forest. Take it, and head gradually uphill along a high fence at the boundary of the park. Cross a bridge over a dry creek bed and follow the signs for the nature trail straight across the gravel path and along the edge of the park. Take the right fork down the hill to the asphalt path that leads from Lake Gardiner. Turn right on the path and follow it. On the right is the Experimental Meadow, a monarch butterfly way station. From here, take either the mowed path that winds through the meadow or stay on the asphalt path along the lake to the Children's Interactive Garden. Past this, turn right at the next intersection. At the tree line, take the dirt trail to the left into the Potomac Valley Native Plant Collection, and pick up a pamphlet with a diagram showing where examples of 16 native trees and shrubs can be found along the trail.

Turn left in front of the second bridge and follow the trail up a gradual incline, back out to the asphalt path. Turn left here to return to the visitor center, following the path around the gazebo and going left again at the next intersection past the carved wooden totem pole and the sign for the azaleas and rhododendrons.

MORE INFORMATION

The park opens at 10 a.m. and closes between 5 p.m. and 8 p.m., depending on the month. There is a $5 entrance fee for adults, $2.50 for children and seniors. Annual passes are available for $25 for an individual and $35 for a family. Visit www.nvrpa.org/park/meadowlark_botanical_gardens or call 703-255-3631.

The park has ample facilities. In addition to the visitor center with a gift shop and educational programs, there is an atrium with an indoor tropical garden that can be rented for weddings and other functions. There are picnic areas, bathrooms, a half-dozen gazebos, and a large parking lot. The park also has a restored eighteenth-century cabin, gardening and horticulture work-shops, and summer concerts.

Plan to pick up a tour map at the visitor center because there is no map of the park online. Also note that plans are underway to connect Meadowlark to Washington & Old Dominion Trail (Trip 43).

APPENDIX:
FURTHER READING

HUMAN HISTORY

Carton, Evan. *Patriotic Treason: John Brown and the Soul of America*. New York: Simon & Schuster, 2006.

> A sympathetic look at Brown that is objective enough to allow for individual reader conclusions, this biography provides perspective on the man, his family, and his ethics.

Chambers, John Whiteclay II. *OSS Training in the National Parks and Service Abroad During World War II*. Washington, D.C.: National Park Service, 2008.

> Covers the creation of the Office of Strategic Service, how the parks were converted into spy training facilities, and the details of training activities in camps as well as in local towns and businesses. Available online at www.nps.gov/history/history/online_books/oss/index.htm.

Ewing, Heather. *The Lost World of James Smithson: Science, Revolution, and the Birth of the Smithsonian*. New York: Bloomsbury USA, 2007.

> A fascinating, deeply researched journey into Smithson's late-Enlightenment world and the optimistic spirit of its scientific vanguard; the greatest contribution to date to our knowledge of the Smithsonian's benefactor.

Henson, Matthew. *A Negro Explorer at the North Pole*. Montpelier, Vt.: Invisible Cities Press, 2001 (reprint).

> Henson's autobiography, originally published three years after the successful expedition to the Pole, tells the full story that Peary wouldn't—or couldn't—such as the discrimination Henson faced for most of his life.

Johnson, Dolores. *Onward: A Photobiography of Matthew Henson*. Washington, D.C.: National Geographic Children's Books, 2005.

Tells a strong story and provides rare photos of Henson and Peary's expeditions and of the Inuit guides who helped them reach the Pole. Geared toward young people, but worth a read by anyone.

Mayer, Henry. *All on Fire: William Lloyd Garrison and the Abolition of Slavery.* New York: W.W. Norton & Company, 2008.

A powerful read that shines much-needed light on the abolition movement, especially noteworthy here for its in-depth treatment of John Brown and his plots.

McIntosh, Elizabeth P. *Sisterhood of Spies: The Women of the OSS.* New York: Dell Publishing/Random House, 1998.

Although the female members of the Office of Strategic Service don't seem to have trained in Prince William Forest or Catoctin Mountain parks, this is a compelling, entertaining set of tales by a female OSS and CIA veteran.

McPherson, James M. *Battle Cry of Freedom: The Civil War Era.* New York: Oxford University Press USA, 2003.

An excellent in-depth, one-volume overview of the events leading up to, and the political and military conflicts of, the War Between the States.

Rountree, Helen C., ed. *Powhatan Foreign Relations, 1500-1722.* Charlottesville, Va.: University of Virginia Press, 1993.

One of the very few published books touching upon the Piscataway people and their lands, traditions, migrations, and relations with neighboring tribes.

Smith, Richard Harris. *OSS: The Secret History of America's First Central Intelligence Agency.* Guilford, Conn.: Lyons Press, 2005.

Considered by many to be the authoritative work on the OSS's creation and operations, it tells of interagency rivalries as well as behind-the-lines derring-do.

Stone, Robert, director. *American Experience: The Civilian Conservation Corps* (DVD). PBS Home Video, 2009.

Documents the reasons behind the CCC's creation, and the impacts on its members nationwide. Many interviews with CCC veterans.

Tayac, Gabrielle, and Schupman, Edwin. *We Have a Story to Tell: The Native Peoples of the Chesapeake Region.* Washington, D.C.: National Museum of the American Indian Education Office, 2006.

An educator's guide geared toward high school students, with depth and insight into the historical and current-day challenges faced by regional tribes.

NATURAL HISTORY

Allaby, Michael. *Temperate Forests* (Biomes of the Earth Series). New York: Chelsea House, 2006.

A general textbook on flora and fauna for Grades 7 and up, with good basic information on beavers, riparian zones, and more.

Choukas-Bradley, Melanie. *City of Trees: The Complete Field Guide to the Trees of Washington, D.C.* 3rd ed. Charlottesville, Va.: University of Virginia Press, 2008.

Astonishingly in-depth and invitingly written, this guide spotlights the plants—and the larger-than-life personalities—that have made Washington the beautiful city it is today.

National Geographic Society. *Wild Animals of North America*. Washington, D.C., National Geographic Society Book Division, 1998.

A beautiful pictorial look at beavers and other wildlife, with entertaining informational tidbits.

Reed, John C. Jr., Sigafoos, Robert S., and Fisher, George W. *The River and the Rocks: The Geologic Story of Great Falls and the Potomac River Gorge*. Washington, D.C.: United States Geological Survey, 1970.

The classic study of Great Falls geology, fascinating and not too technical. Available online at www.nps.gov/history/history/online_books/grfa/contents.htm.

INDEX

A

Accokeek, MD, trips near, x–xi, 47–50
American Chestnut Land Trust, viii–ix, 20–24
American Indians, 50–52, 199
Anacostia River, hikes along, 129–133
Antietam National Battlefield, x–xi, 67–70
ants, 99
Appalachian Mountain Club (AMC), 256–259
Appalachian Trail (AT), hikes along, 165–166, 184, 230
Arlington National Cemetery, 121–122
Arlington, VA, trips near, xii–xiii, 113–122

B

bald eagles, 42, 46, 168, 171
Battle Creek Cypress Swamp Sanctuary, 15
Beallsville, MD, trips near, x–xi, 95–98
beavers, 193
Berwyn Heights, MD, trips near, x–xi, 57–61
Bethesda, MD, trips near, x–xi, 84–87
bicycling
    in District of Columbia, 137
    in Maryland, 10–11, 19, 50, 61, 74, 106, 110
    in Virginia, 162, 205–209
Billy Goat Trail, x–xi, 89–93
bird-watching, 10, 32, 57, 167–173. *See also* individual species
Black Hill Regional Park, x–xi, 75–78
Black Rock Regional Park, 28
bonsai trees, 126–127
Brown, John, 229, 232–233
Bull Run Mountains Natural Area, xiv–xv, 177–180
Bull Run–Occoquan Trail, xiv–xv, 210–214

Bull Run Regional Park, 210
butterflies, 75–78

C

Calvert Cliffs State Park, viii–ix, 12–15
Camp David, 66
camping, xxvii, 38, 56, 66, 102
Canada geese, 7
canal boat rides, 93
canoeing. *See also* kayaking
    in Maryland, 6, 24, 27, 50, 78, 110
    in Virginia, 168, 172, 175, 191, 214
Capital Crescent Trail, x–xi, 84–87
Capitol Building, 149
Catoctin Mountain Park, x–xi, 62–66
Cedarville State Forest, viii–ix, 16–19
Chapman's Mill, 180
cherry trees, 144–146
Chesapeake Bay Critical Area Driving Tour, 11
Chesapeake & Ohio (C&O) Canal, 31, 89–94, 141, 231
chestnut trees, 20
Civilian Conservation Corps (CCC), 226–227
Civil War sites, 67–70, 121–122, 175–176, 231, 235–240
Clarksburg, MD, trips near, x–xi, 75–78, 99–102
Clinton, MD, trips near, viii–ix, 38–41
Clopper Lake, viii–ix, 25–28
Colesville, MD, trips near, x–xi, 79–83
College Park, MD, trips near, x–xi
Colvin Run Mill Park, 209
Cosca Regional Park, viii–ix, 38–41
Croom, MD, trips near, viii–ix, 7–11
cross-country skiing, ix, xi, xiii, xv, 66

Cross County Trail, xiv–xv, 205–209
Cunningham Falls State Park, x–xi, 62–66

D

Delaplane, VA, trips near, xiv–xv, 181–185
Dickerson, MD, trips near, x–xi, 71–74
District of Columbia, trips in. *See* Washington, D.C., trips in
dogs, ix, xi, xiii, xv
Dumbarton Oaks estate, 141
Duval Tool Museum, 11

E

East Potomac Park, xii–xiii, 142–148
Elkridge, MD, trips near, x–xi, 103–106
Etlan, VA, trips near, xiv–xv, 224–228

F

fishing
    in Maryland, 6, 10, 27–28, 38–41, 44–45,
        48, 60–61, 66, 106, 110
    in Virginia, 176, 181–183
Flag Ponds Park, 15
footwear, xxiv
Fort Circle Trail, 133
Fort Hunt Park, xiv–xv, 220–223
Fraser Preserve, xiv–xv, 197–200
Frisbee golf, 28, 172
further reading, 247–249

G

geology, 189
Georgetown, District of Columbia, xii–xiii,
    84–87, 118–122, 138–141
Germantown, MD, trips near, viii–ix, 25–28
Glen Echo Park, 93
Gravatt, Flippo, 20
Great Falls, geology of, 189
Great Falls (MD), x–xi, 89–93
Great Falls (VA), xiv–xv, 186–191
Greenbelt, MD, trips near, x–xi, 53–56
Greenbelt Park, x–xi, 53–56
Greenway Trail, 25
Greenwell State Park, x–xi, 107–110
G. Richard Thompson Wildlife Management
    Area, xiv–xv, 181–185

H

Hains Point, xii–xiii, 147
Harpers Ferry, WV, trips near, xiv–xv,
    229–234
Hawk's Reach Nature Center, 102
Haymarket, VA, trips near, xiv–xv, 177–180

Hemlock Overlook Regional Park, 210
Henson, Matthew, 81
Hollywood, MD, trips near, x–xi, 107–110
Holy Rood Cemetery, 140
horseback riding
    in District of Columbia, 137
    in Maryland, 6, 25, 38, 41, 95–98, 110
    in Virginia, 214
hunting
    in Maryland, 6, 15, 18–19, 24, 110
    in Virginia, 181
Huntley Meadows Park, xiv–xv, 192–196
Hybla Valley, VA, trips near, xiv–xv, 192–196

I

insects, xxv, 99

J

Jefferson Memorial, 147
Jug Bay Natural Area, 11

K

kayaking, 27, 50, 78, 110, 172, 191. *See also*
    canoeing
Kenilworth Aquatic Gardens, xii–xiii,
    129–133
kids, trips recommended for, ix, xi, xiii, xv, 34
kudzu, 101
Kunzang Palyul Choling Buddhist temple,
    32

L

Lake Artemesia, x–xi, 57–61
Largo, MD, trips near, viii–ix, 33–37
Laurel, MD, trips near, viii–ix, 42–45
Leave No Trace principles, xxvi–xxvii
Leesylvania State Park, xii–xiii, 173–176
Lilypons Water Gardens, 74
Lincoln Memorial, xii–xiii, 121, 155
Little Bennett Regional Park, x–xi, 28,
    99–102
Lorton, VA, trips near, xii–xiii, 168–172
Lusby, MD, trips near, viii–ix, 12–15

M

Magruder Trail, 28
Manassas, battle of, 235–236, 239–240
Manassas National Battlefield Park, xiv–xv,
    235–238
Manassas, VA, trips near, xiv–xv, 235–238
Maryland, trips in, viii–xi, 1–112
Mason Neck State Park, xii–xiii, 168–172
Matthew Henson Trail, x–xi, 79–83

McKee-Beshers Wildlife Management Area, viii–ix, 29–32
McLean, VA, trips near, xiv–xv, 215–219
Meadowlark Botanical Gardens, xiv–xv, 241–245
Merkle Wildlife Sanctuary, viii–ix, 7–11
Middleham Chapel, 15
Monocacy Natural Resource Management Area, 6, 74
Mount Vernon Trail, xiv–xv, 220–223
Mount Vernon, VA, trips near, xiv–xv, 220–223

N
National Arboretum, xii–xiii, 123–128
National Mall, xii–xiii, 149–153
Northeast Branch Trail, x–xi, 57–61

O
Occoquan Water Trail, 214
Office of Strategic Services, 162
Old Rag Mountain, xiv–xv, 224–228

P
Paris, VA, trips near, xii–xiii, 164–167
Patapsco Valley State Park, x–xi, 103–106
Patowmack Canal, 186
Patuxent Research Refuge, viii–ix, 42–46
Patuxent River State Park, viii–ix, 3–6
Peace Park, 32
Piscataway Indians, 51–52
Piscataway National Park, x–xi, 47–50
playgrounds, 15–16, 38, 56, 147
Pohick Bay Regional Park, 172
poison ivy, xxv
Poolesville, MD, trips near, viii–ix, 29–32
Potomac Heritage Trail, xii–xiii, 113–117, 186–190
Potomac River, hikes along
    in District of Columbia, 113–122, 168–172
    in Maryland, 29–32, 47–50, 89–93
    in Virginia, 173–176, 186–191, 220–223
Potomac Scenic Heritage Trail, 219
Prince Frederick, MD, trips near, viii–ix, 20–24
Prince William Civil War Heritage Trail, 176
Prince William Forest Park, xii–xiii, 159–162
public transportation, trips accessible by, ix, xi, xiii
    in District of Columbia, 113–153
    in Maryland, 8, 53, 57, 84

Q
Quantico, VA, trips near, xii–xiii, 159–162

R
Riverbend Park, xiv–xv, 186–191
rock climbing, 74
Rock Creek Park, xii–xiii, 134–137
rock scrambles, 65, 89–91, 224–228
Roosevelt, Franklin D., 226

S
safety considerations, xxiii–xxv
sakura, 144–145
Scott's Run Nature Preserve, xiv–xv, 215–219
Seneca Creek State Park, viii–ix, 6, 25–28
Sharpsburg, MD, trips near, x–xi, 67–70
Shenandoah National Park, 224–228
skiing. *See* cross-country skiing
Sky Meadows State Park, xii–xiii, 164–167
Smithson, James, 152–153
Smithsonian Museums, 151–154
snowshoeing, ix, xi, xiii, xv
spies, 162–163
Sugarloaf Mountain, x–xi, 71–74
Sunshine, MD, trips near, viii–ix, 3–6
swimming spots, 13, 66, 103–106, 108–110

T
Theodore Roosevelt Island, xii–xiii, 113–117
Thurmont, MD, trips near, x–xi, 62–66
trip planning, xxi–xxvi
Tyson's Corner, VA, trips near, xiv–xv, 241–245

U
U.S. Botanic Garden, 151

V
Vienna, VA, trips near, xiv–xv, 205–209
Viers Mill, MD, trips near, x–xi, 79–83
Virginia, trips in, xii–xv, 157–245

W
Waldorf, MD, trips near, viii–ix, 16–19
Warrenton, VA, trips near, xiv–xv, 201–204
Washington & Old Dominion Trail, xiv–xv, 205–209
Washington, D.C., trips in, xii–xiii, 113–158
waste disposal, xxvii
waterfall hikes, 62–66, 103–106. *See also* Great Falls
Watergate Hotel, 120

water lilies, 129–131
Watkins Regional Park, viii–ix, 33–37
wetland hikes, 7–9, 34–35, 129–133, 192–196, 243–244
whooping cranes, 42
Wildcat Mountain Natural Area, xiv–xv, 201–204

wildflowers, 35, 71, 75, 128, 181–183, 197–199, 241
wildlife research, 42–45
Woodbridge, VA, trips near, xii–xiii, 173–176
Woodstock Equestrian Park, x–xi, 95–98
World War II Memorial, 154–155

ABOUT THE AUTHORS

STEPHEN MAURO has lived in the Washington, D.C., area for 17 years and hikes extensively there. He is an assistant editor for *Aviation History* and *Wild West* magazines and helps maintain the Weider History Group website www. historynet.com.

BETH HOMICZ qualified for her Washington, D.C., tour guide license in 1994, and has led more than 15,000 people around the capital city. She is an alumna of Georgetown University and a former columnist for *Destinations* magazine; her writing has also appeared in the *Washington Post*. She is currently working on a historical novel about the Underground Railroad.

Appalachian Mountain Club

Founded in 1876, the AMC is the nation's oldest outdoor recreation and conservation organization. The AMC promotes the protection, enjoyment, and understanding of the mountains, forests, waters, and trails of the Appalachian region.

People

We are more than 100,000 members, advocates, and supporters; 16,000 volunteers; and more than 450 full-time and seasonal staff. Our 12 chapters reach from Maine to Washington, D.C.

Outdoor Adventure and Fun

We offer more than 8,000 trips each year, from local chapter activities to major excursions worldwide, for every ability level and outdoor interest—from hiking and climbing to paddling, snowshoeing, and skiing.

Great Places to Stay

We host more than 140,000 guests each year at our lodges, huts, camps, shelters, and campgrounds. Each AMC destination is a model for environmental education and stewardship.

Opportunities for Learning

We teach people the skills to be safe outdoors and to care for the natural world around us through programs for children, teens, and adults, as well as outdoor leadership training.

Caring for Trails

We maintain more than 1,500 miles of trails throughout the Northeast, including nearly 350 miles of the Appalachian Trail in five states.

Protecting Wild Places

We advocate for land and riverway conservation, monitor air quality and climate change, and work to protect alpine and forest ecosystems throughout the Northern Forest and Mid-Atlantic Highlands regions.

Engaging the Public

We seek to educate and inform our own members and an additional 2 million people annually through AMC Books, our website, our White Mountain visitor centers, and AMC destinations.

Join Us!

Members support our mission while enjoying great AMC programs, our award-winning *AMC Outdoors* magazine, and special discounts. Visit www.outdoors.org or call 800-372-1758 for more information.

APPALACHIAN MOUNTAIN CLUB
Recreation • Education • Conservation
www.outdoors.org

The AMC Washington DC Chapter

STARTED IN 1984, this is the southernmost chapter of the Appalachian Mountain Club. Its 2,400 members—mostly from Washington, D.C., Maryland, and northern Virginia—engage in various activities, including day-hiking, backpacking, paddling, biking, and social get-togethers. The chapter also organizes conservation initiatives and offers education and leadership opportunities.

To view a list of AMC activities in Washington, D.C., Maryland, northern Virginia, and other parts of the Northeast, visit trips.outdoors.org.

AMC BOOK UPDATES

AMC BOOKS STRIVES TO KEEP OUR GUIDEBOOKS AS UP-TO-DATE as possible to help you plan safe and enjoyable adventures. If after publishing a book we learn that trails have been relocated or route or contact information has changed, we will post the updated information online. Before you hit the trail, check for updates at www.outdoors.org/publications/books/updates.

While hiking or paddling, if you notice discrepancies with the trail description or map, or if you find any other errors in a book, please let us know by submitting them to amcbookupdates@outdoors.org or in writing to Books Editor, c/o AMC, 5 Joy Street, Boston, MA 02108. We will verify all submissions and post key updates each month. AMC Books is dedicated to being a recognized leader in outdoor publishing. Thank you for your participation.

AMC BOOKS & MAPS

EXPLORE THE POSSIBILITIES

More Books from the Outdoor Experts

AMC Guide to Winter Hiking & Camping

BY LUCAS ST. CLAIR AND YEMAYA MAURER

Exploring the outdoors in winter is exhilarating when you have the right skills. This guide will help you to experience the special allure of hiking and backpacking during the snowy season, with a focus on preparation, safety, outdoor stewardship, and fun.

ISBN: 978-1-934028-12-4
$16.95

AMC's Best Day Hikes Near Philadelphia

BY SUSAN CHARKES

This easy-to-use guide will help families, tourists, and local residents explore eastern Pennsylvania, New Jersey, and Delaware year-round, from lesser-known locations to area favorites, including several hikes on the Appalachian Trail.

ISBN: 978-1-934028-33-9
$18.95

North Carolina Hiking Trails, 4th Edition

BY ALLEN DE HART

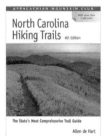

This guide includes the most comprehensive trail information for North Carolina hikers of all ages, interests, and abilities. Inside you'll find detailed descriptions of trails in national forests, state and city parks, historic sites, and other great locations.

ISBN: 978-1-929173-47-1
$22.95

Quiet Water New Jersey & Eastern Pennsylvania

BY KATHY KENLEY

Great for families, anglers, canoeists, and kayakers of all abilities, *Quiet Water New Jersey & Eastern Pennsylvania* features 80 trips, covering the best calm water paddling in the region.

ISBN: 978-1-934028-34-6
$19.95